D1006092

India

A SHORT HISTORY

Andrew Robinson

India

A SHORT HISTORY

12 illustrations

 Thames & Hudson

India: A Short History © 2014 Thames & Hudson Ltd, London

All Rights Reserved. No part of this publication may be reproduced
or transmitted in any form or by any means, electronic or mechanical,
including photocopy, recording or any other information storage and
retrieval system, without prior permission in writing from the publisher.

First published in 2014 in hardcover in the United States of America by
Thames & Hudson Inc., 500 Fifth Avenue, New York, New York 10110

thamesandhudsonusa.com

Library of Congress Catalog Card Number 2013950854

ISBN 978-0-500-25199-7

Typesetting by Servis Filmsetting Ltd, Stockport, Cheshire

Printed and bound in India by Replika Press Pvt. Ltd

CONTENTS

PREFACE

Contemporary India attracts the attention of the world. Yet, only a few decades ago, the subcontinent was largely ignored by outsiders. Writing in the early 1960s, the future Nobel laureate V. S. Naipaul famously termed India *An Area of Darkness* after his first disillusioning sojourn in his ancestral land. In the mid-1970s, when I first arrived in India from Britain, before going to university, to teach science in a school in the Himalayas and see the country, I knew practically nothing of its history and culture, despite India's historic, two-century relationship with Britain. In my school history classes, I had briefly studied Robert Clive, Warren Hastings and the foundation of the British empire in India in the mid-18th century, but the history of the Mughal empire, Hindu kingdoms, the empire of Asoka, the life of the Buddha and the spread of Buddhism, or the ancient Indus Valley civilization was a blank – not to mention the story of Mahatma Gandhi and the end of empire in the subcontinent.

The same indifference was commonplace during the colonial period, before India's independence from Britain in 1947, perhaps surprisingly. In 1925, the historian of India Edward J. Thompson (father of E. P. Thompson) regretted that 'British lack of interest in India is no new thing' in a controversial little book, *The Other Side of the Medal*, published by Leonard and Virginia Woolf's Hogarth Press, intended to ruffle more than half a century of imperial complacency with news of hitherto concealed British atrocities against Indian civilians during the uprising of 1857–58 known to the British as the Indian Mutiny. 'It has been notorious, and a theme of savage comment by Indians, that the Indian Debate in the House of Commons has been regarded with indifference by the few who attended, with contempt by the many who stayed away', Thompson noted. A century earlier, in 1833, at the time of a crucial British parliamentary debate about the government's effective nationalization of the East India Company, the MP and historian Thomas Babington Macaulay – shortly to set sail for India from London as a high government official – regretted 'the strange indifference of all classes of people, members of Parliament, reporters and the public to Indian politics'. However, he also privately admitted to his family his own profound ambivalence towards India: 'Am I not in fair training to be as great a bore . . . as the greatest?' For all his praiseworthy dedication to improving the educational and legal systems of India, Macaulay would himself come to epitomize British indifference to Indian culture. He had polyglot gifts in European languages, but never bothered to learn any Indian language during his four-year stint in India. In his much-quoted Minute on Education, written in Calcutta in 1835, Macaulay asserted: 'who could deny that a single shelf of a good European library was worth the whole literature of India and Arabia'.

Indifference persisted through the 1980s, more or less. When I worked for Granada Television at the time of the making of *The Jewel in the Crown*, the justly acclaimed drama serial set near the end of the British Raj, the production staff looked at India chiefly through colonial-period spectacles – both on screen and off. When I published a biography of India's most internationally acclaimed living cultural figure, Satyajit Ray, in 1989, there were many reviews; but the London and New York film critics were plainly not much interested in Indian culture – only in Ray's artistry as a film director, as being worthy of comparison with, say, Jean Renoir's, Vittorio de Sica's or Robert Flaherty's. The editor of the film magazine *Sight and Sound* (for which I was then writing), despite having revered Ray's films since the classic Apu Trilogy of the 1950s, had nevertheless not felt the desire to visit an Indian film festival – perhaps because she suspected that India's prosaic urban reality and Indian filmgoers' apparent addiction to song and dance would not chime with Ray's enchanting vision of his country. As Ray himself candidly remarked to me in London in 1982: 'the cultural gap between East and West is too wide for a handful of films to reduce it. It can happen only when critics back it up with study on other levels as well. But where is the time, with so many films from other countries to contend with? And where is the compulsion?'

At the beginning of the 1990s, however, the tide began to turn, fairly rapidly, cresting in the first decade of the new millennium as something of an India wave. There were many reasons: empires had gone out of fashion; former servants of the Raj were dead or dying off; younger westerners free from colonial baggage were travelling extensively in India, not just to the usual tourist spots such as Delhi and Rajasthan; some were even marrying Indians and settling there; young India-based writers were being published in the West to considerable acclaim; 'Bollywood' films were becoming partially known to non-Indians. Most important of all, a diaspora of Indian citizens and people of Indian origin was making its mark in Europe, North America and other parts of the globe in business, the media and the professions, especially medicine, science and technology, including information technology. At the same time, within India, following the government's liberalization of the country's commerce after 1991, the economy began to grow fast, averaging just over six per cent per annum during the rest of the decade. The flourishing of the Indian diaspora and of India's own economy made Europeans and Americans curious about the country as a whole, and provided the compulsion – Satyajit Ray's word – to understand the sources of this unfamiliar success.

The sea change was symbolized by the commercial triumph in 2008–09 of a multi-Oscar-winning movie, *Slumdog Millionaire*, which owed almost as much to Bollywood as to Hollywood cinema. The film was not to my taste, but there was no denying its public appeal in both East and West – if that old polarity can any longer be said to mean much in our globalized world. Back in the 1970s, such a British-directed production about India would have provoked outrage from the Indian government and almost every Indian for its lurid revelling in Indian poverty and squalor – as happened with the Indian government's banning in India of Louis Malle's mammoth documentary, *Phantom India*, in 1970, after it was shown on BBC Television. Even Ray's prize-winning Apu Trilogy suffered severe criticism in the Indian parliament in the early 1980s for its projection of Indian poverty to audiences in Europe and America. Now, instead of old-fashioned patriotic outrage, *Slumdog Millionaire*'s worldwide success was greeted in India with nearly unanimous applause. The film's go-getting message, that even a slum kid from Mumbai with some brains could make a million in a TV quiz show – and in real life get to step on the red carpet in Hollywood – jibed with the brash confidence of India's newly rich middle class. After all, the film was based on an English-language novel written by one of their own, a successful Indian diplomat.

The upsurge of interest in India prompted the publication of scores of non-fiction books. Naipaul began the trend in 1990 with *India: A Million Mutinies Now,* by interviewing a wide variety of 'unknown' Indians (to recall the title of Nirad C. Chaudhuri's remarkable 1951 memoir, *The Autobiography of an Unknown Indian*) and narrating their personal histories. Writers, journalists, political activists, business people and academics from many fields – both Indians and non-Indians – followed on. Whereas the first decade or so of these books, including Naipaul's, was understandably optimistic about India, emphasizing its refreshing prominence, later books veered towards pessimism. For example, in *Accidental India*, the India-based economic analyst Shankkar Aiyar argued that almost all of the beneficial economic changes in independent India – including the agricultural 'green revolution' of the 1960s, the economic liberalization of 1991 and the software revolution of the 1990s – happened as a result of 'accidents', not government planning: often they arose from crises forced upon India by incompetent official policies. 'Governance in India, in 2012, is a sham and a shame', summarized Aiyar. 'In every crisis . . ., the common thread is the inability of successive governments to think imaginatively and act decisively. India deserves better.' Few present-day Indian commentators would disagree with that last remark.

Virtually all of the books restricted themselves to India of the past century or two – that is, the British colonial period and after. Most also focused on politics and economics, underplaying India's intellectual, religious and artistic life. Still to be written was an introductory, non-academic history of India since the Indus Valley civilization of the third millennium BC, tackling its significant aspects rather than striving for the completeness of a textbook, and paying as much notice to individuals, ideas and cultures as to the rise and fall of kingdoms, political parties and economies. Although Indian democracy is certainly a remarkable achievement, worthy of study and at times even of celebration, despite its longstanding failures and perversions of justice, India's political system does not – at least in my view it *should* not – define the country's importance to the world, whatever politically minded pundits may instinctively believe. Indian history deserves better than an exclusive focus on politics and economics (or indeed the prejudices of a Macaulay).

India: A Short History aims to steer a middle path between polarized reactions to India, whether positive or negative. Indian history is undeniably full of fascinating extremes; but a historian must try to view them *sub specie aeternitatis*. For me personally, the book is also an attempt to understand somewhat better a civilization that has changed my life.

NOTE ON NOMENCLATURE

Since this is a history book, recently changed Indian spellings of place-names, such as Mumbai (previously Bombay), are not used, except where appropriate in describing present-day India. Personal names and terms taken from Indian languages follow common usage, without being entirely consistent, for example Asoka (rather than Ashoka) but *dharma* (rather than *dhamma*); diacriticals have been omitted.

INTRODUCTION

Startling material wealth has long been a feature of India. Ancient Rome's taste for Indian luxuries is proved by the enormous numbers of Roman gold coins found in southern India. Writing in the first century AD in his *Natural History*, Pliny the Elder complained of the 'drain' caused by Indian luxuries on the Roman economy, and deplored the fact that Rome and India had been 'brought nearer by lust for gain'. The Buddhist cave paintings of Ajanta, created in the first millennium AD, lost in the jungles and rediscovered by the British in the early 19th century, depict lavish personal adornments. The Muslim invaders of India in the eleventh century, such as the Afghan, Mahmud of Ghazni, brought home vast loot by stripping Hindu temples of gold and jewels. The reputation for splendour of the courts of the Great Mughals in the 16th and 17th centuries – symbolized by the jewel-encrusted Taj Mahal built by the Emperor Shah Jahan – attracted the attentions of European traders: first the Portuguese, then other European nations. In 1700, the heyday of the Mughal empire, India's share of world GDP, at 24.4 per cent, almost equalled Europe's share, 25 per cent. Indian wealth underpinned the rise of the British East India Company and the foundation of the British empire in India in the 18th century; by the 1780s, European Calcutta was justifiably known as the 'City of Palaces'. During the British Raj, Indian princes became bywords for opulence and excess. Today, rather than the feudal maharajas, there are ostentatious Indian business moguls who number among the world's richest men – along with institutionalized corruption on a scale so unbridled it threatens the stability of the nation. In 2008, the combined net worth of the four richest Indians in *Forbes* list of billionaires equalled 16 per cent of India's total GDP.

Grinding poverty seems always to have been a fact of Indian life, too. In the 5th or 6th century BC, 'Prince' Siddhartha Gautama, before his enlightenment as the Buddha, was painfully shocked by the poverty and disease beyond his palace walls. In the 3rd century BC, India's first great ruler, the Mauryan emperor Asoka, established what can be called the world's first welfare state, inspired by Buddhism. As the caste system became more rigid under Hindu rulers guided by the values of the highest caste, the Brahmins, the poorest became outcastes from society, in due course known as untouchables (rechristened Harijans by Gandhi, and now generally known as Dalits). Famines regularly afflicted British India from the time of Clive in the 1760s until as late as 1943. In the first half of the 20th century, Mahatma Gandhi deliberately adopted the dress of the poor and focused much of his activism on poverty alleviation. In 1971, Prime Minister Indira Gandhi, having just abolished the privy purses of the Indian princes, won a landslide election victory with the Hindi slogan 'Garibi Hatao' ('Abolish Poverty'). 'Indeed, even today, after twenty years of rapid growth,' the economist Amartya Sen warned in 2011 in an Indian news magazine, 'India is still one of the poorest countries in the world, something that is often lost sight of, especially by those who enjoy world-class living standards thanks to the inequalities in the income distribution.' Only sixteen countries outside Africa had a lower gross national income per capita than India: Afghanistan, Cambodia, Haiti, Iraq, Kyrgystan, Laos, Moldova, Nepal, Nicaragua, Pakistan, Papua New Guinea, Tajikistan, Uzbekistan, Vietnam and Yemen. 'This is not exactly a club of economic superpowers', commented Sen, who was awarded a Nobel prize in 1998, chiefly for his work on famines and poverty.

It is a cliché that India has long been, and still is, a land of inequality and extremes of wealth and behaviour. Acceptance of inequality may be the main reason why India eventually rejected Buddhism and its philosophy of social equality and moderation during the first millennium AD – but not Jainism, a religious movement contemporaneous with Buddhism, which fostered the accumulation of great wealth along with the practice of rigorous asceticism. Endemic disparity is part of India's uniqueness and fascination, and must form an essential theme of any history.

In the arts, for instance, India has produced some of the world's most unique and refined literature, sculpture, painting, music, songs and dance. Poems, plays and novels in several languages by writers such as Kalidasa (Sanskrit), Kabir (Hindi), Rabindranath Tagore (Bengali) and R. K. Narayan (English); the sculpture of the Sun Temple at Konarak in Orissa and the Chola bronze statues of Tamil Nadu; the murals of Ajanta, the Rajput miniature paintings and the contemporary paintings of Binode Bihari Mukherjee; the ragas of Ravi Shankar and Ali Akbar Khan; Bharata Natyam and Kathakali dancing – to name just a few Indian artistic achievements – are recognized contributions to universal culture, which have exerted a powerful influence on 20th-century non-Indian artists, such as the photographer Henri Cartier-Bresson, the sculptor Antony Gormley, the novelist Graham Greene, the musician George Harrison and the poet W. B. Yeats. In the cinema, Satyajit Ray, the first Indian to win an Oscar for his lifetime achievement, was praised by leading artists from all regions of the world, including his fellow film directors, at the same time as being loved by ordinary audiences in his native Bengal for his films' warmth, humour and penetrating honesty. From Japan, the director Akira Kurosawa even said: 'Not to have seen the cinema of Ray means existing in the world without seeing the sun or the moon.' And yet it is also true that most of the output of India's film industry, which is the biggest in the world, is now (after its increasing commodification in recent decades) among the tawdriest in the world, even when compared with the trashiest of Hollywood films. The Himalayan peaks and the monotony of the north Indian plain can sometimes seem like metaphors for the behaviour and achievements of the subcontinent's human inhabitants.

A second great theme for a history must be the interaction of India with other cultures, whether towards the east and south, in China, Japan, Southeast Asia and Sri Lanka, or towards the west, in the Islamic world, ancient Greece and Rome, and modern Europe.

Buddhism formed a vital part of Chinese history from the 1st to the 11th century AD and of Japanese history from the 6th century until today. Whether it reached China from India via a maritime route and was first practised in southern China, in the Yangtze River and Huai River region, or it arrived via the overland routes of the Silk Road and was first practised in western China, at the Han dynasty capital Luoyang, has long been disputed. But certainly the spread of Buddhism led to the printing of the world's earliest dated printed book, *The Diamond Sutra*, a Buddhist text published in Chinese in AD 868, which was discovered in the Caves of the Thousand Buddhas near Dunhuang on the Silk Road and brought to the British Museum in 1909. In Sri Lanka and Southeast Asia – Burma, Thailand, Cambodia, Indonesia and some other countries of the region – Indian Buddhist and Hindu influence is obvious in their art and architecture, for example at Anuradhapura (Sri Lanka), Pagan (Burma), Angkor Wat (Cambodia) and Borobudur (Indonesia), despite much debate about how this influence actually occurred. While the old theories of conquest and colonization of an uncultured Southeast Asia by Indian traders, followed by their marriage to local women, have been abandoned, the formation of states in these areas during the mid-first millennium AD is intelligible only by reference to the spread of Buddhism (in its two major traditions, Mahayana and Theravada) and Hinduism from India.

In the West, Indian influence arrived considerably earlier. The Roman historian Eusebius claimed that learned Indians visited Athens and conversed with Socrates in the 5th century BC. Asked to explain the object of his philosophy, Socrates is said to have replied: 'an inquiry into human affairs'. One of the Indians burst out laughing and asked: 'How can a man grasp human things without first mastering the Divine?' This early example

14

of an East–West encounter may be apocryphal (though Alexander the Great definitely encountered Indian philosophers in the 4th century BC), but it is certain that Buddhists from India visited ancient Alexandria. In the 3rd century AD, the Christian theologian Clement of Alexandria was the first Greek writer to mention Buddha by name (as 'Boutta'). Clement also declared, tendentiously, that the Greeks acquired their philosophy from these 'barbarian' visitors. Some centuries later – by the 9th century, at the latest – the decimal place-value system, including a symbol for zero, was indubitably invented by anonymous Indian mathematicians and passed on to Arab mathematicians, who gave it to Europe around 1200, where the ten symbols became known as 'Arabic numerals': India's greatest practical gift to the world. In the 15th century, the Indian folk tales known in Sanskrit as the *Panchatantra* were translated into Latin and thence into modern European languages, forming the basis of Jean de la Fontaine's second book of *Fables*, published in 1678. In the late 18th century, British scholars working in India learned Sanskrit – most notably Sir William Jones, who discovered the Indo-European language family (including Sanskrit, Greek and Latin) in the 1780s – and began to translate ancient Indian works of literature, law and philosophy; these had a significant impact on the German Romantics, including Immanuel Kant, Johann Wolfgang von Goethe and Arthur Schopenhauer. This was followed in the mid-19th century by the European rediscovery of Indian Buddhism – both as archaeology at magnificent sites such as Sanchi and Sarnath, and as a living philosophy in Sri Lanka, Burma and Tibet.

The converse influence – of the Middle East, Islam and Europe on India – is of course profound. From archaeological evidence, we know there was trade between ancient Mesopotamia and the first urban Indian culture, located in the Indus Valley, as early as the turn of the third millennium BC. Thereafter came the Aryan migrations from Iran into India in the midsecond millennium BC; the Greek influence on northwest India – around the time of Alexander's invasion and thereafter – in the late first millennium

BC; the invasions of Muslim warriors in the early second millennium AD; the rise of the Mughal power after 1526; and the European colonial period in the late second millennium. In addition, India was invaded from the east, from the direction of Burma, by a Tai/Shan people who established the Ahom dynasty in Assam in the early 13th century. The Ahoms successfully resisted Mughal domination in the 17th century and ruled the Brahmaputra Valley for an impressive six centuries until their conquest by the British in 1826.

Scholars by no means agree on which aspects of Indian history and civilization should be regarded as indigenous to the subcontinent and which were the result of outside influences. The European colonial period is perhaps the most controversial, being closest in time and emotion, but even the Aryan migrations continue to provoke impassioned debate, fuelled by Hindu nationalists, who resist the scholarly consensus of a foreign, Aryan origin for Hinduism. What cannot be denied is the complexity of the European influence on India, including the development of the country's system of parliamentary democracy, introduced by the British in the 1930s. Gandhi, Jawaharlal Nehru, independent India's first prime minister, B. R. Ambedkar, the leader of India's untouchables, and Tagore, India's first Nobel laureate, each openly recognized the vital role played by European thought in their own lives: for example, John Ruskin's *Unto This Last* (Gandhi), Fabian socialism (Nehru), western political philosophers (Ambedkar) and English Romantic poets (Tagore). Gandhi even selected a slogan, 'Do or Die', as his mantra for the mass agitation of the 1942 Quit India movement, which he had adapted from Alfred Tennyson's phrase 'do and die' in 'The Charge of the Light Brigade'. In the 1980s, Satyajit Ray frankly said that he thought of himself as '50 per cent western'. Today, the economic revival of India, relying on international trade and information technology, would almost certainly have proved impossible without the widespread use and prestige of the English language in India, bequeathed as part of the British colonial legacy.

Given such complexity of influences, India presents some formidable challenges to historians. To begin with, how are they to accommodate India's traditional indifference to the kind of European historical writing conceived during the European Enlightenment – the very period in which Britain colonized India? For instance, *The History of the Decline and Fall of the Roman Empire* by Edward Gibbon.

In 1924, having read during a spell in a British-Indian jail some of the leading European historical works, including Gibbon's, Gandhi declared: 'I believe in the saying that a nation is happy that has no history'. He added: 'our Hindu ancestors solved the question for us by ignoring history as it is understood today and by building on slight events their philosophical structure.'

In the midst of the Second World War, Gandhi published an article in the newspaper he edited, entitled 'How to Combat Hitlerism', which unwittingly explained the meaning of his above remarks. This was in June 1940, just after the totally unexpected, shocking but comparatively blood-less fall of France to the German army. Gandhi asked: 'What will Hitler do with his victory? Can he digest so much power?' Gandhi's view was as follows: 'Personally he will go as empty-handed as his not very remote pre-decessor Alexander. For the Germans he will have left not the pleasure of owning a mighty empire but the burden of sustaining its crushing weight.' Instead of imperial Britain and other free European nations choosing to offer violent resistance to a coming German invasion, Gandhi recom-mended they offer non-violent resistance. 'Under non-violence only those would [be] killed who had trained themselves to be killed, if need be, but without killing anyone and without bearing malice towards anybody', Gandhi claimed – no doubt thinking of his own non-violent campaigns against the British empire in India during the 1920s and 1930s. 'I dare say that in that case Europe would have added several inches to its moral stature. And in the end I expect it is the moral worth that will count. All else is dross.'

Of course, Gandhi's advice was not taken by Winston Churchill and the British nation. After more German military victories, in early 1942 Gandhi speculated in a further article, 'Suppose Germany Wins', on a German invasion of India. 'If the Nazis come to India, the Congress will give them the same fight that it has given Great Britain. I do not underrate the power of *satyagraha* [literally, 'truth-force', but often translated as passive resistance],' he wrote. 'Imperialism has kept its grip on India for more than 150 years. If it is overthrown by a worse type of rule, the Congress can have the negative satisfaction of knowing that no other "ism" can possibly last beyond a few years even if it establishes a foothold in India.' He ended with a reference to shattering legendary Indian military events believed to have occurred in the same era as the Trojan War during the internecine struggle between the victorious Pandavas and the defeated Kauravas in the epic, *The Mahabharata*:

> Personally I think the end of this giant war will be what happened in the fabled Mahabharata War. *The Mahabharata* has been aptly described . . . as the permanent History of Man. What is described in that great epic is happening today before our very eyes. The warring nations are destroying themselves with such fury and ferocity that the end will be mutual destruction. The victor will share the fate that awaited the surviving Pandavas. The mighty warrior Arjuna was looted in broad daylight by a petty robber. And out of this holocaust must arise a new order for which the exploited millions of toilers have so long thirsted. The prayers of peace-lovers cannot go in vain. *Satyagraha* is itself an unmistakable mute prayer of an agonized soul.

Gandhi's attitude to history, as stated here, in many ways suggests the difficulties of writing a history of India. For the Mahatma was certainly no historian, despite being one of the handful of figures in Indian history known to the entire world. Without apparent irony, Gandhi saw no difficulty in telescoping Adolf Hitler and Alexander of Macedon into fellow tyrants, despite their separation by more than two millennia and two utterly different cultures. He felt able to equate German Nazism with British imperialism, despite their evident dissimilarity – both in their political foundations and in their use of violence against unarmed civilians. (Hitler, in conversation with a former British viceroy of India, Lord Halifax, in the late 1930s, advised the British to shoot Gandhi and his fellow Congress party leaders. Instead, the British jailed them. 'Had the British authorities not behaved like honourable officers and gentlemen, Gandhi's non-violent campaigns would never have been possible', admitted one of the jailed leaders, Minoo Masani.) Moreover, Gandhi saw no obstacle in comparing the mythical battles of the ancient *Mahabharata* with 20th-century technological warfare. Above all, he read history as a morality tale, dominated by eternal spiritual values, rather than as the temporal rise and fall of rulers, merchants and empires.

Throughout the span of Indian civilization, Indians have been inclined to a view of history resembling that of Gandhi. They include Tagore, who wrote some essays on Indian history, and even, in some important respects, Nehru, who wrote significant historical books while he was in and out of various colonial jails, notably *The Discovery of India*, published in 1946. There Nehru approvingly quotes these words about the distant past written by Tagore: 'I love India, not because I cultivate the idolatry of geography, not because I have had the chance to be born in her soil, but because she has saved through tumultuous ages the living words that have issued from the illuminated consciousness of her great ones.' On the whole, over the centuries, Indians have shown a puzzling lack of curiosity about the facts of history, whether ancient or more recent; and a disinclination to record important events in written form. How else to account for the astonishingly outdated and impoverished presentation of history in key Indian museums, and for the dearth of biographies of Indians, even of leading figures in the independence movement, other than Gandhi and Nehru? The chief biography of Ambedkar, for example, was first published many decades ago, in 1954, when its subject was still alive. Where a biography does exist, it often lacks historical context and tends towards the hagiographical.

In the 1970s, Satyajit Ray faced this problem while making his period drama in Urdu based on a story by Prem Chand, *Shatranj ke Khilari* (*The Chess Players*), about the controversial British military annexation of the north Indian state of Oudh (Awadh) in 1856 – a pivotal event in the build-up to the uprising of 1857. 'People just didn't know anything about the history of Lucknow and its nawabs,' explained Ray. Purely to educate his Indian audience, he felt obliged to add a 'documentary' prologue to the film. This prologue encapsulated, in a palatable and entertaining way (using cartoons), the history of Lucknow during the Mughal and British period. For his extremely detailed historical research on the mid-19th century in Oudh, Ray had to rely almost exclusively on contemporaneous British sources, including memoirs and biographies, and on a visit to former imperial archives kept in London, in the absence of more than a handful of Indian sources.

Professional historians of India – whether non-Indian or Indian – are handicapped by a lamentable lack of indigenous records for the period preceding the Muslim chroniclers, that is, before AD 1000. A. L. Basham was vexed by 'the annoying uncertainty of much ancient Indian history' in his highly influential study, *The Wonder That Was India*, first published in 1954. D. D. Kosambi claimed that 'India has virtually no historical records worth the name' in *The Culture and Civilisation of Ancient India*. John Keay, in his *India: A History*, opens with the comment: 'Histories of India often begin with a gripe about the poverty of the available sources.' Romila Thapar, a former student of Basham, repeats his complaint in her *Early India*: 'The chronology of the earlier part of Indian history is notoriously uncertain compared to that of China and the Mediterranean world.' The earliest, really substantial, non-Muslim source comes from Assam: the chronicles of the Ahom conquerors, dating from the early 13th century, who had 'a keen historical sense', notes Edward Gait in his history of Assam. Indeed, India's lack of written history might almost be regarded as a third theme of this book.

There are very early readable records from ancient Mesopotamia (in cuneiform) and from ancient Egypt (in hieroglyphs); they date from the early third millennium BC. For ancient Greece and ancient China, records date from the second half of the second millennium BC, written in Mycenaean Linear B and the Shang character script, respectively. Not so for ancient India. The exquisitely carved seal script of the Indus Valley civilization dates from the second half of the third millennium BC, long before the Shang records; but the script is tantalizingly undeciphered, despite much effort by scholars since it was discovered in the 1920s by British and Indian archaeologists (in what is now Pakistan). Until it is deciphered, the earliest readable materials from the Indian subcontinent date only from the 3rd century BC, that is, the relatively brief stone inscriptions of the great emperor Asoka, who ruled most of the subcontinent; while the earliest archaeological remains – other than those found in the Indus Valley – are not much older than those of Asoka, besides being of no great significance. Indo-European linguistic evidence, however, shows that the origin of Sanskrit is much older than the inscriptions of Asoka written in Magadhi Prakit. Sanskrit may have been spoken and memorized as early as the first centuries of the second millennium BC; but if the sacred language was written down, the records have not survived.

As a direct consequence of this dearth of written evidence, it is impossible to specify the date of composition in Sanskrit of the earliest Hindu scriptures, the *Vedas* of the second millennium BC, or of the later epics, *The Mahabharata* and *The Ramayana*, with an accuracy better than perhaps half a millennium. As for the dates of the earliest known historical figure in India, Siddhartha Gautama, these vary by more than a century, depending upon which source one consults – without any prevailing consensus. There is no argument that the Buddha lived for eighty years, according to the Buddhist scriptures. But according to the Sri Lankan Buddhist tradition, he died in 544 BC (hence the international celebration of the Buddha's 2500th death anniversary in 1956), whereas according to some modern scholars of

Buddhism the date of his death lies around 483 BC, while others favour a date as late as 400 BC (contemporary with the death of Socrates). Part of the chronological problem is that the dating of the Buddha depends on the dating of his admirer Asoka, which is somewhat uncertain.

Pursuing this catalogue of chronological uncertainty, three or four centuries after Asoka another important ruler and patron of Buddhism, Kanishka, is thought by some scholars to have acceded to the throne in AD 78 – year zero of the Indian national (Saka) calendar; however, others place Kanishka's accession as late as 144. The dates of ancient India's greatest writer, the Sanskrit poet and playwright Kalidasa – much admired by the poet and playwright Goethe – are usually given as some time in the late 4th to mid-5th century AD; but we can be certain only that Kalidasa lived some time between the 2nd century BC and AD 634! Another celebrated writer, the Tamil poet and philosopher Thiruvalluvar, lived some time between the 2nd century BC and the 8th century AD. Even the date of completion of India's most famous monument, the Taj Mahal, is not precisely known (not to mention the names of its architects, which were not recorded in the chronicles of the Mughal emperor Shah Jahan): it lies somewhere between 1643 and 1648.

The shortage of early evidence leaves Indian history open to conflicting interpretations, which are sometimes motivated by modern political agendas. Hindu nationalists, such as those of the Bharatiya Janata Party (BJP), who came to power in New Delhi in the late 1990s, not surprisingly dislike the idea that the most prestigious Indian language, Sanskrit, is an Indo-European language deriving from the language of the Aryans; they therefore attempt to maintain that the language of the undeciphered Indus Valley script – which is indubitably indigenous – must be Sanskrit, against the dominant scholarly consensus that the Indus language is likely to be related to the Dravidian languages (such as Tamil) spoken in the subcontinent before the arrival of the Aryans. There is argument, too, about the extent to which the empire of Asoka was Buddhist or Brahmin in its orientation; this feeds into a debate about whether Brahmin intolerance of Buddhism was, or was not, the chief cause of the mysterious evanescence of Buddhism from the land of its birth, during the first millennium AD. This in turn raises the question of the supposed Hindu tolerance of other religions, and the vexed question of Hindu–Muslim relations in India during the second millennium AD, beginning with the raids into India of Mahmud of Ghazni from AD 1000 and culminating in the partition of India in 1947.

At times, as Hindu nationalists claim, there was unquestionably active persecution of Hindus by Muslim invaders and rulers. At other times, though, peaceful cooperation prevailed, along with a remarkable synthesis of Hindu and Muslim cultures, for example in music and painting – most famously under the Mughal emperor Akbar in the second half of the 16th century and in Lucknow in the decades before 1857, where the flamboyant king of Oudh, Wajid Ali Shah, went so far as to dress up as a Hindu god (as shown in *The Chess Players*). Eventually, of course, in the 1940s, the two-nation theory predominated, and the subcontinent was bloodily partitioned into India and Pakistan, leaving India as chiefly Hindu but with a very substantial Muslim minority – in fact virtually the same size today as the entire Muslim population of Pakistan, about 180 million people (exceeded only by the number of Muslims in Indonesia and in Bangladesh).

Historians have been picking over the reasons for the partition of India ever since 1947. The catastrophic loss of status of Indian Muslims with the collapse of the Mughal empire in the mid-18th century, the divide-and-rule policy of the British Raj (now favouring Hindus, now favouring Muslims), the arrogance of the Congress party's high command led by Nehru, and the intransigence of the Muslim League led by Mohammed Ali Jinnah, all played a part. And so, perhaps, did historians themselves. Romila Thapar pins some blame on the *History of British India* of 1818 written by the Scottish historian and philosopher James Mill, who never visited India. This was the first book to periodize Indian history into the Hindu civilization, the Muslim civilization (including the Mughal empire) and the British period. '[Mill's] division of the Indian past . . . has been so deeply embedded in the consciousness of those studying India that it prevails to this day. It is at the root of the ideologies of current religious nationalisms', laments Thapar. 'It has resulted in a distorting of Indian history and has frequently thwarted the search for causes of historical change other than those linked to a superficial assessment of religion'. Thapar herself is more inclined towards secular, economic interpretations of Indian events.

In any nation, historians search for both continuities and discontinuities between the past and the present – whether for intellectual and academic purposes or for emotional and patriotic reasons. Colonialism reinforced this desire, as Indian nationalists sought from history rational explanations for their domination by the British, and also consolation and strength to fight for their freedom from colonialism.

Gandhi drew inspiration from *The Mahabharata*, as we know. Nehru looked to the ancient edicts of Asoka carved on imperial inscriptions all over India, such as: 'All sects deserve reverence for one reason or another. By thus acting a man exalts his own sect and at the same time does service to the sects of other people.' He chose the sculpted lion capital of the Asokan pillar inscription at Sarnath as the symbol of the new government of India in 1947, and the capital's 24-spoked Buddhist wheel, the *dharmachakra*, as the emblem on the Indian flag (replacing the 1930s image of the spinning wheel favoured by Gandhi). A recent president of India, the nuclear missile scientist A. P. J. Abdul Kalam, born and brought up during the independence movement, claimed in 2012: 'Freedom and democracy have all along been an integral part of India's culture', as far back as the local assemblies (known as *sabhas* and *samitis*) in the putative 'village republics' of ancient India. 'Our choice of a democratic political system on achieving Independence was therefore an automatic continuation of the ethos that had always been there in Indian culture', claims Kalam.

But this factually unsubstantiated attitude to the past and present raises problems for Indian historians writing in a less nationalistic age. How influential has the political and religious tolerance of, say, Buddha, Asoka and Akbar really been in the later history of India? Did it survive in a meaningful sense into the 20th century?

One looks in vain for a single reference to these three great historical figures in *The Idea of India* published by Sunil Khilnani in 1997, and finds no significant reference to them in a far lengthier study, *India after Gandhi*, by a second historian of modern India, Ramachandra Guha, published in 2007. In general, argues Khilnani, supported by Guha, the period of colonialism should be seen not as a continuity in Indian history, but as a discontinuity. 'Contrary to India's nationalist myths, enamoured of imme-morial "village republics", pre-colonial history little prepared it for modern democracy', writes Khilnani. 'Democracy was established after a profound historical rupture – the experience, at once humiliating and enabling, of colonialism . . .'.

Amartya Sen, by contrast, in his 2005 collection, *The Argumentative Indian*, promotes both Asoka and Akbar as exemplary figures of Indian tol-erance, hugely influential in their lifetimes and also long after their deaths, even in today's India. Unlike Khilnani and Guha – but quite like Kalam – Sen is determined to locate the beginnings of Indian democracy not in the British colonial period but in ancient India, starting with the Buddhist councils held some time after the death of the Buddha, the largest of which is associated with Asoka. Sen argues: 'Asoka's championing of public discus-sion has had echoes in the later history of India, but none perhaps as strong as the Mughal emperor Akbar's sponsorship and support for dialogues between adherents of different faiths . . . In the deliberative conception of democracy, the role of open discussion, with or without sponsorship by the state, has a clear relevance.'

Sen and Guha have disagreed publicly over the significance of pre-colonial Indian history to a post-colonial nation. Sen argues that a 'historical disjunction' between the two periods 'does not do justice to India's past or present', whereas Guha argues for the existence of just such a disjunction, and elects to begin his history of modern India with the colonial period. Their difference of opinion is somewhat ironic, given that Sen, born in the early 1930s, actually experienced colonialism, whereas Guha, born in the late 1950s, grew up in independent India. One might perhaps have expected Sen to view the colonial period as a historical discontinuity, Guha to see it as a continuity.

Such contradictions are typical not only of colonial and post-colonial India, but also of Indian history taken as a whole, as we shall see in this book. They bring to mind what Satyajit Ray said when asked how he felt about the British heritage in India, which he had so subtly (and ambivalently) portrayed in *The Chess Players* – using a game, *chaturanga*, which was invented in classical India in the 6th century AD, then exported to Persia as *shatranj* and hence to medieval Europe, where it was subsequently modified, made faster, and eventually reimported into colonial India as the modern game of chess. After a long pause for thought, Ray responded: 'It's a very, very complex mixed kind of thing. I think many of us owe a great deal to it. I'm thankful for the fact that at least I'm familiar with both cultures and it gives me a very much stronger footing as a film-maker, but I'm also aware of all the dirty things that were being done. I really don't know how I feel about it.'

ONE The Indus Valley Civilization

THE INDUS VALLEY CIVILIZATION

When the first Hindu nationalist government, led by the Bharatiya Janata Party, came to power around the beginning of the new millennium, it set about rewriting India's history. Revised school textbooks, by biddable historians, were required, essentially to promote the antiquity, dominance and independence from foreign influence of Hinduism.

Indian history was now claimed to have started in the third or fourth millennium BC with the beginnings of Hinduism among people indigenous to the subcontinent – in deliberate contradiction of the scholarly consensus since the 19th century that Aryan 'invaders' of the subcontinent migrating from the northwest in the mid-second millennium BC were the originators of the Indo-Aryan, Vedic religion that gave rise to Hinduism in the first millennium. For the most extreme of Hindu fundamentalists, all so-called Muslim structures in India are really the work of Hindus. Even the Taj Mahal is believed once to have been 'Tejo-Mahalaya', a Shiva temple, by 'many a visitor, who is at pains to put his foreign fellow visitors right about the origin of the building', writes the leading scholar of the history of the Taj, Ebba Koch.

One of the controversial textbook revisions introduced by the National Council of Educational Research and Training at this time was to rename India's earliest urban culture, the Indus Valley civilization, as the 'Indus-Saraswati' civilization. There is some support among reputable archaeologists and scholars for such a change. The ancient Saraswati River apparently dried up in the second millennium and its course no longer exists above ground

– unlike, evidently, the Indus River – but part of the Saraswati's course has been identified by some scientific surveys with an existing river (Ghaggar-Hakra), east of the Indus, which flows intermittently during the monsoon through the desert on both sides of the India-Pakistan border, and is densely lined by ancient sites of the Indus Valley civilization. However, for Hindu nationalists, the Saraswati River is important not so much for its disputed geography as for the fact that it is prominently mythologized in the *Vedas*, the oldest and most sacred of the Hindu scriptures. 'Foremost mother, foremost of rivers, foremost of goddesses, Saraswati. In thee, Saraswati, all generations have their stars', proclaims one of the hymns of the *Rigveda*, the oldest of the *Vedas*. Long after the period of the *Vedas*, Saraswati became the name of the Hindu goddess of knowledge, music, arts and science. Thus, renamed the Indus-Saraswati civilization, the Indus Valley civilization might conceivably be trumpeted as the forerunner of the Vedic civilization, which is the indisputable fountainhead of the Hindu religion and also, according to the nationalists, of ancient Indian mathematics and science. Over the past century and more, some of them have claimed to discern in the *Vedas* calculations of the speed of light, allusions to high-energy physics and even the outlines of advanced technology of our own times, such as aeroplanes.

However, this new theory immediately stumbled against serious historical obstacles. The most obvious characteristics of the archaeological remains of ancient cities and towns in the Indus Valley and surrounding areas, which we shall describe shortly, bear no evident relationship to the pastoral, semi-nomadic society described in the *Vedas*. The language of the Indus Valley civilization, so far as it can be understood from analysis of the undeciphered Indus script, seems to have little in common with Sanskrit, the unquestioned language of the *Vedas*. Moreover, to unbiased eyes, the *Vedas* contain no sophisticated mathematics – unlike certain elements of the Indus Valley civilization – and precious little in the way of scientific knowledge.

In need of bolstering evidence, Hindu nationalist historians appealed to a new book, *The Deciphered Indus Script*, written by two Indians with some linguistic and scientific credentials. The book's authors, N. Jha and N. S. Rajaram, made astounding claims, announced to the Indian press with a fanfare in 1999 and published in 2000. The Indus script was apparently even older than had been thought (the mid-third millennium BC), dating back to the mid-fourth millennium, which would make it the world's oldest readable writing, predating Mesopotamian cuneiform and Egyptian hieroglyphs. It employed some kind of alphabet, two millennia older than the world's earliest-known alphabets from the Middle East. Perhaps most sensationally of all, at least for Indians, its inscriptions could be read in Vedic Sanskrit; one of them was found to mention the Saraswati River, albeit obliquely ('Ila surrounds the blessed land').

Astonishing further support for the Hindu nationalist view seemed to come in the form of an excavation photograph from the 1920s showing a broken Indus seal inscription depicting the hindquarters of an animal, accompanied by four signs. The book's authors claimed that the animal was a horse, as shown in a 'computer enhanced' drawing published by them; and that the signs could be read, in Vedic Sanskrit, as '*arko ha as va*', which they translated as 'Sun indeed like the horse'. Another Indus inscription – the longest inscription so far discovered (as recently as 1990) – they translated as: 'I was a thousand times victorious over avaricious raiders desirous of my wealth of horses!'

But horses were unknown to the Indus Valley civilization, almost all scholars had long maintained, since horses were not depicted among the many animals (including buffaloes) shown on its seals and in its art, and no horse bones had been discovered by excavators – or at least no bones that convinced zooarchaeologists specializing in horse identification. Horses are generally thought to have arrived in northwestern India only with the horse-drawn chariots of the Aryans; certainly, in later history, Indian armies imported their horses from outside India. Horses are, however, abundantly mentioned in the *Vedas*. If, after all, horses did feature in the Indus inscriptions, was this not important evidence that the creators of the inscriptions and of the *Vedas* were one and the same – indigenous – people?

The arguments in *The Deciphered Indus Script* would probably have been ignored by most people, as had happened with literally dozens of failed Indus script decipherments announced since the 1920s by both Indian and non-Indian scholars, including eminent figures in their field like the Egyptologist Flinders Petrie. But on this occasion, because of their potentially explosive educational and political implications, the book attracted widespread attention, both in India and internationally.

Within months, the authors' claims of a successful decipherment were easily demonstrated to be nonsense in articles for national news magazines in India written by scholars, notably Iravatham Mahadevan, the leading Indian expert on the Indus script, Asko Parpola, the leading non-Indian expert, and Michael Witzel, a professor of Sanskrit at Harvard University, with his collaborator Steve Farmer. Mahadevan termed the so-called decipherment 'completely invalid . . . a non-starter'. Witzel and Farmer's chief article was entitled 'Horseplay in Harappa', in reference to Harappa, the best-known city of the Indus Valley civilization. They demonstrated beyond question, even for non-specialists, that the supposed Indus alphabet was so absurdly flexible that it could be manipulated to produce almost any translation that the authors might desire. Furthermore, the supposed Indus Valley horse – after comparison of the broken seal photograph with photographs of various similar-looking, but more complete, Indus seals – was shown to be a 'unicorn' bull of a type commonly depicted in the inscriptions. The horse image had to be a hoax created by one of the book's authors, an Indian-born, US-trained engineer with experience of computer drawing (and a taste for Hindu nationalist propaganda), as he more or less admitted under questioning by Indian journalists.

The entire, farcical, episode might seem too trivial to dwell on here. Yet, as Witzel and Farmer presciently concluded in 2000: 'If reactionary trends in Indian history find further political support, we risk seeing violent repeats in the coming decades of the fascist extremes of the past.' Despite theirs and other scholars' exposure of this particular book's intellectual bankruptcy, the new Indian school textbooks introduced in 2002 referred to 'terracotta figurines' of horses in the 'Indus-Saraswati civilization', and continued to do so until the fall of the BJP-led government in 2004, when the textbooks were withdrawn by the incoming Congress-led government. More important, the idea that the language of the Indus Valley civilization is Sanskrit or Indo-Aryan, and of local origin, continues to enjoy wide support in India, to the consternation of most scholars trained in Indo-European linguistics.

Unfortunately, the Indus Valley civilization has always suffered – and probably always will suffer – from a paucity of evidence and an excess of speculative interpretation, compared with the well-endowed and well-documented ancient civilizations of Mesopotamia, Egypt and China. It was lost to the world even at the time of Alexander the Great. When Alexander's emissary, Aristoboulus, visited the area in 326 BC, he found 'an abandoned country, with more than a thousand towns and villages deserted after the Indus had changed its course'. It was not mentioned again in historical records for over two thousand years. In the early 1920s, an Indian archaeologist, R. D. Banerji, out searching for non-existent victory pillars put up by Alexander on his retreat from India, stumbled across the true significance of the ruin mound at Mohenjo-daro ('mound of the dead'), which is now in Sindh province of Pakistan. His discovery, and a similar discovery 350 miles away at Harappa (also now in Pakistan), would double the recorded age of Indian civilization from 250 BC (the inscriptions of Asoka) back to about 2600 BC.

Excavation proved to be a challenge from the very beginning; indeed, most of the sites of the Indus Valley civilization are unexcavated today for lack of resources. Even at Mohenjo-daro and Harappa, only the central area has been excavated, leaving extensive areas of these cities unknown. At Mohenjo-daro, later structures, including a ruined Buddhist stupa dating from the centuries after Alexander, stood on top of the so-called 'citadel' (though it lacks fortifications), while the rest of the city was largely buried by deep alluvial deposits laid down by the floods of the Indus River. At Harappa, a Muslim cemetery and a modern town covered much of the ancient city, which had been quarried for its ancient bricks by the town's inhabitants and, much more destructively, by 19th-century railway contractors in need of vast quantities of brick rubble.

Notwithstanding, a team under Sir John Marshall, director general of the Archaeological Survey of India, immediately began excavating at both sites in the early 1920s. 'Not often has it been given to archaeologists, as it was given to [Heinrich] Schliemann at Tiryns and Mycenae, or to [Aurel] Stein in the deserts of Turkestan, to light upon the remains of a long-forgotten civilization,' Marshall wrote excitedly in 1924 in the *Illustrated London News*. 'It looks, however, at this moment, as if we are on the threshold of such a discovery in the plains of the Indus.' Since then, over almost a century of study, archaeologists from many countries have identified about a thousand settlements belonging to the Indus Valley civilization in Pakistan and northwest India, covering an area of 300,000 square miles (approximately a quarter the size of Europe), with a population of one million people. This was the most extensive urban culture of its time, larger than either the ancient Mesopotamian or Egyptian empires of the third millennium BC.

Most of the settlements were villages, but five were major cities. Harappa and Mohenjo-daro were comparable with cities like Ur in Mesopotamia and Memphis in Egypt in the mature period of the Indus civilization, that is, between about 2600 and 1900 BC according to radiocarbon dating. (Its beginnings are naturally older; indeed there is impressive evidence of village habitation in northwest India dating as far back as 7000 BC at Mehrgarh.)

The Indus Valley cities cannot boast grand pyramids, palaces, temples, statues and graves, or hordes of gold. But their society, fed by the waters of the Indus, appears to have been remarkably prosperous, storing food in granaries filled by two growing seasons in agriculture: in the winter, they grew barley, wheat, oats, lentils, beans, mustard, jujube and linen; in the summer during the monsoon, millets, cotton, sesamum, melons, jute, hemp, grapes and dates. The civilization certainly traded with Gujarat, northern Maharashtra, Afghanistan, the Persian Gulf and Mesopotamia, where Indus jewelry, weights, seals and other objects have been excavated; and the trade with Mesopotamia seems to have been chiefly in favour of the Indus Valley (which was apparently known as Meluhha in cuneiform records), since very few objects from Mesopotamia have been found in the Indus Valley. Its cities' well-planned streets, bathrooms and advanced drainage – including what is termed the Great Bath at Mohenjo-daro – put to shame all but the town planning of the 20th century AD, as proudly noted by Jawaharlal Nehru in his *Discovery of India* after he had twice visited Mohenjo-daro in the 1930s. Some of its ornaments, such as the necklaces of long, finely drilled, biconical carnelian beads found as far afield as the royal cemetery of Ur, rival the treasures of the Egyptian pharaohs for loveliness and technical sophistication. Experiments show that each bead could have taken up to two weeks to produce; a necklace might have required a year. Its remarkable system of standardized weights – consisting of stone cubes and truncated spheres – based on a binary system for small quantities and a decimal system for large quantities, was unique in the ancient world; the system provided the weight standards for the earliest Indian coins, issued in the 7th century BC; and it is, amazingly, still used in traditional markets in Pakistan and India. The inspiration seems to have been the weight of a seed of a particular creeper, equivalent to 1/128th part of the basic Indus weight unit: known as the *ratti*, this is still used by Indian jewellers. In addition, the Indus seals are exquisitely carved miniature works of art: 'little masterpieces of controlled realism, with a monumental strength in one sense out of all proportion to their size and in another entirely related to it', enthused the Indus excavator Mortimer Wheeler. And of course the unde-ciphered Indus script has long been one of the most tantalizing mysteries of the ancient world. Numerous problems of the Indus civilization might be solved at a stroke, if only its script could be read, as can Babylonian cuneiform and Egyptian hieroglyphs.

Indus Valley archaeology has come a long way since the 1920s. Yet, it has so many unanswered fundamental questions that the Indus Valley civilization still risks being regarded as the dowdy poor cousin of ancient Mesopotamia, Egypt and China, and as a receptacle for speculative theories, some of them motivated by current Indian political agendas, as discussed above.

What type of authority held together such an evidently organized, uniform and far-flung society, which apparently managed without palaces, royal graves and rulers, temples, icons and priests, fortifications, military weapons and warriors? No unambiguous evidence for any of the above has been found in excavations – unlike, of course, in ancient Mesopotamia, Egypt and China. We simply do not know the answer to this question, although most scholars assume that the civilization was a federation with some kind of unifying central administration, rather than consisting of independent 'village republics' with a shared culture.

The puzzling absence of evidence for luxurious palaces and powerful rulers, combined with the overwhelming evidence for diverse specialization in sophisticated crafts, and the apparent emphasis on (ritual?) bathing, has led some scholars to attribute the origin of the Hindu caste system to the Indus Valley civilization. However, the Indian concept of caste involves more than simply social class, craft and career specialization and an aristocracy of relatively austere priests; it depends on an underlying philosophy of a cosmic order, expressed in the concept *rita* in the *Rigveda*, where the first indisputable hint of the concept of caste appears (as we shall see), which foreshadows the later, better-known concept of *dharma*, the eternal law of the cosmos. Since the Indus inscriptions cannot be read, nothing definite can be said about Indus philosophy, and whether it had a comparable concept.

Other scholars wonder if the apparent absence of war marks the beginning of the Indian tradition of pacifism and non-violence, inaugurated by the Buddha and epitomized in modern times by Gandhi (who was born in the region covered by the Indus Valley civilization). Here, the archaeological evidence is more decisive, given the lack of evidence for the defensive fortifications, military weapons and mutilated corpses found in other ancient civilizations. Wheeler's powerful conviction in the 1940s that he had discovered evidence at Mohenjo-daro of a massacre of defenders – perhaps at the hands of attacking Aryans – has now been conclusively disproved by careful analysis of the find spots and conditions of the skeletons; they were not killed in war but may have been victims of a disease, such as malaria. That said, it seems inherently improbable that any civilization could sustain itself for more than half a millennium without the need for coercion and fighting. Certainly, the violent struggles of subsequent Indian history, including that of the *Vedas* and the early Buddhist period, provide no warrant whatsoever for believing that non-violence is intrinsic to India.

As for the enigmatic Indus religion, there are undoubtedly images on the seals of humanlike figures and animals with clear echoes in later Hinduism. One of these images, showing a 'yogic' figure with folded legs wearing a horned headdress surrounded by a tiger, an elephant, a water buffalo and a rhinoceros, was influentially dubbed 'proto-Shiva' by its discoverer Marshall. 'In the religion of the Indus people there is much, of course, that might be paralleled in other countries', Marshall wrote. 'But taken as a whole, their religion is so characteristically Indian as hardly to be distinguished from still living Hinduism.' Nehru, though not personally attracted to religion, eagerly agreed with Marshall. While admitting 'many gaps and periods about which we know little', Nehru claimed to see 'an underlying sense of continuity . . . It is surprising how much there is in Mohenjo-daro and Harappa which reminds one of persisting traditions and habits – popular ritual, craftsmanship, even some fashions in dress.' An interesting example is the *swastika* symbol, first seen on Indus Valley objects, and still used as a good luck symbol on the walls of Indian homes.

Whether Marshall was right or not about the Indus religion remains a matter of interpretation and dispute. Consider the discovery at many Indus sites of the sacrificial hearths known as fire altars, which were at first doubted but are now accepted. At Kalibangan, these consist of clay-lined pits containing ash, charcoal, the remains of a clay stele and terracotta cakes; at Lothal, a terracotta ladle with smoke-marks was found near such a hearth. Such discoveries recall the Hindu ritual of libation of the five products of the cow (milk, sour milk, melted butter, urine and dung) in the presence of a fire as offerings to a clay lingam in the worship of Shiva. A parallel with the Vedic fire ritual is striking, too. In the *Vedas*, the heated milk is considered to be the sun or the sun's seed poured into the womb. 'Surya (the sun) and Agni (the fire) were in the same receptacle [*yoni*, meaning 'womb']. Thereupon Surya rose upwards. He lost his seed. Agni received it . . . he transferred it to the cow. It (became) this milk.' But while there can be no doubt that such sacrifice at fire altars was integral to the Vedic religion, there is no proof that the excavated Indus Valley hearths are fire altars in the Vedic sense. 'The similarities have been overemphasized and the shared elements of fire and animal sacrifice are too common, being found in many religions, to be a culturally diagnostic link', notes Jane McIntosh in her account of the Indus Valley civilization, *A Peaceful Realm*. Religion is notoriously tricky to reconstruct with confidence without scriptures – which are plentiful for the Vedic religion, but of course non-existent (or anyway indecipherable) for the Indus religion.

The crux of the problem in penetrating the Indus Valley civilization remains its undeciphered script. So it is worth returning to the subject in slightly more detail, in order to grasp what is understood about the script. Unlike ancient Egyptian and Mayan hieroglyphs, Mesopotamian cuneiform, Shang (Chinese) characters and Mycenaean Linear B – all of which can now be read with varying degrees of completeness – the Indus script appears not on walls, tombs, statues, stelae, clay tablets, papyri and codices, but rather on seal stones, pottery, copper tablets, bronze implements and ivory and bone rods, found scattered in the buildings and streets of Harappa, Mohenjo-daro and other urban settlements. No doubt it was written, too, on perishable materials, such as the bark and palm fronds traditionally used for writing in India. The seal stones are the most numerous of the inscriptions and are justly celebrated for their exquisiteness and unique style of carving (achieved using a burin, probably a flint tool with an angled blade, comparable with a modern scalpel). Once seen, they are never forgotten.

About 3,700 inscribed objects are known, 60 per cent of them on seals, but some 40 per cent of these are duplicate inscriptions, so the useful total for the decipherer is not as large as it seems. More were found in the 1990s, but it is not an abundant corpus, especially as the inscriptions are brief: the average has fewer than four signs in a line and five in a text, the longest only twenty-six signs divided along the three sides of a terracotta prism. Many of the seals carry a boss on the back with a hole drilled in it, suitable for a string. Very likely, they were worn around the neck of a person, whose signature was spelt out on the seal. In addition to the signs, many seal stones are engraved with an often-detailed intaglio of animals. These are generally recognizable – buffaloes, elephants, rhinoceroses, tigers and zebus, for instance, though no horses, as already noted, and curiously no cobras, monkeys or peacocks – but some are fantastic or chimerical, including a one-horned bull, which the early excavators promptly dubbed a 'unicorn' (a creature legendarily originating in India). Unidentified anthropomorphic figures, sometimes seated in yogic postures, also feature and may be gods and goddesses. Many scholars, beginning with Marshall, have suggested that some of these figures are precursors of the Hindu deities, as mentioned earlier.

Most decipherments of ancient scripts have proved feasible because the language of the script proved to be related to a known language: for instance, the language of the Egyptian hieroglyphs was related to the Coptic language, that of Babylonian cuneiform to Semitic languages, that of Mycenaean Linear B to archaic Greek, that of the Mayan glyphs to modern

Mayan languages and that of the Shang characters to modern Chinese. But even before the related language has been detected, it is always possible to make some progress in decipherment by internal analysis of inscriptions, without taking a stab at guessing the underlying language.

In the case of the Indus script, by internal analysis scholars have settled the direction of writing and reading (overwhelmingly, right to left); they have established an approximate number of signs (425, plus or minus 25) and a sign list on which there is considerable agreement; they have agreed on some of the numerals (one to seven appear to be written with one to seven short strokes, suggesting a base-eight system, although larger numbers seem to use a decimal system); and they have shown – by comparing repeated sequences of signs in different inscriptions – that inscriptions containing these sequences are likely to be segmentable into what may be discrete words. Beyond this, though, there are yawning disagreements between the most distinguished of scholars, for example on how to interpret the iconic nature of many signs. The most frequent sign of all is ᴜ. To the Finnish scholar Asko Parpola, this shows the head of a horned cow seen from the front; to the American Walter Fairservis, a pot with handles; and to the Russian Yuri Knorozov (the key player in the recent Mayan decipherment), a pipal tree. Each has his reasons. As Parpola was obliged to admit in his massively erudite survey of attempts to decipher the Indus script: 'Many of the signs . . . are so simplified and schematic that it is very difficult to understand their pictorial meaning unambiguously and objectively.'

Other informed speculations about the script have depended on the assumption that the Indus language is Dravidian, so we shall now very briefly review the evidence concerning the complex issue of what the language may be. In doing so, we must discount the possibility that the language has completely died out, if we are to make any progress – an assumption for which there is some rationale, given the exceptional linguistic continuities of Indian civilization as a whole. We shall also discard a second possibility, that the Indus language is related to the Munda languages of central and (mainly) eastern India, a part of the Austro-Asiatic family that covers most of the languages of Southeast Asia, because this theory receives little support from linguistic evidence and no support from archaeology. That leaves us with the Indo-Aryan hypothesis, which favours the Sanskrit language, and the Dravidian hypothesis, which favours the languages of south India, such as Tamil.

Archaeologically, the evidence is adverse to the Indo-Aryan/Sanskrit connection, as already discussed. However, archaeology provides no definite support for the Dravidian connection either, although the chance discovery in 2006 in a pit in Tamil Nadu of a Neolithic stone celt apparently bearing four signs of the Indus script is certainly intriguing. Geographically, Sanskrit has the edge over Dravidian, since Sanskrit was the classical language of north India (like Latin in Europe), while today's Dravidian speakers belong almost exclusively to south India, far away from the Indus Valley region. That said, an important and fascinating caveat arises. Pockets of Dravidian languages exist in north India, such as Kurukh and Malto, and one of these languages, Brahui, spoken by around 300,000 nomadic people in Baluchistan (western Pakistan), is significantly close to the Indus Valley. These Dravidian speakers are presumably remnants of a Dravidian culture once widespread in the Indian subcontinent before it was submerged in the north by encroaching Indo-Aryans during the second millennium BC – pools left by the receding tide, so to speak – although it is conceivable that modern Brahui speakers could be descended from people who migrated to their present locations from the south. There is disagreement about this, but in general it seems improbable that a people would migrate from the relatively clement plains of India into the rugged and hostile mountains of Baluchistan. 'If the Brahuis were not the indigenous inhabitants of Baluchistan, who were?' asks Parpola, reasonably enough. 'Certainly not the Baluch, who came from northern Iran in the 10th century AD or later.'

The Dravidian hypothesis is therefore favoured over the Indo-Aryan by a majority of scholars, though in no sense proven. On the working assumption that it is correct, they try to look for sensible links between the meanings of words in early Dravidian languages such as Old Tamil, and the iconic and iconographic signs and images on the Indus seals and other inscribed Indus Valley objects, taking help from cultural evidence about Dravidian civilization and its religious beliefs and archaeological evidence about the Indus Valley civilization.

The simplest example – and still the most intuitively convincing one – was first suggested by the Jesuit Father Henry Heras (who lived in India) in the 1950s. The word for fish in almost all Dravidian languages is 'mīn'. In many Dravidian languages 'mīn' also means 'star'. Could the very frequent 'fish' sign on the Indus seals have been pronounced *mīn* but have had the dual meaning 'fish' and 'star', which, as Parpola demonstrates, is an emblem of divinity and can thus stand for 'god'? The 'fish' sign could then be part of a theophoric name – a very common occurrence in Indian culture, where people are often named after gods and goddesses, for instance, Rama, Krishna, Ganesh, Indira, Lakshmi and Arundhati.

One could object to this: why is the star not represented pictorially too, like the fish? We are used to representing a star with a few short lines crossing at a point ('twinkling', so to speak), but this is just our particular convention, which happens to distinguish all other stars from our sun, which we generally represent with a small circle with 'rays' sticking out of it. It is quite conceivable that the Indus Valley writers could have chosen a different, and more subtle, approach based on a homophony in their language between the Indus words for fish and for star that English does not possess. (An English parallel might be 'son' and 'sun'.) As Robert Caldwell, the bishop of south India who published the first grammar of the Dravidian language family in 1856, beautifully observed: 'Who that has seen the phosphorescence flashing from every movement of the fish in tropical seas or lagoons at night, can doubt the appropriateness of denoting the fish that dart and sparkle through the waters, as well as the stars that sparkle in the midnight sky, by one and the same word – viz., a word signifying that which glows or sparkles?' On certain Indus Valley pottery, drawings of fishes and stars (pictured as small circles with 'rays' sticking out) appear as a closely integrated artistic motif, which appears to support the idea of the drawings' linguistic equivalence.

Several scholars have extended this approach to other Indus inscriptions with ingenuity based on their knowledge of Dravidian languages and Indian culture, most notably Parpola. But it can at best be highly speculative, in the absence of any proof that the Indus language is Dravidian, and at worst it can fall into absurdity, as happened with the fanatical espousal of the Sanskrit hypothesis in *The Deciphered Indus Script* discussed earlier. As Parpola himself frankly states in his *Deciphering the Indus Script*: 'It looks most unlikely that the Indus script will ever be deciphered fully, unless radically different source material becomes available' – such as a large haul of substantial inscriptions from some newly unexcavated Indus sites, or perhaps the Holy Grail of decipherment: a bilingual 'Rosetta Stone', perhaps written in both the Indus script and Mesopotamian cuneiform (given the trading links between the Indus Valley and Mesopotamia). 'That, however, must not deter us from trying', says Parpola.

In all this uncertainty, one aspect of the script, so far unmentioned, is certain. Once the Indus script ceased to be used in the early part of the second millennium BC, with the decline of the Indus Valley cities, it was never revived. Its signs bear no resemblance at all to the next writing that appeared in India, after a vast gap of a millennium and a half, that is, the Brahmi and Kharosthi alphabetic scripts used to write the inscriptions of Asoka in the 3rd century BC. At least in respect of its script, there is a decided discontinuity between the Indus Valley civilization and later Indian culture.

The reasons for the disappearance of the civilization after 1900–1800 BC are, however, obscure. Among its early excavators, the idea of an invasion by the Aryans was favoured – mainly on the evidence of the *Rigveda*, which vividly describes the destruction of the ninety-nine forts of the dark-skinned

Dasas by Indra, the god of war. But there is no archaeological evidence to identify such literary forts with the excavated 'citadels' of Indus Valley cities, nor the literary Dasas with the people of the Indus Valley civilization. More likely is an environmental explanation. A possible human-made hazard was deforestation caused by over-grazing with cattle or the burning of wood in brick-making and copper-smelting. Natural hazards could include changes in river systems brought about by tectonic activity in the Himalayas. This could have caused the drying up of the Saraswati River, and, perhaps, prolonged flooding of the Indus River and salination of the fields used for crops, as has happened in Pakistan with disastrous impact in modern times. If so, not only agriculture but also the navigability of the Indus, and hence river-borne trade – for example, with Mesopotamia – would have declined; moreover, water-borne diseases, such as malaria and cholera, would have spread. Even a major earthquake cannot be ruled out, given the record of earthquakes in the region in modern times, as recently as 2001 in the case of a highly destructive shock in Gujarat. But it has to be admitted that there is no compelling evidence for any of these environmental explanations. Most probably, the decline of the Indus Valley civilization was gradual and the result of a combination of factors, including changes in hydrology, floods, diseases and an increasing rejection of central authority, perhaps due to migrations of foreigners from the northwest.

TWO

Vedas, Aryans and the Origins of Hinduism

VEDAS, ARYANS AND THE
ORIGINS OF HINDUISM

Unlike the physical legacy of the Indus Valley civilization, the oral literature memorized and compiled in the *Vedas* and their associated later scriptures during the second and first millennium BC forms part of everyday life for modern Hindus, whether in its original form or reinterpreted by the many subsequent reform movements in Hinduism. No Hindu marriage ceremony would be complete without the incantation of Sanskrit verses from the *Rigveda*, accompanied by the performance of Vedic rituals in the presence of a sacred fire. Ayurveda, the still-popular traditional system of Indian medicine, basing itself on ideas of balance in the bodily system – as in the ancient Greek medical concept of the balance of the four humours – and emphasizing diet, herbal treatment and yogic breathing, is derived from verses in the first and the last of the *Vedas*, the *Rigveda* and the *Atharvaveda*. The origins of the Indian caste system, which divided Hindu society into four basic castes (from the Portuguese word for 'race, lineage or breed'), are first mentioned in a famous verse of the *Rigveda*. This describes the Primeval Man at the Creation and how his body was dismembered into the four *varnas* (Sanskrit for 'colours'). From his mouth came the priest, from his arms the warrior, from his thighs the trader and from his feet the servant. In Hindu society, the priests belonged of course to the Brahmin *varna*, the warriors to the Kshatriya *varna*, the traders, cultivators and herders to the Vaishya, and the servants and serfs to the Shudra. Even anti-Brahmin feeling – a perennial theme in Indian history – occurs in certain verses of the Vedic literature that satirize unthinking and gluttonous Brahmins. In any controversy about Hindu values, the authority – or otherwise – of the *Vedas* is likely to be invoked, today almost as much as in the past.

During the early 19th century, for instance, Hindu society in British-ruled Bengal was split over the longstanding and increasingly common custom of *sati* (suttee), in which widows immolated themselves by climbing onto the funeral pyres of their deceased husbands, sometimes voluntarily but often through coercion. Did *sati* have religious sanction, or was it simply a murderous solution welcomed by unscrupulous relatives faced with the problem of an unwanted woman?

Orthodox Bengali Hindus claimed that a certain verse in the burial hymns of the *Rigveda* supported *sati*. This states: 'Let these women, whose husbands are worthy and are living, enter the house with ghee (applied) as collyrium (to their eyes). Let these wives first step into the pyre, tearless, without any affliction and well adorned.' Although this verse nowhere mentions widowhood, it does mention a funeral pyre. Yet, the very next verse of the *Rigveda*, which unambiguously mentions widows, explicitly states that the widow should *not* forfeit her own life with the death of her husband. 'Rise, come unto the world of life, O woman – come, he is lifeless by whose side thou liest. Wifehood with this thy husband was thy portion, who took thy hand and wooed thee as a lover.'

The leading Bengali social reformer of the period, Rammohun Roy, despite being himself a Brahmin, decided to overlook the first of these verses in the *Rigveda*, and appeal instead to somewhat later commentaries on the *Vedas*, the philosophical and esoteric *Upanishads*, as well as to the religious prohibition of suicide and to rational and moral arguments, so that he could support a government move in Calcutta to eradicate widow-burning in Bengal. The abolition of *sati* became law in 1829, although the governor-general, Lord Bentinck, remained convinced that 'the conventional belief of every order of Hindoos, with few exceptions, regards it as sacred.' Sure enough, soon after the legislation was passed, some prominent orthodox Bengalis in Calcutta founded an institution called the Dharma Sabha for the purpose of repealing the act; but in 1832, their petition to the government in London not to interfere with this Hindu custom was dismissed, partly as a result of the arguments of Roy. However, cases of *sati* continued to be reported long after its official abolition.

Later in the 19th century, it became clear to scholars that the confusion about the meaning of the *Rigveda* on such a vital issue had arisen because one consonant of a Sanskrit word, *yomiagne*, in the first verse above, meaning 'fire' (or 'pyre', in this burial context), had been changed from the original word, *yomiagre*, meaning 'house'. Therefore, the second sentence of the verse should properly read as follows: 'Let these wives first step into the house, tearless, without any affliction and well adorned.' Probably, the alteration was a deliberate, mischievous interpolation by those who supported *sati*; but it might have been a scribal error in successive copyings of the manuscript. Yet, sad to report, the claim of Rigvedic support for *sati* has refused to die, even in the 21st century. In 2002, a widow committed *sati*, and two others attempted to do so, in the state of Madhya Pradesh. A senior Indian diplomat felt stirred to write a newspaper article, headlined 'The Rigveda: widows don't have to burn', explaining the true scriptural position, and ended with this appeal to fellow Hindus: 'If greedy people incite a widow to commit suicide on the pyre of her husband, let us not say or believe that widow burning is sanctified by the *Rigveda* or by Hinduism.'

The confusion created by these two verses hints at intractable difficulties and obscurities in the way of translating the *Rigveda* and other very early Indian scriptures, which translators have complained about since the time of the Sanskrit scholar and comparative philologist Friedrich Max Müller and his pioneering series, Sacred Books of the East, published in English in the late 19th century. In 1938, Rabindranath Tagore, when asked to advise on an ongoing British translation of the *Upanishads*, which he had been reading in Sanskrit since boyhood, remarked to its British publisher: '*Upanishads* in some of their parts are incomprehensible owing to the symbolic language used which has utterly lost its significance. These portions should have been avoided, for grammar and lexicon are no proper guide to them and there are no means whatever today for realizing their spirit.' The leading present-day Vedic translator, Wendy Doniger, confesses: 'Like the Englishman who announced that he preferred English to all other languages because it was the only language in which one said the words in the order that one thought of them, one feels that the *Rigveda* poets are not saying the words in the order that *they* thought of them, let alone the order that we would think of them.' The fact that the two Rigvedic verses bearing on the issue of *sati* are actually in sequence – and so should presumably enjoy a logical connection – is actually of little assistance in understanding their meaning, explains Doniger. 'Perhaps the single factor that tends to interfere most with the poetry throughout the *Rigveda* is the fragmentary quality of the work. Not only is each hymn a separate statement (though some work well together), but each verse stands on its own and often bears no obvious relationship with the verses immediately preceding and following it', she writes. 'This discontinuity – which is, ironically, the one continuous thread in the *Rigveda*, the one universal semantic feature – tends to produce a kind of poetry that can be overpowering in the intensity of the separate forces that it juxtaposes but disconcerting to anyone looking for a sustained mood.'

The opacity inherent in the *Vedas* for modern readers leaves them open to widely differing interpretations. Earlier, we contrasted the agricultural and urban society of the Indus Valley civilization, and its plethora of specialized crafts and long-distance trade, with the pastoral, semi-nomadic society that most scholars have perceived in the *Vedas*. But for Hindu nationalists, keen to stress the continuities between the archaeological evidence of the Indus Valley civilization and the literary evidence of the Vedic culture, this contrast is simply false in the light of the available evidence. Thus S. P. Gupta, the archaeologist who proposed the name Indus-Saraswati civilization for the Indus Valley civilization, claims that the Vedic culture, like the Indus-Saraswati civilization, had 'many centres, many craft specializations, many mining activities, many trade routes, and many talents for management of long-distance trade', and that 'the Vedic people were also metallurgists', though Gupta wisely stops short of claiming that the people were also literate, since there is not even a glimmer of a notion of writing in the *Vedas*, despite the many contexts where a reference to script might be expected to occur. The reason why this congruence between the Vedic and Indus bodies of evidence is not more widely accepted is because of scholarly prejudice against it, Gupta alleges. Almost all translators of the *Vedas*, from Max Müller to Doniger, have chosen to emphasize only cattle-keeping as the mode of economic life described in the *Vedas* and to 'dishonestly suppress', says Gupta, the references that prove Vedic awareness of other, non-pastoral, economic activities.

There may be something to Gupta's view – but not very much, if we consider the basic content matter of the *Vedas* and leave aside the nuances of translating particular phrases. In Doniger's detailed index and glossary for her (admittedly selective) edition of the *Rigveda*, there are very occasional references to villages, but none at all to towns and cities; there are references to crafts such as weaving and leather work, but none to brick and jewelry making; there are very occasional references to iron, but none to metallurgy or mining; and there are occasional references to journeys and even to boats and ships (though the ships are probably metaphorical), but none at all to merchants and trade, whether long-distance or not – not to mention no references to complex weights and measures, such as those found in the Indus Valley civilization. Beyond reasonable dispute, the overwhelming majority of the *Rigveda*'s verses concern sacrifices, rituals and gods, generally named, with many references to nature and natural phenomena, creation, women, animals (especially cows and horses), pastoral life, chariots, war and death.

This is not to say that the people of the Indus Valley civilization were entirely unlike those of the Vedic period. For example, the Indus Valley people gambled. Numerous of their clay gaming boards and dice made of simple split reeds, cowrie shells, clay and stone cubes, and finely carved ivory rods with circles incised on each face, have been excavated. And so did the Vedic people, as described in the following verses, seven and eight, of the *Rigveda*'s powerful 'Gambler's Lament' (in Doniger's translation):

> The dice goad like hooks and prick like whips; they enslave, deceive and torment. They give presents as children do, striking back at the winners. They are coated with honey – an irresistible power over the gambler./ Their army, three bands of fifty, plays by rules as immutable as those of the god Savitri [the god of the rising and setting sun]. They do not bow even to the wrath of those whose power is terrifying; the king himself bows down before them.

In addition, the Vedic people probably lived in small settlements, practised some degree of agriculture (ploughs are occasionally referred to), employed carpenters and metal workers to make and repair their wheeled chariots, fashioned precious adornments for their women and supported traders who made journeys from village to village. But these things and activities were not sufficiently extensive or permanent to leave any remains behind today, or at least nothing that archaeologists have discovered – except for the Vedic peoples' oral literature. Whatever Hindu nationalists may wish, no amount of special pleading can marry up the society described in the *Vedas* with the Indus Valley archaeological remains.

There are 1,028 hymns in the *Rigveda*, the oldest of the *Vedas*, arranged in ten sections. Most of the *Samaveda* consists of transposed parts of the *Rigveda*. The *Yajurveda* deals with the correct way for priests to perform the sacrifices required by the gods. The tone of the *Atharvaveda* is different from the preceding three; it consists mainly of magical spells and incantations, including medical spells. Within the four *Vedas*, scholars have distinguished strata: subsections of the whole apparently drawn from different periods and various sources in Vedic society (which helps to explain the fragmentary quality that bedevils translation).

The principal Vedic gods are beings known as *devas*, the 'shining ones', and not surprisingly they are associated mostly with the sky and the heavens, rather than with the ground, the soil and the mysteries of fertility. The union of the Vedic Sky Father, Dyaus Pitar (compare Greek Zeus Pater, Latin Jupiter), with Mother Earth provides the earliest creation myth in the *Rigveda*. But we do not hear much about Dyaus, whose place is taken by Varuna, guardian of the sacred law and cosmic order (*rita*). Varuna, with his thousand eyes ever watchful for wrongdoing, is one of the Vedic gods who always behaves ethically. But then Varuna, in his turn, gives way to Prajapati, the Lord of Creatures, who, in the form of the Primeval Man, is dismembered to form the phenomenal world, including the four castes. Other gods include Mitra, the god of integrity and friendship, who is closely linked with Varuna; Surya, the sun god; Agni, the god of fire, who consumes sacrificial offerings and thereby conveys them from men to the gods; Soma, who is both a god and an elixir of immortality, made from the juice pressed from a hallucinogenic plant (perhaps a mushroom); and in the afterlife, Yama, the god of death, who presides over the spirits of the dead. There are also important goddesses, such as the goddesses of Earth, the dawn (Ushas) and speech (Vac). Most important of all, however, is the warrior Indra, god of war and god of weather, with many of the characteristics of Zeus and Thor, as shown in his exploits. Indra kills the demon Vritra by wielding his thunderbolt, and thereby releases the waters of life. He rescues the sun from another demon (possibly a reference to a solar eclipse) with the help of the high priest. He destroys the walled fortresses of the enemy known as the Dasas. He is borne by an eagle to heaven and returns with Soma for men and gods. And he regularly overdoes the drinking of Soma in noisy wassails.

Many of the gods' names first seen in the *Rigveda* continue in later Hinduism, for example Varuna, Surya, Agni, Yama and Indra, though with varying degrees of importance attached to them compared to their Vedic originals. But there is little sign in the Vedic pantheon of the two greatest gods of 'classical' Hinduism: Shiva and Vishnu. The Vedic storm god, Rudra, 'in whom are later incorporated other ideas in the Hindu

conception of Shiva, is a turbulent god more to be propitiated than peti-
tioned,' notes the Indo-Aryan specialist Thomas Trautmann, while Vishnu
in Vedic literature is 'a dwarf who with three giant strides wins the earth, air
and sky for the gods and consigns the demons to the nether world.' Indeed,
few of the Vedic deities became the major gods and goddesses of Hinduism,
and only one of the major deities, Surya, kept a central position in later
Hindu art as a dynastic deity. Objectively viewed, there is no great connection between the Vedic gods and the gods of modern Hinduism, despite the
high regard for the *Vedas* among current Hindus.

This evolution of the gods between Vedic times and the appearance
of classical Hinduism in the first millennium AD raises the question of the
date of composition of the *Vedas*. Max Müller, working on his translation
of the *Rigveda* in the mid-19th century, was the first scholar to provide
an estimate. He suggested that the search should begin with the date of
the Buddha in the 6th century BC, and then reckon back from this, on
the assumption that Buddhism – which regards certain doctrines first put
forward in the *Upanishads* as axiomatic – emerged from the full development of successive strata of Vedic texts. These texts begin with the *Rigveda*,
the *Samaveda*, the *Yajurveda* and the *Atharvaveda*, and are followed by
the later collections and commentaries: first the hymn collections known
as the *Samhitas*, then the prose texts explaining the Vedic mythology and
sacrificial rituals known as the *Brahmanas*, and finally the prose philosophical works known as the *Upanishads*. Allotting two or three centuries to the
development of each of these three strata, Max Müller posited an approximate date for the *Rigveda* of 1200 BC, which was for a long time taken to be
reasonable, if entirely unproven.

Today's estimated date generally lies somewhat earlier than this, in
the period 1500–1200 BC. The argument for it depends on epigraphical
evidence discovered in the early 20th century, not in India but in eastern
Turkey, at Bogazkale, the site of the ancient capital of the Hittite empire,
whose official language was Indo-European. The document in question

relates to the kingdom of the Mitanni, which existed in the period from about 1500 BC to about 1360 BC in northern Mesopotamia, in what is now northern Syria and southeastern Anatolia. It is a treaty between the king of the Mitanni and the king of the Hittites, written in cuneiform, dateable to around 1380 BC on the basis of reliable king-lists of the region, in which the Mitannian king calls upon the gods of the Mitanni to guarantee his promises to the Hittite king. Although the chief language of the treaty is not an Indo-European one (it is Akkadian, a Semitic language used as a lingua franca in Mesopotamia), the part dealing with the gods mentions Arunashshil, Mitrashshil, Indara and Nashattiyanna – names that are remarkably close to the names of the Vedic gods Varuna, Mitra, Indra and Nasatyas, which of course are Indo-European. The names of Mitannian princes, some numerals and some technical terms for horse training are also recognizable in Vedic Sanskrit. The explanation for these surprising linguistic resemblances appears to be that the Mitannian elite, like the Hittite rulers, were Indo-European speakers.

But how could two groups located as geographically far apart as northern Mesopotamia and northwest India seem to have spoken closely related languages? The reason must be that both languages – that of the Mitannian elite and the Sanskrit (Indo-Aryan) of the Vedic peoples – were derived from a common proto-Indo-European source. While this fits with the theory of the dispersion of the ur-Aryans and the creation of the Indo-European language family, it is surprising to scholars that the above-mentioned names of the Mitannian gods resemble Vedic gods more closely than they resemble the names of Zoroastrian gods in the ancient Avestan language of Iran. The Mitannian god Nashattiyanna is equivalent to the Vedic god Nasatyas and to the Zoroastrian god Naonhaitya. Yet, not only is Iran geographically much closer to India than is northern Mesopotamia, the very name of the country, Iran, means 'land of the Aryans' in Persian and has been in use since antiquity. In fact, the affinity between Vedic Sanskrit and Avestan has been demonstrated to be closer than that between any other two branches of the Indo-European language family – so much so that the idea of a common ancestry for ancient Indians and ancient Iranians, with a common culture and a common language, is established beyond doubt. (For example, both Hindus and Zoroastrians have a sacred-thread ceremony marking the second 'birth' of a child as a full member of his religious community.)

There seem to be two possible explanations for the surprising similarity in the names of the Mitannian and Vedic gods. Either the ur-Aryans migrated southwards from their original homeland – wherever that was, perhaps on the steppes of southern Russia – into the area of the Mitannian kingdom *before* the Indo-Iranian language split into Iranian (Avestan) and Indian (Sanskrit); if so, then any subsequent changes in the Iranian language – such as the name Naonhaitya – would not be reflected in the Mitannian language. Or, some Indians, *after* the Indo-Iranian split, migrated far across the Iranian plateau into the area of the Mitannian kingdom, bringing their Vedic language with them. Although considerable linguistic evidence exists, it is probably insufficient to decide between these two incompatible hypotheses. But there can be little hesitation in declaring that the date of composition of the *Rigveda* in Sanskrit cannot be much earlier than the date of the Mitannian-Hittite cuneiform treaty, *c.* 1380 BC.

This suggests a gap of several centuries between the decline of the Indus Valley civilization in the early part of the second millennium BC and the rise of the Indo-Aryan Vedic culture in the middle of the millennium – rather than the earlier idea of an Aryan invasion from the west that destroyed the Indus Valley cities. Although there is no archaeological and little linguistic evidence to illuminate what actually happened in this period, it seems more probable than not that Indo-European-speaking migrants came in their chariots from Iran to India through the mountain passes of what is now Afghanistan and Pakistan. They populated first the northwest and then the north of the subcontinent – the valley of the river Ganges – and in the process encountered, and sometimes fought with, the area's existing Dravidian-speaking inhabitants. This collision, rather than some military subjugation of the Indus Valley cities, might account for the Vedic god Indra's attacks on the fortresses of the Dasas (Sanskrit for 'slaves') mentioned in the *Rigveda*.

The paucity of evidence did not (and does not) inhibit scholars and others from erecting a precarious structure of theory concerning the origin and development of the Indo-Aryans, which continues to wobble in the fierce winds of opinion. This is hardly surprising, given that some of the foundations of the structure were originally fashioned along racial lines, and depend on an over-interpretation of the *Rigveda*, involving a mere two passages about the dark skin of the Dasas, and a single, disputed, passage about their possibly flattened, 'primitive', noses.

What Trautmann, in his *Aryans and British India*, calls 'the racial theory of Indian civilization' was constructed by European Indologists and some scientists – such as the British ethnographer H. H. Risley, who oversaw the 1901 census of India – in the late 19th century and early 20th century. The idea that races could define civilizations was then in its heyday, and ethnicity was widely assumed to be intimately linked with language, despite a few warnings to the contrary. In outline, the racial theory proposed that the fair-skinned, Indo-European-speaking, Aryan invaders were civilizers of the dark-skinned, non-Indo-European-speaking, Dasa aboriginals, and thereby the source of all that was finest in subsequent Indian history and culture, especially classical Hinduism. The higher the caste, the greater the proportion of Aryan blood, thought Risley. Thus, when a newly built Indian Institute at Oxford University was opened in 1883, it carried a Sanskrit inscription with the following official English translation: 'This Building, dedicated to the Eastern sciences, was founded for the use of Aryas (Indians and Englishmen) by excellent and benevolent men desirous of encouraging knowledge.' The late Victorian racial theory had sanctioned the dubious translation of Sanskrit 'Arya' as including both races, not just the Indian.

At its most inclusive and sophisticated, the racial theory was a vision that inspired the Oxford-based Max Müller for decades until his death in

1900, during which he spoke out against both anti-Semitism in Europe and the denigration of Indians by the British in India. While lecturing 'on the science of language' before a capacity audience at London's Royal Institution, he enthused about the Aryan 'clan' and their Indo-European origins as follows:

> Before the ancestors of the Indians and Persians started for the south, and the leaders of the Greek, Roman, Celtic, Teutonic, and Slavonic colonies marched towards the shores of Europe, there was a small clan of Aryans, settled probably on the highest elevation of Central Asia, speaking a language, not yet Sanskrit or Greek or German, but containing the dialectic germs of all; a clan that had advanced to a state of agricultural civilization; that had recognized the bonds of blood, and sanctioned the bonds of marriage; and that invoked the Giver of Light and the Life in heaven by the same name which you may still hear in the temples of Benares, in the basilicas of Rome, and in our own churches and cathedrals.

For the British living in India, the racial theory held obvious appeal. It meant that they could pride themselves on following in the footsteps of the ancient Indo-European-speaking invaders with a modern civilizing mission, and could also attribute the best of Indian civilization to outside influences. Less predictably, the theory also appealed to many educated Indians, especially to high-caste Brahmins. For it offered them the consolation of being elevated to be 'Aryan brethren' (a favourite concept of Max Müller), in other words fellow members of the Indo-European-speaking family, rather than offspring of inferior, Dravidian-speaking aboriginals. As a result, Max Müller, despite never having visited India, came to be regarded by leading Indians of the time, such as Swami Vivekananda, as India's greatest well-wisher in the West. 'Gratified by the discovery of their proud historical pedigree, India's aspiring nationalists embraced the Aryans as readily as did Europe's cultural supremacists', comments John Keay in his history of India. In due course, the Aryan idea would prove as attractive to many Indians for the promotion of racial brotherhood with Europeans in India as it was to Nazi theorists for the promotion of racial hatred in Europe.

Indeed, the theory gave a fillip to turn-of-the-century Hindus of several different persuasions. It legitimized orthodox Hindus to become more dogmatic and intolerant about their religion. It encouraged reformist Hindus inspired by Christianity, such as Tagore, to clothe their religious life under the cover of Upanishadic teachings. It impelled Hindus with less intellectual confidence to accept their religion from dubious European interpreters such as the Theosophists, led by the Russian spiritualist Madame Blavatsky. And lastly, it induced the half-Europeanized part of the Hindu intelligentsia, such as the followers of the back-to-the-*Vedas* movement known as the Arya Samaj, 'to bolster up a peculiarly xenophobic nationalism, without any realization of its spiritual value', writes Nirad C. Chaudhuri in his biography of Max Müller.

The progeny of this last group live on today in the form of the Hindu nationalists, who still have a love-hate attitude towards European and American praise for their religion. Of course their arguments have changed during the intervening century. They know that the racial theory of civilizations is now widely discredited, along with the 19th-century notion that a race must be linked with a particular language – in a globalized world where more Indians in India speak English than the entire indigenous population of England. Moreover, the discovery of the Indus Valley civilization (in the 1920s) has fundamentally altered our understanding of India's prehistory. Today's Hindu nationalists, instead of embracing a foreign influence in the Vedic religion, strongly deny it, along with the concept of Aryan migrations into India. However, they still cling to a racial theory of Indian civilization by maintaining that Vedic Sanskrit, the supposed language of the first Indians, originated not in some Indo-European-speaking homeland such as the south Russian steppes but in India, among the natives of the Indus Valley civilization.

Yet, even if the nationalists and a few more serious scholars may choose to deny the Aryan migrations, they cannot simply wish away the compelling evidence for an Indo-European family of languages. First presented by Jones to the Asiatic Society in Calcutta in 1786, the Indo-European concept has withstood the scrutiny of more than two centuries of scholarship in both the West and India. To give three simple examples out of hundreds of striking resemblances between Sanskrit and European languages, the Sanskrit word for 'father' is *pita*, while the Greek word is *pater*; the Sanskrit for 'wife' is *gna*, while the Greek is *gyne*; and the Sanskrit for 'two' is *dva*, while the Greek is *dyo*. A more complicated example is the Sanskrit word *cakra*, which means 'wheel'; it is thought to have originated from a proto-Indo-European word pronounced something like *kwekulo*, which was also the ancestor of the Greek for 'wheel', *kuklos*, and the Old English word *hweogol*, from which modern English 'wheel' is derived.

That said, there is little agreement between scholars on how the postulated Indo-European linguistic changes came about through migration of actual language-speakers. In the discouraging words of a detailed 2001 survey, *The Quest for the Origins of the Vedic Culture: The Indo-Aryan Migration Debate* by Edwin Bryant: 'how the cognate languages got to be where they were in prehistory is as unresolved today, in my mind, as it was two hundred years ago when William Jones announced the Sanskrit language connection to a surprised Europe.' And yet, short of postulating that the first speakers of the proto-Indo-European language were born in ancient *India*, rather than on the Russian steppes, and arguing that some of them then migrated from India westwards towards Europe – a fantasy for which there are no grounds archaeologically and almost no grounds linguistically – there must have been an actual migration of Indo-European-speaking people into India from the northwest to account for the resemblances between so many Asian and European languages. By what route, under what conditions, and at what date these migrations occurred, are questions that will continue to be debated until such time as more solid evidence may be discovered.

THREE Buddha, Alexander
and Asoka

BUDDHA, ALEXANDER AND ASOKA

In the 6th century BC, Indian history begins to free itself from the silence of the archaeological excavations in the Indus Valley and from the myths and dubious traditions of the Vedic literature. The written record is yet to come into existence, or at any rate it has not survived. However, we now encounter not only the first historical Indian figure but also the person who, 'even if judged only by his posthumous effects on the world at large . . . was certainly the greatest man to have been born in India', as the historian A. L. Basham notably describes Siddhartha Gautama, the Buddha.

Rabindranath Tagore went even further than this in his praise. Towards the end of his life, in a moving speech honouring the birthday of the Buddha, Tagore described him as 'the greatest man ever born on this earth'. He recalled a visit to the Mahabodhi Temple at Bodhgaya in Bihar, the place of the Buddha's enlightenment under a *bodhi* tree, where he saw a poor Japanese fisherman who had travelled across the seas from Japan 'to expiate for some misdeed'. As Tagore observed the fisherman, 'Evening passed slowly into the solitude and silence of midnight, and still he sat with folded hands repeating with intense concentration, *Buddham saranam gacchami*: In the Buddha do I seek my refuge.' Tagore also recalled his visit to the Buddhist temple at Borobudur in Java, where he saw the celebrated stories depicting everyday life in ancient India and the nativity of the Buddha, known as the *Jatakas*, 'carved in hundreds of images round the stupa, each a perfect specimen of the sculptor's art, chiselled with loving care and infinite pains.'

In many parts of northern India, there are ancient Buddhist stupas – some of them built by Asoka to honour the Buddha's ashes – and other Buddhist monuments, including the stupa built on top of the ruins of the city of Mohenjo-daro. The highest concentration of these remains is in the birthplace of Buddhism, which now occupies part of the Indian states of Bihar and Uttar Pradesh plus a small part of Nepal (where Siddhartha Gautama was actually born). Indeed, Buddhist stupas, not Hindu temples, are the oldest surviving religious architecture in India. The Buddhist religious remains from the period 200 BC to AD 200 so far discovered by archaeologists outnumber by far those belonging to early classical Hinduism and to Jainism. At the best preserved of these sites, the stupa and gateways of Sanchi in the state of Madhya Pradesh – which are superbly sculpted with stories from the *Jatakas* – building began in the 3rd century BC and carried on until the 6th or 7th centuries AD. At the Ajanta caves in the state of Maharashtra, the Buddhist murals – many of which are among the greatest works of Indian art – were painted from about 200 BC over a period lasting for well over half a millennium, until perhaps as late as AD 650. (Some scholars favour an earlier date for the caves' abandonment, 480.) 'Was ancient India "Hindu" or Buddhist?' asks Gail Omvedt in her study *Buddhism in India*. 'Art and architecture testify that it was overwhelmingly Buddhist for over a millennium.'

Nonetheless, by the early 19th century, when Europeans first began to investigate these Buddhist remains, the living religion had vanished from its homeland and from the rest of India, except for Assam, the foothills of the Himalayas and Kashmir. It had to be reconstructed by European scholars – who encountered hardly any living Buddhists – from surviving Buddhist texts; and then popularized by writers such as Edwin Arnold in *The Light of Asia*, his bestselling biography of the Buddha, published in 1879, which tailored its subject's life to a Victorian British readership steeped in the Christian gospels. An extraordinary and revealing historical fact is that not a single Buddhist text was preserved in Bihar and Uttar Pradesh, whether written in the Pali or the Sanskrit languages. References to this vanished Indian literature by modern scholars rely on Buddhist manuscripts that were preserved in monasteries in Sri Lanka, Tibet and China. Today Buddhism (like Jainism) is very much of a minority religion in India: less than 1 per cent of the population is Buddhist, compared with three times as many Indians who are Christians. Even the worldly-cum-spiritual emperor Asoka, whose ethical government seems to have been much inspired by the Buddha's teachings, cannot be said to be a living presence in India, apart from the use of Asoka's sculpted lion capital from Sarnath on banknotes and government documents as the national emblem of India – despite the high respect for Asoka and the Buddha shown by Nehru. His house as prime minister in New Delhi, Teen Murti, had an image of the Buddha in almost every room, including a photograph of a Buddha image on the table next to his bed; and he named his daughter Indira Priyadarshini Nehru, her second name meaning 'Beloved-of-the-Gods': the favourite title adopted by Asoka in his edicts.

In *The Discovery of India*, Nehru writes of the mid-20th-century relationship between Hinduism, Jainism and Buddhism as follows:

> Jainism, a rebel against the parent religion and in many ways utterly different from it, was yet tolerant to caste and adapted itself to it; and so it survives and continues in India, almost as an offshoot of Hinduism. Buddhism, not adapting itself to caste, and more independent in its thought and outlook, ultimately passes away from India, though it influences India and Hinduism profoundly.

Modern visitors to such popular Buddhist sites as the Mahabodhi Temple at Bodhgaya, and Sarnath where the Buddha first began to teach his followers the *dharma* (*dhamma* in Pali), cannot fail to notice that the vast majority of the pilgrims have come from Asian countries outside India, in particular Burma, China, Japan, Korea, Sri Lanka, Taiwan, Thailand

and Tibet, which have living Buddhist traditions, and from Europe and the United States; Indian visitors make up a small minority. In fact, it is possible to visit the less prominent of the ancient sites on the Buddhist 'circuit' in Bihar and Uttar Pradesh without seeing Indian pilgrims – rather as if, in the Catholic world, one were to see no Italian Catholics worshipping in the great cathedrals of Italy, only groups of Irish, Spanish and Portuguese, South Americans and Filipinos. Buddhism did not begin to make a comeback in the heartland of the subcontinent until the mid-1950s (a decade after Nehru wrote the above words), when Ambedkar, the leader of the untouchables, having convinced himself that the first untouchables were really Buddhists outcasted by Hindu society, underwent a conversion from Hinduism to Buddhism at a controversial public ceremony in Maharashtra just months before his death. Hundreds of thousands of other untouchables, who wished to escape the oppressive restrictions put upon them by orthodox Hindu society, underwent conversion at the same time. About three quarters of the Buddhists in present-day India are Dalits, while the remaining quarter are concentrated in Assam and the Himalayan regions, including Dharamsala, the headquarters of the Tibetan community in exile.

The complex historical relationship between Buddhism and Hinduism is encapsulated in the complicated story of the Mahabodhi Temple. Its beginnings as a Buddhist shrine go back to Asoka's time, but the structure of the present-day building dates from much later than this: the 5th or 6th century AD. Yet even in the mid-7th century, when a Buddhist pilgrim from China, the celebrated Xuanzang, toured parts of India and visited Bodhgaya, he found the site to be virtually engulfed in drifting sand dunes. By the time a Tibetan translator and Tantric Buddhist named Dharmasvamin visited in about 1234, he saw the shrine in great disrepair following damage to it by recent Muslim invaders. On the door he observed an image of Shiva, which he imagined to be a guardian deity from the Tibetan Buddhist pantheon. 'It was just as likely evidence of an increased level of Hindu activity at the shrine', suggests the anthropologist Alan Trevithick in his history of the

Mahabodhi Temple. The temple was finally abandoned by its Buddhist monks in the 15th century, and taken over by local Hindus probably some time in the 17th century. They dedicated it to Vishnu in the form of 'Buddha Dev' – Vishnu's ninth incarnation, according to classical Hinduism. But all memory of its original Buddhist significance was apparently lost. A British servant of the East India Company conducting a statistical survey, who reached Bodhgaya in 1811 and questioned the leader of a group of Hindu ascetics living in the partially restored ruins, was told by the man that he had been in complete ignorance of Buddhism until quite recently, when some emissaries sent by the king of Ava (in Burma) had informed him of Bodhgaya's sacred importance to the Burmese.

At this time, British officials and scholars themselves knew virtually nothing of Buddhism. After a British army officer out hunting accidentally discovered the Ajanta caves in western India in 1819, there was speculation that the mysterious paintings had been created by unknown conquerors who had sailed to India from Egypt. From the 1840s onwards, though, after the decipherment of Asoka's edicts by James Prinsep and others – beginning with Asoka's title, Piyadassi (Priyadarshini in Sanskrit) – and the discovery in Tibet of Buddhist texts in Sanskrit, Tibetan, Chinese and Mongolian, Eugène Burnouf and a select group of European scholars developed some understanding of the Buddha and much admiration. Later in the 19th century, British archaeologists led by Alexander Cunningham set about renovating the Mahabodhi Temple. Soon, Bodhgaya began to be visited by practising Buddhists from Sri Lanka, Burma and other Buddhist-dominated countries, led by an evangelical Sri Lankan monk, Anagarika Dharmapala, who founded the Mahabodhi Society in 1891, with the express aim of reclaiming the temple at Bodhgaya from the Hindus. This led to an acrimonious struggle between local Hindus and foreign Buddhists over the management of the temple, ending in 1949 with some Bihar government legislation (supported by Nehru) that established a joint management committee with a mix of Hindu and Buddhist members and a Buddhist superintendent in charge of the temple rituals. In the debate over the legislation one local politician, a Brahmin and a major landowner, while attempting to justify continued Hindu domination, argued, quite typically for a high-caste Hindu: 'After all – what were Hindus? – they were neither Shaivas, Jains, Buddhists nor other branches of religion but were inheritors of one great Aryan culture.' During the second half of the 20th century, the new managerial arrangement between Hindus and Buddhists, though sometimes fraught, led to a startling revival of Buddhist attendance at Bodhgaya, including the international crowds that flocked to see the Dalai Lama on his regular visits to teach, and to a huge boost in temple donations by Buddhists.

Tempting as it may be to conclude from the story of the Mahabodhi Temple that Hinduism, fuelled by undoubted Brahminical antipathy towards Buddhism, must have been the chief enemy of Buddhism within India, in truth the mystery of Buddhism's disappearance from the land of its birth appears to be more puzzling. Unlike in Europe, with its battles between Catholic and Protestant theologians and kingdoms, there was never any overt political, or indeed military, struggle between Hinduism and Buddhism in India. The explanation for Buddhism's decline appears to have more to do with the diminishing appeal to Indians of its social, political and philosophical outlook, even if the precise reasons for this diminishing are controversial.

To understand what may have transpired and why, we need to consider how Buddhism, and simultaneously Jainism, may have arisen in the societies of the middle Gangetic basin valley in the mid-first millennium BC. As the initially tribal Vedic culture of the second millennium BC spread from its upper Gangetic source eastwards down the Ganges valley, it appears to have become weaker. Although it influenced the political and religious forms of the middle Ganges, they departed from the original Vedic culture in new directions. Inevitably, archaeological evidence for this transformation is lacking (there are no excavated remains of any Gangetic settlements from this period); conclusions have to be drawn from textual sources, that is, from late Vedic (Upanishadic) and early Buddhist literature.

The dominant early Vedic emphasis in the *Rigveda* on sacrificial rituals, for example, which was suited to an essentially pastoral, semi-nomadic, tribal society in the second millennium, must have been less attractive to later, settled societies practising agriculture, commerce and urban living, which naturally preferred to use their economic surplus for building and trading, as well as for individual pleasure. Moreover, unnecessary animal slaughter in sacrifices seems to have become increasingly offensive to people. This hypothesis would account for an obvious change of emphasis in the youngest Vedic texts, the *Upanishads*, in which the concept of sacrifice is interpreted by their Brahmin authors more philosophically than in the *Vedas*, so as to ritualize the entire round of life for an individual – both from day to day and from birth to death. It would also fit with the consistent criticism of animal slaughter found in the Buddhist texts, and especially in the Jain texts, which from the outset promoted non-injury to living beings (*ahimsa*) and vegetarianism.

The geographical setting of the *Upanishads* was probably the three, newly founded, neighbouring eastern kingdoms of Kosala, Kashi (the ancient name for Varanasi/Benares) and Videha, all in the middle Gangetic basin, on the evidence of certain names in the texts, for example Janaka, a king of Videha, and Yajnavalkya, a Brahmin adviser to Janaka, both of whom are mentioned in the *Brihadaranyaka Upanishad*. It is also clear that a king such as Janaka – in the manner of monarchs through-out history seeking new prestige – competed with other kings to attract noted Brahmins from the original, upper Gangetic heartland of the Vedic culture to his eastern court. Not only did the mere presence of Brahmins at court lend legitimacy to a ruler, the Brahmins would also be encouraged by the king to indulge in philosophical discourse and debate with other Brahmins, with substantial prizes awarded to the victors. Sage Yajnavalkya is said to have defeated in argument the best of the established Vedic theologians, including even the great sage Uddalaka Aruni, who is vilified in the *Brihadaranyaka Upanishad.*

A fourth kingdom, Magadha, east of Kashi, with its capital at the fortress of Rajagriha, was the least dominated by Brahmins. Unsurprisingly, the Brahmin authors of late Vedic literature were contemptuous of the Magadhans. In the *Atharvaveda*, notes Trautmann, a medicinal spell 'wishes fever away to the peoples of Magadha and their eastern neighbours of Anga (Bengal) along with other undesirables.' But in due course Magadha would become by far the most influential of these four kingdoms.

The jostling for power between the middle Gangetic kingdoms – frequently referred to in the early Buddhist texts – provided the setting for the rise of three contemporaneous religions of renunciation in the 6th century: Buddhism, Jainism and Ajivikism, the last of which survived in India until about AD 1400. Both Siddhartha Gautama and Vardhamana the Mahavira (Great Hero), founder of Jainism, were born in the princely class. The first belonged to the Sakya tribe, who were under the sway of Kosala, and was born in the foothills of Nepal, while the second was born in Videha; little is known of the origins of Makkhali Gosala, the Ajivika teacher.

Asceticism and renunciation have roots in India at least as old as the *Rigveda*, which mentions visionaries known as *munis* who went about without speaking, either naked or in orange rags and with their hair matted. By the 6th century, in the eastern kingdoms, such ascetics had become commonplace, presumably in reaction against increasing materialist values among the rulers, merchants and general population. Some of them lived as celibate hermits in the forests; others were wandering beggars and preachers; still others practised harsh penances involving extreme heat and cold, or sat in silent meditation. Collectively, they were known as Shramanas, meaning 'renouncers'.

The Shramanas utterly rejected the authority of the Vedic tradition and its keepers, the Brahmins. So much so, that traditionally the Brahmana (Brahmin) and the Shramana are compared to the cobra and the mongoose.

For the two groups differed profoundly over the purpose of human existence. The Brahmin was enjoined by the *Vedas* to procreate a son in order to perpetuate the ancestral cult, whereas the Shramana took a vow to observe lifelong celibacy so as to be released from the otherwise endless cycle of rebirth.

The Buddha, by contrast, enjoined for the ordinary person neither the sacrificial worship of gods in the Vedic tradition nor the asceticism of the Shramanas, but rather a path of mental discipline and moderation. And of course he rejected the Vedic caste system and the dominant status of Brahmin priests. The kernel of his teaching is contained in the *Dhammacakkapavattana Sutta*, the 'Sermon of the Turning of the Wheel of the Law', which the Buddha is said to have preached (after his enlightenment at Bodhgaya) to his first disciples at Sarnath, near Benares. It includes the 'Four Noble Truths' and the 'Noble Eightfold Path'. Since these two are accepted as basic tenets by all Buddhist sects – and since they sum up the Buddhist world view – it is worth quoting them verbatim (though in a somewhat abridged form). They begin with the introductory phrase characteristic of Buddhist texts:

Thus have I heard. Once the Master was at Benares, at the deer park called Isipatana. There the Master addressed the five monks:

'There are two ends not to be served by a wanderer. What are those two? The pursuit of desires and of the pleasure which springs from desires, which is base, common, leading to rebirth, ignoble and unprofitable; and the pursuit of pain and hardship, which is grievous, ignoble and unprofitable. The Middle Way of the Tathagata [one of the titles of the Buddha, meaning "He who has thus attained"] avoids both these ends; it is enlightened, it brings clear vision, it makes for wisdom, and leads to peace, insight, full wisdom and Nirvana. What is this Middle Way? . . . It is the Noble Eightfold Path – Right Views, Right Resolve, Right Speech, Right Conduct, Right Livelihood, Right Effort, Right Recollection and Right Meditation. This is the Middle Way. . . .

'And this is the Noble Truth of Sorrow. Birth is sorrow, age is sorrow, disease is sorrow, death is sorrow, contact with the unpleasant is sorrow, separation from the pleasant is sorrow, every wish unfulfilled is sorrow – in short all the five components of individuality are sorrow.

'And this is the Noble Truth of the Arising of Sorrow. [It arises from] thirst, which leads to rebirth, which brings delight and passion, and seeks pleasure now here, now there – the thirst for sensual pleasure, the thirst for continued life, the thirst for power.

'And this is the Noble Truth of the Stopping of Sorrow. It is the complete stopping of that thirst, so that no passion remains, leaving it, being emancipated from it, giving no place to it.

'And this is the Noble Truth of the Way which Leads to the Stopping of Sorrow. It is the Noble Eightfold Path – Right Views, Right Resolve, Right Speech, Right Conduct, Right Livelihood, Right Effort, Right Recollection and Right Meditation.'

By the beginning of the 5th century BC, during the lifetime of the Buddha (if we accept that he died in the 480s), Kosala, located at the confluence of the Ganges and the Yamuna Rivers, was the most powerful of the eastern kingdoms, having absorbed Kashi and several tribal states on its northern borders (now in Nepal), including the Buddha's Sakya tribe. Videha, to the east, on the northern bank of the Ganges, was by now controlled not by a king but by a tribal confederacy dominated by the Vrijjis and the Licchavis. Magadha, south of Videha on the southern bank of the Ganges, was overshadowed by Kosala and Videha, though able to dominate further to the east, in Anga (Bengal) and Assam.

Within less than half a century, however, Magadha succeeded in absorbing Kosala and Videha. The two key figures in the Magadhan success were the energetic Bimbisara, an admirer of the Buddha, and Bimbisara's son, also known to the Buddha, Ajatasattu, who murdered his father and seized the throne of Magadha around 490 BC. Ajatasattu then fought a series of wars with Kosala and Videha and, according to the Buddhist tradition, undermined the Vrijjian confederacy with the help of his wily chief minister. By pretending to have fallen out with Ajatasattu, the minister persuaded the Vrijjis to give him refuge in their capital Vaisali and then, once he was inside their city, fomented trouble among them. Having now taken over Videha and gained access to the Ganges, Ajatasattu shifted his capital from Rajagriha to Pataliputra (modern Patna) on the river, which gave control of all riverborne trade to Magadha's growing empire. By the time Ajatasattu died around 460 BC – murdered by his son, according to the Buddhist tradition (though the Jain tradition differs) – his power extended from the Bay of Bengal to the Nepal Himalayas. Subsequent Magadhan rulers continue to be remembered for their bloody dynastic successions and their unscrupulousness in pursuing territory, as well as for their wealth and their upstart origins. By the time that Alexander the Great's army appeared on the Indian scene in 326 BC, the Nanda dynasty of Magadha, with its great capital at Pataliputra, was ruling the largest empire yet seen on the subcontinent. Having either destroyed or subjugated all earlier kingdoms, Magadha controlled the whole Ganges basin, indeed all of northern India east of the Indus basin, excluding Rajasthan, Sindh, Punjab and the northwest, where tribal rule remained dominant.

The Greek invaders never engaged with the Magadhan empire. After crossing the Indus River and reaching the Jhelum River (known to the Greeks as the Hydaspes), Alexander outwitted and defeated the much larger, elephant-mounted army of a warlike king of the Punjab, Porus (a name probably connected with Puru, an old Vedic name), with the loss of perhaps 200 cavalry and 700 infantry, as against 12,000 dead on Porus's side and the seizure of almost all of his elephants. According to Greek sources, Porus – who stood over six feet six inches tall – remained defiant when finally captured, though he was wounded in nine different places. Brought before

Alexander and asked how he wished to be treated, Porus replied: 'As befits me – like a king!' An impressed Alexander made Porus a vassal, restored his kingdom and left him in charge of the Punjab. But despite this victory, and much against the desire of Alexander, the Greek army turned back at the Beas River, the border of the mighty Magadhan empire. In effect, the ordinary troops mutinied against their leader's 'seemingly unquenchable thirst for further exploration and conquest', writes Paul Cartledge in his history of Alexander. 'The many years of horrendously tough marching and campaigning, the appallingly dispiriting monsoon rains, chronic homesickness and a heightened fear of the unknown had taken a heavy toll.'

This was not the first time that Greek soldiers had encountered Indian vigour. According to Herodotus, Indians fought in the Persian army during the second Persian invasion of Greece in 479 BC. In 331, the Persian empire under Darius III, while fighting Alexander's forces at the crucial battle of Gaugamela, deployed a small detachment of Indian troops from the west of the Indus with fifteen elephants. After subduing the Persians and a long campaign in Bactria, Alexander, on his way through the Punjab, stopped at the city of Takshashila (modern Taxila in Pakistan), where the king offered no resistance and feasted the Greek army with a Vedic-style sacrifice of 300 oxen. Here, Alexander personally encountered learned Brahmins and naked ascetics, Shramanas, whom the Greeks called gymnosophists – but apparently no Buddhists. Near the banks of the Indus, having captured ten gymnosophists who had helped to inspire rebellion against him, a curious Alexander interrogated them, declaring that he would put to death the first of them who made an incorrect answer. According to the ancient Greek historian Plutarch's much later *Life of Alexander*, Alexander was intrigued by their responses to his questions. The first gymnosophist, when asked 'which, in his opinion, were more numerous, the living or the dead, said that the living were, since the dead no longer existed.' Another, 'being asked which, in his opinion, was older, day or night', replied: 'Day, by one day', and added, upon Alexander's expressing amazement, that 'hard questions must have hard answers.' Yet another, when asked 'how a man could be most loved', replied with pointed bravery: 'If he is most powerful, and yet does not inspire fear.'

Retreating from India, Alexander and his army sailed down the Indus past long-deserted ancient towns and cities on their arduous journey back to Mesopotamia. But they left behind no monuments or remains in northwestern India – unlike Asoka less than a century after Alexander's invasion and the later Indo-Greek kingdoms in the area. Perhaps more surprisingly, 'The name of Alexander is not found in Indian literature', writes A. K. Narain in his history of the Indo-Greeks.

Plutarch claims that Alexander was encouraged by an Indian stripling – known to classical historians as Sandrocottus – to advance across the Beas River and attack the Magadhan empire. Its people would rise against the Nanda dynasty, said the youth, because the Nanda ruler was 'hated and despised on account of his baseness and low birth'. Another classical historian, Justin, states that the boldness of Sandrocottus at some point offended Alexander, who ordered his execution; but that Sandrocottus escaped. 'Some time after, . . . a wild elephant of great bulk presented itself before him of its own accord, and, as if tamed down to gentleness, took him on its back, and became his guide in the war, and conspicuous in fields of battle.' Whether or not all of these stories are true, after the death of Alexander in Babylon in 323, forces led by Sandrocottus were able to defeat the Greek satrapies in northwest India left behind by Alexander and expel the Greeks from India.

Around the same period, Sandrocottus himself defeated the Nanda ruler and became known to Indian chroniclers not as Sandrocottus but as Chandragupta, the first emperor of the Mauryan dynasty of Magadha. Chandragupta Maurya's date of accession is usually given as around 321, though there is considerable uncertainty about this, and about the exact order of his conquests. By the time of his death, however, around 298, he had laid the foundation of an empire, the Mauryan empire, which would grow to cover almost the entire subcontinent under Chandragupta's grandson, Asoka, during the second half of the 3rd century.

Chandragupta's rise to power owed a great deal, according to all Indian traditions, to his much older chief minister, a highly capable but unscrupulous Brahmin possibly born and educated at Takshashila, who had a grudge against the Nanda court. Known variously as Kautilya, Chanakya and Vishnugupta, he is often regarded as an ancient Indian equivalent of Machiavelli, and has also been compared with such modern practitioners and theorists of *realpolitik* as Otto von Bismarck and Henry Kissinger. Appropriately enough, Chanakyapuri is the name of the diplomatic enclave that was built in New Delhi after Independence.

The main source of Kautilya's fame is a treatise on statecraft known as the *Arthashastra*, attributed to him. However, its origin and dating are problematic, as with so many aspects of ancient Indian history. Its very existence was unknown until 1904, when it was discovered by the Sanskritist R. Shamasastry in an archive in south India among a heap of palm-leaf manuscripts. While the *Arthashastra* may possibly be the work of a single author living in the 4th century BC (Kautilya's dates are unknown), most scholars now assume that the original version was revised by others and may not have reached its final form until as late as the 3rd or 4th century AD. One reason is that the text contains references to people and places that were apparently unknown to Indians in the 4th century BC, for instance 'silk and silk-cloth from the land of China'. Another is that the terminology the text uses for government is not generally similar to that of the inscriptions of Asoka but instead came into regular use only after the Mauryan period.

As its basic principle, the *Arthashastra* – a title translated as 'Economics' by Amartya Sen – unabashedly states that 'material wellbeing (*artha*) alone is supreme . . . for spiritual good (*dharma*) and sensual pleasures (*kama*) depend on material wellbeing.' It therefore argues that a ruler has an ethical duty to make *artha* his priority, in order to promote the welfare of his state and people. 'Kautilya, if reborn as an economist today, would be at home with his sensibility in any high-level international meeting of finance ministers', argues the American attorney Bruce Rich in a recent study of Kautilya, Asoka and global ethics. With wealth promotion in mind, the *Arthashastra* discusses economic, social, legal and foreign policy and justifies more or less any kind of government surveillance of, and intrusion into, people's lives, including a vigorous secret service, to which the *Arthashastra* devotes two chapters. For example, petty officials, known as *gopas*, were to be responsible for forty households each; they were expected to keep records of the households' births and deaths, income and expenditure, and even their visitors – all to be permanently recorded in the central archives of a town. How many of the text's recommendations were actually applied is unknown, though it is reported by Megasthenes, a Greek ambassador from the neighbouring Seleucid empire to the early Mauryan court at Pataliputra, that the movements of strangers were carefully monitored and recorded. If the spy-ridden Mauryan state begins to sound somewhat like Communist East Germany, consider instead a comparison with the United States, says Rich. 'The contrast between [Kautilya's] proclaimed goals of social good and the unsavoury methods he sometimes advocated is hardly as glaring as the spectacle of a new country 2200 years later that claimed to be the cradle of human liberty, but that tolerated a system of slavery harsher and more absolute than anything that existed in Kautilya's India.'

The grandson of Chandragupta, the immortal Asoka, came to the throne of Magadha around 269 and died around 232 BC. 'In the history of the world there have been thousands of kings and emperors who called themselves "their highnesses", "their majesties", "their exalted majesties" and so on,' wrote H. G. Wells in *The Outline of History*. 'They shone for a brief moment, and as quickly disappeared. But Asoka shines and shines brightly like a bright star, even unto this day.'

Asoka's first decade as a ruler was dedicated to the ruthless statecraft recommended in the treatise of his grandfather's adviser Kautilya, while the rest of his reign was dominated by the philosophy of non-violence and *dharma* discussed in the discourses of the Buddha. The pivotal event, which caused his volte-face, was his brutal conquest of the Kalinga kingdom in central-eastern India (now Orissa), probably in 261 or 260 BC. His first rock edict, at Girnar, on the western seaboard of India, records that 100,000 Kalingas were slaughtered by the Magadhan forces, half as many again were deported and many more died from other causes. Then, speaking of himself, Asoka writes: 'After the Kalingas were conquered, Beloved-of-the-Gods [King Piyadassi] came to feel a strong inclination towards the Dharma, a love for the Dharma and for instruction in Dharma. Now Beloved-of-the-Gods feels deep remorse for having conquered the Kalingas . . .' Others of the thirty-three edicts, inscribed on rocks and pillars scattered across the subcontinent, extend this message of non-violence, including non-violence to all living creatures, even into the royal kitchens, where the slaughter of most animals was henceforth prohibited. For example, '. . . now with the writing of this Dharma edict only three creatures, two peacocks and a deer, are killed, and the deer not always. And in time, not even these three creatures will be killed.' Carved in one of two scripts, Brahmi and Kharoshti, most of the edicts are written in the north Indian languages of the 3rd century known as Prakrits, but a handful of them, in the Indus valley and beyond, are written in Greek and Aramaic, a lingua franca of the former Persian empire, which exerted a considerable influence on Asoka. (The very idea of rock and pillar inscriptions was surely part-inspired by the great rock and pillar inscriptions of the Persian ruler Darius I, written in cuneiform.)

At the same time, according to the edicts, an excellent and enlightened administration prevailed throughout the empire. Highways were constructed; wells were dug beside them for refreshment; trees were planted to provide shade for travellers and animals. Botanical gardens, the planting of medicinal herbs and hospitals were introduced. As for individual and social relationships, Asoka's 'Dharma' advocated respect for Brahmins, Shramanas, parents, friends and inferiors. Religious bigotry and controversy, such as that between Brahmins, Shramanas, Buddhists and Jains, was discouraged – as Nehru approvingly noted in *The Discovery of India*. Yet, while the tone of Asoka's edicts is always one of persuasion and exhortation, rather than coercion, it appears that the Mauryan state also continued to maintain its army, the death penalty (abolished under some later Indian kings) and judicial torture. Significantly, Asoka's remorse over the conquest of Kalinga is not recorded in the two rock edicts that have been discovered in the area where the slaughter took place.

It seems virtually certain that Asoka was personally drawn to Buddhism. Why else would he have erected so many stupas, along with some inscribed pillars at sites known to be connected with events in the life of the Buddha, including Sarnath and the Buddha's birthplace at Lumbini (now in Nepal)? He is also thought to have convened a major Buddhist Council at Pataliputra in order to resolve certain doctrinal disputes within the Buddhist monastic order, the *sangha*, although Buddhist sources disagree about whether this event actually occurred. What is puzzling, however, is that only a single edict by Asoka refers directly to the Buddha and the *sangha*; and this edict is one of his earliest rock inscriptions. There are frequent references in the edicts to Brahmins, Shramanas and the Dharma, and yet Asoka never states that he means the Buddhist *dhamma*. From his edicts alone, it would be impossible to guess that Asoka was a Buddhist. As a result there is considerable controversy about his government's treatment of Buddhism. Some scholars, such as Abhishek Singh Amar, argue that Buddhism was effectively the state religion of the Mauryan empire under Asoka, but was not officially declared as such for strategic reasons. Others, including Romila Thapar, maintain that Asoka's edicts should be interpreted more literally and believe that he espoused a broader ethic than Buddhism in his governance. Whatever the reality was, it seems that Asoka must have recognized – probably keeping in mind the advice of the essentially secular *Arthashastra* – that Buddhism might not appeal to an influential section of the population of his empire. To have embraced its philosophy officially would most likely have had divisive, rather than unifying, consequences for his unique imperial rule.

FOUR Hindu Dynasties

HINDU DYNASTIES

If the predominant religion of the Mauryan empire in the 3rd century BC cannot be unambiguously described as Buddhist, neither can it be said to have been Hindu – at any rate not in the modern sense of that word. The ancient meaning of 'Hindu' was geographical, not religious: it derived from the Sanskrit word *sindhu*, meaning 'river', specifically the Indus River. The ancient Persians from the time of Darius dropped the 's' and used *hindu* to mean 'pertaining to the region of the Indus' – the area now known as Sindh. In the pioneering map of the world created in the 2nd century AD by the Greek geographer Claudius Ptolemy, the approach to India from the west is marked 'Indiostena regio', Latin for 'region of Hindustan'. Thereafter, the Arabs, who conquered Sindh in the 8th century, gradually extended the meaning of the word to denote the entire region of northern India as 'Hindustan'.

During the first millennium AD, most Indians – other than Buddhists and Jains – identified themselves by their caste or sect. 'The clubbing together of all the castes, non-castes and sects under one label – Hindu – would have been strange to most people and even repugnant to some, since it would have made Brahmins, Shudras and untouchables equal members of a religious community of "Hindus",' observes Romila Thapar. 'This was alien to the existing religions in the subcontinent.' Not until the second millennium did 'Hindu' acquire its current meaning connected with a group religious identity. The earliest use of the term in this sense came in the 14th century, though it was still infrequent, while its earliest

84

citation in the *Oxford English Dictionary* is dated 1655, from the work of a British travel writer who visited the court of the Great Mughal: 'The Inhabitants in generall of Indostan were all antiently Gentiles, called in generall Hindoes.'

The first temples that are recognizably Hindu, which are dedicated to Shiva and Vishnu, did not appear until the Gupta empire of the 4th–6th centuries AD, while the finest ones postdate the Gupta period. For example, the Shiva Temple in a cave on the island of Elephanta near Mumbai, with its classic three-headed (*trimurti*) Shiva sculpture symbolizing creation, protection and destruction, was possibly built under the Kalachuri dynasty, or perhaps under the Chalukya dynasty, in the 6th century. The 'Shore' Temple on the coast at Mahabalipuram in Tamil Nadu, with its three shrines to Shiva and a reclining Vishnu, was built under the Pallava dynasty in the early 8th century. The giant Kailasanath Temple at Ellora in Maharashtra was sculpted out of the living rock by the Rashtrakuta dynasty in the mid-8th century. The Brihadishwara Temple at Thanjavur in Tamil Nadu, with its astonishing pyramidal tower, was constructed by the Chola dynasty in the early 11th century. And the Kandariya Mahadeva temple at Khajuraho in Madhya Pradesh, with its notorious erotic sculptures, was built by the Chandella dynasty in the mid-11th century.

Between the end of the Mauryas in the 2nd century BC and the close of the first millennium AD, there developed what is often called classical Hinduism, involving a multifarious divine pantheon and devotional rituals, scriptures and literature that remain popular in present-day India. Unlike the Vedic religion of the Brahmins, the asceticism of the Shramanas or the austerity of the Buddhists, this religion was suitable for the masses in need of reward, guidance and comfort from offering their devotion to a god. Thus, the ten incarnations of Vishnu, the cult of the Shiva lingam, the *Manusmriti* (Laws of Manu), the *Puranas* (Ancient Stories) and the two epic poems, *The Mahabharata* and *The Ramayana* (the first of which includes the *Bhagavad Gita*), all date from this long period of development of classical

Hinduism, even if their origins must in many cases lie much earlier, in the period when the *Vedas* and the *Upanishads* were composed.

Despite much scholarly effort, there is insufficient evidence to date the completion of the two epics in their latest form, or even to decide whether *The Ramayana* was composed before *The Mahabharata*, or vice versa. *The Ramayana* is sometimes dated to around 300 BC, and *The Mahabharata* to around AD 400, but these dates mean little without specifying which stage in the process of composition they refer to. Yet, as mentioned in the Introduction, the epics have played a key role in forming the conception of 'history' of most Indians – including that of Gandhi. The reason is implied in the preface to *The Mahabharata*, written by its mythical author, Vyasa, who states that:

> This work opens the eyes of the world blinded by ignorance. As the sun dispels darkness, so does Bharata [the epic] by its exposition of religion, duty, action, contemplation, and so forth. As the full moon by shedding soft light helps the buds of the lotus to open, so this Purana by its exposition expands the human intellect. The lamp of history illumines the 'whole mansion of the womb of Nature.'

Of all the writings that have come down from ancient India, the epics have probably had the most lasting influence – not only on the visual and dramatic arts (chiefly in India, though in Southeast Asia, too, on the walls of Angkor Wat in Cambodia and in the shadow puppet plays of Java) but also on the lives of Hindus. In his fascinating study of *The Mahabharata*, *The Difficulty of Being Good*, Gurcharan Das, a successful Indian executive educated at Harvard University, who gave up his business career to become a writer, comments: '*The Mahabharata* is about our incomplete lives, about good people acting badly, about how difficult it is to be good in this world. It turned out to be a fine guide in my quest to make some sort of sense out of life'. In V. S. Naipaul's *India: A Million Mutinies Now*, a Bangalore-based engineer whose grandfather was a Brahmin priest tells Naipaul about the epic's influence at a more populist level:

> Recently [1989] there have been on TV the serials of the epics, *The Ramayana* and *The Mahabharata*. Most of the people on the streets of Bangalore haven't actually read those epics. They haven't read them in the original or in an English version or in any version. They take them for granted; they're there. They would have known the main characters and the broad theme. They wouldn't have known the details; they wouldn't know the inside characters. But the TV serials were an instant success.

Indeed, the televised *Ramayana* – which was transmitted in seventy-eight weekly episodes on the national channel from early 1987 until mid-1988, followed by *The Mahabharata* in ninety-four weekly episodes from late 1988 to mid-1990 – is generally regarded to have been the most popular programme in the history of Indian television, which brought the country to a virtual standstill while it was on screen.

There have been many attempts to translate *The Ramayana* and *The Mahabharata* into European languages since their European scholarly discovery in the 19th century, most recently in an English edition of *The Mahabharata* published by Penguin Classics which, though abridged by its translator John D. Smith, nevertheless runs to some 900 pages. (The original is seven times the length of Homer's *Iliad* and *Odyssey* combined.) Perhaps the most accessible editions are the two 1970s prose versions in drastically abridged form by India's greatest English-language novelist, R. K. Narayan. In his introduction Narayan regards *The Mahabharata* as 'a great tale with well-defined characters who talk and act with robustness and zest – heroes and villains, saints and kings, women of beauty, all displaying great human qualities, super-human endurance, depths of sinister qualities as well as power, satanic hates and intrigues – presented against an impressive background of ancient royal capitals, forests, and mountains.' However, his versions are retellings, rather than translations. 'I have not attempted any translation, as it is impossible to convey in English the rhythm and depth of the original language. The sound of Sanskrit has a hypnotic quality which is inevitably lost in translation. One has to feel content with a prose narrative in a story form.' In truth, reading Narayan's retellings, one cannot help feeling that he was a little out of his depth. The very qualities of preciseness, subtlety and humour in a purely domestic, contemporary setting for which Narayan's own fiction is affectionately cherished, are surely the antithesis of epic poetry about the ancient past that is profoundly concerned with dynastic politics, war and extreme violence.

The Ramayana, reputedly written by the sage Valmiki, is the shorter and simpler of the two epics. It describes the royal birth of Rama in the kingdom of Ayodhya, his tutelage under the sage Vishvamitra, and his winning of Sita, the daughter of Janaka (the king mentioned in the *Upanishads*) by bending Shiva's mighty bow at a ceremony for a girl to choose her husband from a range of suitors, known as a *swayamvara*. But Rama is banished from the court at Ayodhya through an intrigue, and spends fourteen years in exile in the forest with Sita and his favourite half-brother, Lakshmana. There the demon-king of Lanka, Ravana, sends a golden deer to distract Sita's protectors, and abducts her. Imprisoned in his capital, Sita rejects Ravana's attentions without wavering. Rama and his brother make plans to rescue her, and after many adventures form an alliance with the king of the monkeys, Sugriva; with the aid of the monkey-general Hanuman and Ravana's own brother, they attack Lanka. Rama slays Ravana and rescues Sita. In a later version she undergoes an ordeal by fire so as to clear herself of any suspicions of infidelity. But once Rama and his wife are back in Ayodhya, he learns that his people still have doubts about Sita's chastity, and so he banishes her to the forest. There she meets Valmiki and gives birth at his hermitage to Rama's two sons. When the sons come of age, the family is reunited, but Sita, having once more protested her innocence, requests deliverance from the earth, which swallows her up.

The central plot of *The Mahabharata* is a family feud that becomes a civil war, waged between the five Pandava brothers and their far more numerous Kaurava cousins at Kurukshetra, a real place near Delhi in the modern state of Haryana. It begins with the death of a king and a disputed succession between his sons. The elder of two princes, Dhritarashtra, who is blind, is passed over in favour of his brother Pandu. Dhritarashtra has a hundred sons – all named in the epic – the eldest of whom is Duryodhana; but Pandu is prevented from fathering children by a curse. However, his wife Kunti asks the gods to father children in Pandu's name. The gods agree to this request: the god Dharma will father Yudhishthira; the god of wind Vayu will father Bhima; the god Indra, Arjuna; and the twin gods of sunrise and sunset, the Ashvins, Nakula and Sahadeva (also twins, who are born to Pandu's second wife, Madri). When Pandu dies, enmity and jealousy develop between the cousins and force the five Pandava brothers to leave the kingdom. In their forest exile they jointly marry Draupadi, who is born out of a sacrificial fire and is won by Arjuna after he shoots an arrow through a row of targets. They also meet their cousin Krishna (not a Kaurava, but instead related to them via their mother, Kunti), who becomes their friend and companion. Although the Pandavas return to the kingdom, they are again sent into exile after Yudhishthira loses everything to Duryodhana, the eldest of his Kaurava cousins, in a rigged game of dice – this time for twelve years. The feud culminates in a series of great battles, during which, through the *Bhagavad Gita*, Krishna, as charioteer of the archer Arjuna, encourages a morally squeamish Arjuna to do his duty by killing his Kaurava cousins. 'To die in one's duty is life: to live in another's is death.' All the Kauravas die, and the Pandavas are victorious, but on the Pandava side only the five brothers and Krishna survive. Krishna dies when a hunter, mistaking him for a deer, shoots him in his foot – his one vulnerable spot. The five brothers, along with Draupadi and a companionable stray dog, set out for Indra's heaven in the Himalayas. But each of them, one by one, falls en route, leaving only the sinless Yudhishthira to reach the gate of heaven. After passing further tests of his fidelity and constancy, including a refusal to abandon his dog – who is then revealed to be the god Dharma, Yudhishthira's father, in disguise – Yudhishthira is at last reunited with his four brothers and Draupadi, as well as with his cousin enemies, the Kauravas. All now enjoy perpetual bliss.

Only a little over a fifth of *The Mahabharata* is occupied with this central plot. The rest of the epic concerns a wide range of myths and legends, including the romance of Damayanti and her husband, Nala, who gambles away his kingdom as Yudhishthira did, and the legend of Savitri, whose devotion to her dead husband, Satyavan, convinces the god of death, Yama, to restore him to life. There are also descriptions of places of pilgrimage in various parts of India, such as those associated with the Ganges and the Himalayas.

The great length of the two epics and the difficulty of translating them from the Sanskrit cannot alone account for the generally cool western response to them. The physicist J. Robert Oppenheimer, father of the atomic bomb, who knew Sanskrit, famously quoted some words of Krishna to Arjuna in the *Bhagavad Gita* – 'Now I am become Death, the destroyer of worlds' – to describe his feelings after watching the first detonation of the bomb in the American desert in 1945. However, there are precious few other widely familiar references to the Indian epics in western culture. More typical is the Macaulay-like reaction of a young journalist in India, Rudyard Kipling, reviewing in 1886 the early instalments of a sixteen-volume edition of *The Mahabharata* translated by Pratap Chandra Roy, in the pages of the *Civil and Military Gazette*. According to Kipling:

> section after section [of the epic] – with its monstrous array of nightmare-like incidents, where armies are slain, and worlds swallowed with monotonous frequency, its records of impossible combats, its lengthy catalogues of female charms, and its nebulous digressions on points of morality – gives but the scantiest return for the labour expended on its production. . . . [The] bare

outlines of [the epics'] stories are known and sung by the village folk of the countryside, taking the same place as folklore and love ditties; but as living forces, they are surely dead and their gigantic corpses, like whales stranded by an ebbing tide, are curiosities to be regarded from a distance by the curious, and left alone by those who look for any solid return from laborious reading.

Not to be vanquished by the challenge of translation, a century later, in the 1980s (coincidentally at the very same time as the hugely popular Indian television series), the English theatre director Peter Brook and the French writer Jean-Claude Carrière teamed up to create an ambitious stage version of *The Mahabharata* in English, followed by a film, both with an international cast. The Brook production eschewed the unimaginative literalness of the Indian-made television adaptation, but failed to be a masterpiece of dramatic art. Its staging was splendid and ingenious but – despite some wonderful moments – the effect was ultimately an unmoving cavalcade, curiously reminiscent of the great French director Jean Renoir's failure to make sense of Hinduism in his 1951 film, *The River*, even down to Renoir's uncomfortable use of English, a language in which he was no more at home than were many of Brook's actors.

The most clear-sighted modern artist to attempt the presentation of *The Mahabharata* in translation has been the film director Satyajit Ray, who was uniquely placed to view it through both Indian and western eyes. Like R. K. Narayan, Ray had the advantage of knowing the epic from a young age. As a boy, he had heard the whole story read to him by a great-uncle, in a Bengali version for children created by his writer grandfather – including a particular grisly episode involving severed and exploding heads, which the boy Satyajit wanted to hear at least four times. At the same time, Ray was also steeped in European and American cinema, as well as being conversant with English literature. In the late 1950s he read and reread *The Mahabharata*, 'never ceasing to marvel at it', as he said, but feeling that a film could succeed only by concentrating not on action scenes but on 'the personal relationship – so profound and so timeless, and the reflections on war and peace, with their eternal verities.' Yet, after giving a film adaptation much thought over several years in the 1960s, Ray found himself stumped by the problem of how to introduce even the main characters of its sprawling cast to a non-Indian audience, which he assumed would have to see the film to make such a grand subject financially viable. Without solving this, Ray knew, foreign audiences would be as indifferent to a filmed *Mahabharata* as was Kipling to the literary original.

He never solved the problem. 'I gave up for the very good reason that I couldn't establish the relationships for a foreign audience,' Ray said in the 1980s. 'In a film you have to address somebody as an uncle three times at least to establish that he is an uncle.' He was also bothered by the choice of language, especially as he had in mind (like the later Brook) an international cast, including the Japanese Toshiro Mifune, the lead actor in Akira Kurosawa's *Seven Samurai* (1954). 'Bengali wouldn't do,' Ray said, 'and Hindi doesn't sound right when spoken by *Mahabharata* characters. Perhaps English would have been better.' Sanskrit he didn't even consider; Ray's aim, like Brook in his stage production, was to create 'very modern human beings with modern psychological feelings.' That aim, and some particular cinematic possibilities, explain Ray's attraction to filming just the dice game episode of the epic, in which Yudhishthira loses the kingdom to Duryodhana, watched by the Pandavas and the Kauravas. 'It shows all the characters, and all their aspects,' said Ray. 'I don't think I could have tackled the War at all. You see Peter Brook can suggest a whole chariot with just a wheel. In cinema you can't do that kind of thing.'

Mythical as the Indian epics are, their complex plots and confusing structures are undoubtedly a reflection of the complexity and confusion of real dynastic struggles, warfare between petty states and widespread rapine experienced by the subcontinent during the centuries of their composition. The five centuries between the overthrow of the Mauryas in a military coup d'état by their general, Pushyamitra Shunga, who founded the Shunga dynasty in 187 BC, and the ascent to the throne of Magadha by the first Gupta emperor, Chandra Gupta I (not to be confused with Chandragupta, the first Mauryan emperor), in AD 320, are often considered by historians to be a dark period. Shunga rule lasted for about a century, despite an invasion by an Indo-Greek king, Demetrius I of Bactria, which may have reached as far as Pataliputra. Thereafter came a dearth of strong indigenous rulers, weakened by the further invasions from the northwest of three different peoples descended from the mounted nomadic herdsmen of Central Asia: the Scythians, the Parthians and the Yuezhi, who were known in India as, respectively, the Sakas, the Pahlavas and the Kushans. Indian civilization acquired little from the invaders except their cavalry techniques and 'an almost pathological dread of anarchy', writes Basham, expressed in the concept of *matshya-nyaya*, literally 'the way of the fishes' or, in modern parlance, 'dog-eat-dog'.

In the words of *The Ramayana*:

Where the land is kingless the cloud, lightning-wreathed and loud-voiced, gives no rain to the earth.

Where the land is kingless the son does not honour his father, nor the wife her husband.

Where the land is kingless men do not meet in assemblies, nor make lovely gardens and temples.

Where the land is kingless the rich are unprotected, and shepherds and peasants sleep with bolted doors.

A river without water, a forest without grass,
A herd of cattle without a herdsman, is the land without a king.

With which view of kingship and anarchy, *The Mahabharata* concurs:

> A man should first choose his king, then his wife,
> and only then amass wealth;
> for without a king in the world
> where would wife and property be?

The son of Chandra Gupta I, Samudra Gupta, expanded the Gupta kingdom through warfare. He annexed almost all of the small states along the Ganges and Yamuna Rivers, and forced the eastern and northern border kingdoms of Bengal, Kamarupa (Assam) and Nepal to pay tribute to the Guptas, along with the western tribal oligarchies; even the kings of the Indo-Iranian borderlands offered submission to him. In the south, he appears to have exerted less direct influence, but he did send an expedition down the east coast as far as the Pallava kingdom based at Kanchi (Kanchipuram) in Tamil Nadu, and he received the personal submission of the king of Sri Lanka. During the reign of Chandra Gupta II, the son of Samudra Gupta, Saka (Scythian) rule in western India was brought to an end after three centuries. By the beginning of the 4th century – half way through Chandra Gupta II's reign – the Gupta empire covered most of northern India, and what is often considered to be a 'Golden Age' of prosperity for India began, just as the western empire of ancient Rome fell into disarray at the hands of invaders from Central Asia. However, during the second half of the century, India, too, was once again invaded by nomadic peoples from Central Asia, the Hunas (Huns). Skanda Gupta initially achieved victory over the invaders, but during a second wave of Huna invasion in about 500, the Gupta ruler saw his empire splinter as Gupta vassals in the northwest and Rajasthan transferred their allegiances to the Hunas. (Some scholars attribute the mysterious origin of the later 'Rajput' tribes of Rajasthan – so named during the Mughal empire – to the integration of the Hunas into the Hindu military stratum.) Narasimha Gupta, in coalition with another

Indian king, was able to defeat the Hunas and drive them out of India in 528, but the Gupta empire was essentially finished by about 550, although its suzerainty survived in the east, in Bengal, Orissa and Assam, until as late as 570.

The Gupta and the Mauryan empires differed in important respects. For a start, the Gupta empire had no commitment to non-violence, and indeed employed war as a means of expansion. Secondly, it was somewhat smaller, but more importantly, it was much less centralized. The Gupta emperor ruled more through vassal kings, and was less directly in touch with the people, than the Mauryan. One royal panegyric, a compound word of twenty components, titles the emperor as 'binding together the whole world by putting forth his strength and by [accepting] acts of service [from other kings], such as paying personal homage, the presentation of gifts of maidens, and soliciting his charter, sealed with the Garuda-seal, to confirm them in possession of their territories'.

But while the affairs of state were still the Gupta emperor's sole prerogative, the organization of society was not. Socially, the authority of the Brahmins and the taboos of the caste system were more powerful than they had been under the Mauryas, as we might expect given the intervening centuries of development of Hinduism. Under the Guptas, 'the king's recognized duty was to punish the wicked, protect the good, direct men to their appropriate duties (*varnashrama-dharma*), and prevent the intermixture of the various castes. However, the classical Indian king was not to reform society or improve human nature, as Asoka had attempted to do', writes Thomas Trautmann. 'Society, through the system of castes, was largely capable of regulating itself, with minimal interference by the state to restore the balance from time to time.' The importance of caste is shown by the first indisputable evidence of the practice of something like untouchability in this period. According to the memoir of the Chinese Buddhist monk Faxian, who visited Gupta India at the start of the 5th century, the dwellings of a certain caste were segregated from the rest of society;

moreover, members of this caste, on approaching a market or a city, were required to beat a piece of wood so as to announce their presence to those who wished to avoid 'polluting' contact with them – a practice that would persist in parts of India until the 20th century, in the beating of a small leather drum.

The Guptas also placed emphasis on the arts, unlike the Mauryas. Fine gold coins struck by Samudra Gupta portray him as a warrior (wielding a battle-axe, or slaying a tiger) and as a supporter of religion (conducting the Vedic horse sacrifice) but also as a musician (playing the Indian lyre known as the *veena*). The Gupta court patronized poetry, music and other fine arts, and scholarship, including the founding of a university at Nalanda, not very far from Pataliputra. The traditions of central Indian Gupta art seem to have influenced the soft modelling of the figures and the delicacy of the carving in the paintings of the later caves at Ajanta. But alas, there is no direct description of life at the Gupta court in the poems and plays of the greatest literary figure in Sanskrit, Kalidasa. However, on the evidence of his works' refined style, many scholars think that Kalidasa probably flourished some time during the reigns of Chandra Gupta II and his son Kumara Gupta, that is, between 375 and 455.

In the 7th century, however, well after the Gupta empire, one of the greatest masters of Sanskrit prose, Banabhatta (or Bana), becomes a prolific source of information about life in a relatively insignificant northern kingdom. Thanks to Banabhatta's biography, *Harshacarita* (The Deeds of Harsha), and to the Indian travel journal of the Chinese Buddhist monk Xuanzang, historians know more about life in the empire of the Buddhist king Harsha (or Harshavardhana) than they do about life in the Gupta empire, or indeed in any ancient Indian kingdom, including that of Asoka.

Harsha was originally the prince of a small state near Delhi. Over a reign of four decades he assembled an empire stretching along the Gangetic valley from the eastern Punjab to Bengal and Orissa, with allies further west in Kathiawar and further east in Kamarupa (Assam), all of which quickly unravelled after his death in 647. From Xuanzang's account, it is clear that only Harsha's personal presence could have held such an unwieldy empire together. Harsha was constantly on tour with his army, except during the rainy season, every day (except when he was in battle) distributing alms to both Buddhists and Brahmins, hearing the grievances of people against his officials, and residing in temporary grass shelters that were burned after his departure.

Banabhatta – a Brahmin who had lost both his parents at a young age and decided to lead a bohemian life, travelling adventurously to various courts and universities with a group of friends including his two half-brothers by a lower-caste woman, a snake doctor, a goldsmith, a gambler and a musician, before returning home and eventually, after some coolness from Harsha, joining his court – was a camp follower on Harsha's tours. Although his Sanskrit is ornate, as befits a court writer, and he sometimes exaggerates the virtues of the emperor, as is only to be expected, Banabhatta's powers of observation are exact and concrete, and he shows an empathy with the poor that is rarely found in ancient Indian literature. Banabhatta is perhaps the most modern in outlook of all of the Sanskrit writers from the first millennium.

Here, for example, are a few sentences from his gritty description of Harsha's army striking camp to march against the enemy (in E. B. Cowell and F. W. Thomas's translation):

> In front went the field-kitchens of the chief vassals. Standard bearers led the ranks. As the troops left their small huts hundreds of their friends came out to meet them. The feet of the elephants trampled the hovels by the roadside, and the people came out and threw clods at their keepers, who called on bystanders to witness their assaults. Poor families ran from their wrecked and ruined huts. Oxen, bearing the wealth of unfortunate merchants, fled from the hubbub. Clearing a path through the crowd with the glare of their torches, runners led the way for the elephants bearing the women of the

harem. Horsemen shouted to the dogs running behind them. The veterans praised the tall Tangana horses, which trotted so smoothly and quickly that they made travelling a pleasure. Unhappy Southerners upbraided their fallen mules. The whole world was swallowed in dust.

After Harsha, the Indian kingdoms of the late first millennium once again revert to relative anonymity. In the north, in the middle of the 8th century, the Gurjara-Pratihara dynasty rose to power in the middle Gangetic basin once ruled by Harsha, with their capital at Kanauj. Their control was contested by the Pala dynasty, until the Gurjara-Pratiharas defeated the Palas, who nevertheless retained control of Bengal and Bihar, where they were active patrons of Buddhism and of the Nalanda university until the 11th century. When the Gurjara-Pratihara empire itself weakened in the 10th century, one of its vassals established itself as the Chandella dynasty in central India, with its first capital at Khajuraho.

Further south, new dynasties appeared on opposite sides of the peninsula. On the northwestern side, in the Deccan, the Chalukyas of Badami ruled in the time of Harsha, whom they fought under their ruler Pulakeshin II and defeated in 620, agreeing to establish the Narmada River as the boundary between the Chalukya kingdom and Harsha's empire. But in the 8th century the Chalukyas were themselves defeated by the Rashtrakutas, who went on to establish a powerful state that clashed with both the Gurjara-Pratiharas to the north and the rulers of the Tamil country to the south, until the Rashtrakuta dynasty was replaced in the late 10th century by a revived Chalukya dynasty, generally known as the Western Chalukyas (to distinguish them from the Eastern Chalukyas, a buffer state between the Western Chalukyas and the south-eastern Chola empire). On the south-eastern side of the peninsula, the Tamil country and the Coromandel coast, the Pallavas ruled from at least the time of Samudra Gupta's expedition to the south in the 4th century, perhaps even as early as the 2nd century. Pallava rule lasted until the 9th century, when Vijayalaya Chola, who was probably a vassal of the Pallavas, established the Chola kingdom, its name coming from one of the three ancient Tamil kingdoms. The Chola empire, renowned for its bronze sculptures combining simplicity with ornamentation, reached its zenith under Rajaraja and his son Rajendra I in the 11th century, dominating not only much of southern and eastern India but also Sri Lanka and Sumatra, Java and the Malay peninsula – as a result of an unprecedented Chola naval expedition to Southeast Asia.

We may know the names of these Indian dynasties (as well as those of other dynasties of the first millennium AD), and the names of many of their rulers, but we know rather little of their society and thought from their surviving inscriptions. Even so, it is clear from the records that they presided over states that were often stable, substantial and creative. Many dynasties endured for centuries, with their rulers reigning for an average of twenty years: for example, the Eastern Chalukyas lasted for over 400 years, the Palas of Bengal for nearly 400 years, and the Cholas of south India for more than 300 years – a period considerably longer than that of the British empire in India. They also commissioned and embellished some of the greatest of India's Hindu temples at sites such as Badami, Elephanta, Ellora, Khajuraho, Mahabalipuram and Thanjavur, and filled them with treasures. India in the late first millennium certainly did not descend into anarchy, as it did in the dark period between the Mauryas and the Guptas. But neither were its rulers capable of uniting, as they had under Asoka and Chandra Gupta II. And so, when the next great wave of invaders after the Hunas arrived around 1000, western and northern India would prove to be vulnerable to attack.

FIVE

The Coming of Islam

THE COMING OF ISLAM

India's initial encounter with Islam was a peaceful and productive one. The religion came in the shape of Arab merchants landing on the coastlines. Long before the time of the Prophet Muhammad, Arab, Greek and Roman traders had journeyed by boat from ports on the Egyptian coast of the Red Sea such as Berenike along the Arabian and African coasts of the Indian Ocean. In due course they learned how to sail directly across the ocean to India with the summer southwesterly monsoon wind; this method may first have been used by a Greek skipper, Eudoxus of Cyzicus, between 120 and 110 BC, under the guidance of an Indian sailor who had been shipwrecked in the Red Sea and offered his navigational services in Alexandria. Some of the Arab traders settled in the ports of the Malabar coast in south-western India, such as ancient Muziris, where they intermarried with the locals. From the 7th century, after their conversion to Islam, they became a Muslim community in Kerala known as the Moplahs (or Mappilas). Tradition has it – there is no historical evidence – that one of the ruling Chera dynasty of Kerala even converted to Islam during the lifetime of the Prophet and built the first Indian mosque in Kodungallur (Cranganore) in 629, perhaps on the site of today's Cheraman Juma Masjid, a mosque built in the 12th century.

Subsequent Muslim incursions were less peaceful, however. The first Arab (Umayyad) conquest of Indian territory occurred in Sindh, in 711; but the attempted expansion of this Arab empire further into India was successfully resisted by both the Chalukyas and the Gurjara-Pratiharas in the

730s. There was now a hiatus until the late 10th century, when Turkish raids on India from Afghanistan began, led by Mahmud of Ghazni; these raids continued for two centuries until the defeat of Prithviraj Chauhan, leader of the Rajput Chauhan dynasty, by Muhammad of Ghor at the second battle of Tarain, north of Delhi, in 1192. Soon after, the first Muslim government in India was established by Turko-Afghans with its capital in Delhi: the first mosque there was completed in 1198, and what is known as the Delhi Sultanate began on Muhammad of Ghor's death in 1206 with the accession of his slave governor, Qutb-ud-din Aibak. It endured through five successive dynasties, the Mamluks, Khiljis, Tughlaqs, Sayyids and Lodis, although a sultan's average reign was only ten years and often ended squalidly in murderous violence, including the catastrophic sack of Delhi by the Mongol ruler Timur (Tamerlane) in 1398. Then, in 1526, yet another invasion from Afghanistan, this time by Babur, descendant of Timur and Genghis Khan, inaugurated the Mughal empire, which ruled most of India until the mid-18th century.

Thus, for some six centuries, the leading power in India was Muslim, not Hindu. Even after the beginning of British rule in 1757, for many decades the language of government and diplomacy remained Persian, as it had been under the Mughals. At the time of Independence in 1947, undivided India had the largest population of Muslims in the world – larger than the entire Muslim population of the Middle East in the original homeland of Islam – before it split into two nations, India and Pakistan, the first having a Hindu majority but retaining a very substantial Muslim minority. The great question for historians is whether the partition of India was an inevitable outcome of the long and often troubled history of Hindu–Muslim relations in India, or not.

What caused the Hindu rulers of the 11th and 12th centuries to be more vulnerable to the Turko-Afghan attacks than their predecessors had been to the Arab attacks in the 8th century? Historians have advanced various theories since the 19th century, including the enervating effects of tropical climates, the petty rivalries born of feudal loyalties, the inherent divisiveness of the caste system and the unwieldiness of the rulers' elephant-mounted armies. However, all of these factors would presumably have applied during the abortive 8th-century Arab expansion. A more convincing explanation lies in the comparative strength of the later invaders. 'While several factors defeated the Hindu rulers, the overriding elements in the Muslim victory were their advanced military tactics and the tenacity of their Turkic leaders, who from their childhood were nurtured in the guerrilla warfare of the steppes', argues the historian S. A. A. Rizvi. 'If able leadership counted for anything, Mahmud [of Ghazni] and Muhammad [of Ghor] were such leaders.' Moreover, 'Prospects of limitless Indian loot united the tribes'. No doubt Muslim religious zealotry against Hindu idolaters was an additional motivating factor; but while much evidence exists of Muslim iconoclasm, surprisingly little is available for the forced conversions of Hindus to Islam by the invaders.

There can be no question about the scale of the destruction by the Turko-Afghans in India in the three centuries from the time of Mahmud of Ghazni to the death of Alauddin Khilji in Delhi in 1316 – if we judge from the accounts of Muslim chroniclers, such as al-Biruni, who was a contemporary of Mahmud. Between 1001 and 1027 Mahmud made seventeen great raids on India, carrying back to Ghazni enormous quantities of loot, as well as slaves, from palaces and Hindu temples in the west and north of India, as far apart as the great Shiva temple at Somnath in Kathiawar, the cities of Kanauj and Mathura in the Ganges valley, which were captured and plundered, and the central Indian kingdom of the Chandellas (not to mention Mahmud's plundering of cities with 'heretic' Muslim populations such as Multan in the Punjab and Rey in Iran). At Somnath, Mahmud ordered the upper part of the Shiva lingam to be broken and the remainder to be taken to Ghazni, 'with all its coverings and trappings of gold, jewels and embroidered garments', writes al-Biruni. 'Part of it has been thrown into the hippodrome of the town . . . Another part . . . lies before the door of the mosque of Ghazni, on which people rub their feet to clean them from dirt and wet.' In the 1190s, the first mosque in Delhi, named Quwwat-ul-Islam (Might of Islam), with its famous victory tower known as the Qutb Minar, was constructed by Qutb-ud-din Aibak from the reassembled pillars, capitals and lintels of no fewer than twenty-seven Hindu and Jain temples (as noted in a Persian inscription on the mosque's gateway). In 1309–11, after Malik Kafur, a slave who became general of the army of Alauddin Khilji, had campaigned southwards as far as Madurai in Tamil Nadu, his army eventually returned to Delhi with booty consisting of 612 elephants, 20,000 horses, 96,000 *man* of gold (estimated to be 241 metric tons) and countless boxes of jewels and pearls, one of which was said to have been the Koh-i-noor diamond – as recorded by the historian Ziauddin Barani, who was personally present in Delhi. Barani writes in his chronicle: 'The old inhabitants of Delhi remarked that so much gold had never before been brought into Delhi. No one could remember anything like it, nor was there anything like it recorded in history.'

Scholarship and libraries suffered, too, under the Turko-Afghan assaults. The great university at Nalanda in Bihar, founded under the Gupta dynasty, appears to have been ransacked and its library burnt by the forces of Muhammad Bakhtiyar Khilji around 1193, according to a contemporary Persian historian, Minhaj Siraj – though he does not specifically name Nalanda, referring only to the destruction of a city in western Bihar that was found to be a place of study. In 1234–35, the travelling Tibetan trans-lator Dharmasvamin (who had noted the invaders' damage at Bodhgaya) was an eyewitness when Nalanda, now reduced to just two monasteries with seventy monks, was attacked. A 17th-century Tibetan authority on Buddhism in India, Taranatha, refers to three separate attacks in the same period, in which 'the Turks conquered the whole of Magadha and destroyed many monasteries; at Nalanda they did much damage and the monks fled abroad' (chiefly to Tibet), or were massacred. Partly as a result of such Turko-Afghan depredations, Buddhist manuscripts disappeared altogether from India, as we know; and as much as 90 per cent of the extant Sanskrit literature postdates 1200 and was written in the Indian regions unaffected by the Muslim conquest, such as Kerala, according to an estimate by a modern Sanskrit scholar.

Even from this one example of Nalanda, it is clear that the sources on the looting and destruction of cities are not always specific and to some extent differ, besides having their own possible biases. When it comes to the totality of Hindu temple desecration by Muslim invaders and rulers, the debate becomes seriously contentious and distinctly politicized. Hindu nationalists such as Sita Ram Goel and other contributors to a two-volume work published in the 1990s, *Hindu Temples: What Happened to Them*, have compiled a list from historical sources – both Hindu and Muslim, contemporary and retrospective – 'of 2000 Muslim monuments built on the sites and/or with the materials of Hindu temples'; others claim to have found as many as 60,000 instances of temple desecration. By contrast, the historian of Indian Islam, Richard Eaton, in his book challenging such claims, *Temple Desecration and Muslim States in Medieval India*, argues for a mere eighty 'reasonably certain' cases of desecration based on a strict reliance on 'contemporary or near-contemporary epigraphic and literary evidence' for the period 1192–1729. Eaton explains:

> Undoubtedly, some temples were desecrated but the facts in the matter were never recorded, or the facts were recorded but the records themselves no longer survive. Conversely, later Indo-Muslim chroniclers, seeking to glorify the religious zeal of earlier Muslim rulers, sometimes attributed acts of temple desecration to rulers even when no contemporary evidence supports their claims. As a result, we shall never know the precise number of temples desecrated in Indian history.

In 1990, the Hindu nationalist BJP launched a so-called 'Rath Yatra' (a term normally denoting a Hindu chariot festival) at the Somnath Temple in Gujarat, the site of the temple desecrated in 1026. The idea was that the BJP's air-conditioned Toyota van, decorated as a Hindu *rath* (chariot), would journey from Somnath across northern India towards Ayodhya in Uttar Pradesh, the birthplace of Lord Rama according to *The Ramayana*. There, said Hindu nationalists, an ancient temple dedicated to Rama had been obliterated in 1528 by the construction of a mosque on the authority of the first Mughal emperor Babur. This political stunt had a major impact in galvanizing electoral support for the BJP. It also prepared the way for the violent demolition of the mosque in Ayodhya, known as the Babri Masjid, by a crowd of activists at the end of 1992 – an act that divided Indians and alerted the world to the growing power of Hindu nationalism.

'The destruction of the mosque was justified by some groups as the Hindu reply to Mahmud's iconoclasm', notes Romila Thapar in her *Somanatha: The Many Voices of a History*. 'Such a view is historically untenable, because apart from other factors, it nullifies the events that took place in and around Somanatha [Somnath] during the intervening thousand years.'

The historiography of the Somnath Temple's desecration is unexpectedly confusing and complex. Turko-Persian and Arab writers, including al-Biruni, discuss Mahmud's raid, but give conflicting accounts, even on the question of whether the idol was a lingam or some other kind of image. Al-Biruni is definite about a lingam, as mentioned above, and some writers concur with him; other early writers refer to an idol of a pre-Islamic goddess of southern Arabia, Manat, or to an anthropomorphic figure stuffed with jewels. Al-Kazwini, writing in the 13th century, fails to describe the idol's form but provides a long and incredible account of how it floated in mid-air without any visible means of support, perhaps because it was made of iron and its canopy was an ingeniously contrived lodestone, as one of the raiding party suggested to Sultan Mahmud. 'Whoever beheld it floating in the air was struck with amazement, whether he was a Mussulman or an infidel.'

Among Hindus, no contemporary or near-contemporary local source refers to the raid, other than a passing mention in a Jain text, so it clearly did not outrage Hindus at the time it occurred. It was still unmentioned two centuries later, in the mid-13th century, during the rule of the Chalukya-Vaghela dynasty, when the town authorities gave permission for a mosque to be built in the vicinity of the temple by a Muslim shipping magnate with trading connections in Somnath, one Nuruddin Firuz from Hormuz in Persia. The local raja, the town's elite and the Brahmin priests of the temple all welcomed this proposal, according to a lengthy bilingual inscription in Sanskrit and Arabic drawn up by the Persian merchant, which details the gift of land from the temple estate for the construction of the mosque. There is no hint in this document of any earlier ill-feeling between Hindus and Muslims at Somnath.

Indeed, the very first historical reference to any Hindu outrage at Mahmud's raid comes, strangely enough, from a heated debate over the Somnath Temple in the British Parliament in 1843. The governor-general of India, Lord Ellenborough, had issued a controversial proclamation to the chiefs and princes of northern and western India. In a clear attempt to curry favour with Hindus, and to repudiate the Afghan Muslims with whom Britain was then at war, Ellenborough ordered the original gates of the Somnath Temple, which Mahmud had supposedly carted away to Ghazni in 1026, to be restored to the temple, with the express intention of avenging an 800-year-old insult to Hindu pride. But rather than evoking a positive response in India from the princes and Hindus in general, the British proclamation instead provoked a battle in London, with a flight of rhetoric from Macaulay in the House of Commons attacking Ellenborough, not only for advocating shameful Hindu idolatry of an unmentionable kind (phallus worship) but also for employing the language of an Indian potentate rather than an English imperialist. Why, said a mocking Macaulay, should Ellenborough not imitate the Indian princes by sitting cross-legged, allowing his beard to grow to his waist, wearing a turban and riding about Calcutta 'on a horse jingling with bells and glittering with false pearls'? Although a parliamentary motion to censure Ellenborough was defeated, he was recalled from India a year later, partly as a result of his misjudged Somnath Temple proclamation.

From now on, the historical desecration of the temple began to acquire its modern symbolic resonance. In the 1860s, the mysterious idol was incorporated into the plot of Wilkie Collins's hugely successful mystery novel, *The Moonstone*, in the form of the Yellow Diamond. 'Of all the deities worshipped in the temple, the moon-god alone escaped the rapacity of the conquering Mohammedans. Preserved by three Brahmins, the inviolate deity, bearing the Yellow Diamond in its forehead, was removed by night, and was transported to the second of the sacred cities of India – the city of Benares', writes Collins. In reality, the controversial gates in Ghazni were apparently retrieved by the British and brought back to India, but discovered to be of non-Indian workmanship (made from Afghan deodar, not the alleged Indian sandalwood) and discreetly relegated to a storeroom in the Agra Fort. Yet, a century or so later, in 1951, there was a report from Peshawar in Pakistan that millions of Afghan tribesmen were willing to prevent the return of the gates from Afghanistan to India. Prime Minister Nehru felt obliged to inform the prime minister of Pakistan that the story was completely false: 'In fact nobody knows if there are any such gates anywhere and nothing of the kind is being sent from Afghanistan to India.' In her book on Somnath, Thapar notes a recent claim that the gates are now part of an unidentified *haveli* (private mansion) in Rajasthan. 'The claim to the identity of the gates will doubtless be revived from time to time.'

On the whole, concludes Eaton from his careful study of the records, desecration of temples was motivated far more by politics than by religion. In other words, when a Hindu dynasty was overthrown by military force, a temple that was particularly identified with the ruler's power –

typically because it housed an image of his state-deity (usually Vishnu or Shiva) – tended to be looted and destroyed by the invaders. Temples that were not identified in this way, or which had been abandoned by their royal patrons, were normally left alone. The Somnath Temple, which had long been closely associated with royal power in Gujarat, was therefore targeted for desecration in 1026, and subsequently by Alauddin Khilji in 1296, by two different sultans of Gujarat in 1375 and 1451, and yet again by the Mughal emperor Aurangzeb in 1701. But the temples of the Chandella dynasty at Khajuraho were left undesecrated (despite their explicit sexual imagery), because their royal patrons appear to have abandoned them before the appearance of Turko-Afghan armies in the area in the early 13th century. A further example of such differing treatments comes from Benares under Mughal rule. In 1659, Aurangzeb, despite his well-known religious orthodoxy, ordered local officials to prevent the harassment of Brahmin priests in charge of the temples in the sacred city: 'you must see that nobody unlawfully disturbs the Brahmins or other Hindus of that region, so that they might remain in their traditional place and pray for the continuance of the Empire.' Yet only ten years later, in 1669, Aurangzeb ordered the demolition of the most important Hindu temple in Benares, the Vishvanath Temple, and the construction of a mosque on the site. This was punishment for a rebellion of landholders in Benares, whom Aurangzeb suspected of assisting the escape from Mughal detention of his arch-enemy, Shivaji, the leader of the Marathas (Mahrattas), a warrior caste found predominantly in the Deccan (modern Maharashtra). Among the prime suspects was the great grandson of Raja Man Singh, who had almost certainly built the Vishvanath Temple in the previous century.

Cooperative Hindus formed part of government and administration under the Delhi Sultanate, though much less so than they would under the Mughals. In Delhi, and also in the sultanate's provincial capitals, the court consisted principally of Turks, Afghans and Persians, with few

Indians. 'Ethnic as much as religious exclusivity made the Delhi regime totally alien to most of India's peoples', notes John Keay.

At the apex of power was the Turko-Afghan military aristocracy, who occupied the chief military and political offices of the kingdom. They ruled through a group of Iranian Muslim administrators, many of whom were glad to escape the disaster inflicted on Iran in 1258 by the Mongol invasion that destroyed Baghdad and finished the Abbasid caliphate. These Iranians knew that the Delhi Sultanate made 'a practice of honouring strangers, and showing affection to them, and singling them out for governorships or high dignitaries of state', in the words of the Moroccan traveller Ibn Batuta, who worked as a judge in Delhi under the fabulously rich and bloodthirsty Sultan Muhammad bin Tughlaq in the 1330s. Thus, thanks to Mongol rule in Iran, and to the wealth and generosity of the military aristocracy in Delhi, India gave employment to a steady stream of émigré Iranian Muslims literate in the Persian language who became judges, land revenue officers and bureaucrats, scholars and teachers, poets and artists. This continued to be true under the Mughals and, for a short while, even under the British. It is these Indo-Persian chroniclers – both grateful to and nervous of their generous Turko-Afghan patrons in Delhi – who must bear some of the responsibility for the British colonial division of Indian history into the 'Hindu' and 'Islamic' eras. With the important exception of Akbar's courtier Abu'l Fazl, most of the chroniclers took it for granted that Indian history began with the advent of Indo-Muslim rule in 1192.

How then, given the separation between the Muslim rulers and the non-Muslim ruled in these centuries of Muslim dominance, did India come to acquire such a substantial Muslim population? Liaisons and marriages between Turkish, Afghan and Persian men and Indian women certainly occurred, as happened in the growth of Kerala's Moplah community (and between early British colonialists and Indian women in the 18th and early 19th centuries). These naturally contributed to the numbers of Muslims in the cities. So, too, did the conversion of Indians to Islam. But it appears that the process of conversion was far from the stereotype of the invading Muslim warrior converting the Hindu infidel under threat of imminent death.

There are three common theories to explain the conversion of Indians to Islam. The first, involving military force, was favoured by Orientalist scholars in the late 19th and early 20th centuries, who identified Islam as a religion of the sword. But the evidence for it is weak. In Indo-Persian chronicles, it is true that there are frequent phrases about the conquered like 'they submitted to Islam' and 'they came under submission to Islam', which suggest that the Indians changed their faith under coercion. Read in context, however, the passages in which these phrases occur generally refer not to religion but to submission to the state or its army. Furthermore, and more convincing, the areas of India where there are most Muslims are not the areas that came most directly under the rule of the Delhi Sultanate and the Mughal empire, as one would expect from this theory, but rather the areas on the fringes of Indo-Muslim rule, in eastern Bengal (present-day Bangladesh) and the western Punjab. In addition, forced conversion of large numbers of Indians would have created a reservoir of resentment – a potentially disastrous policy for the vastly outnumbered Turko-Afghan elite.

A second theory involves political patronage and careerism. The idea here is that Indians converted to Islam in exchange for favours granted by the ruling class, for instance promotion within the administration or relief from taxes. Non-Muslims under the Delhi Sultanate were liable for a poll tax (*jizya*) and a heavy tax on agricultural land (*kharaj*), whereas Muslims paid no poll tax and a much lower rate of tax on agricultural land. Census records from the 19th century note that many Hindu landholding families had earlier declared themselves to be Muslims in order to avoid imprisonment for non-payment of *kharaj*, or to keep ancestral lands in the family. But again this theory stumbles on the fact that conversions to Islam were highest not in regions near the centres of political patronage in Delhi and the provincial capitals but in peripheral regions. Moreover, it is by no means clear that a new convert was financially better off than he had been as a Hindu. Although a Muslim was exempted from paying *jizya* and *kharaj*, he was liable for *zakat*, a tax based on a man's wealth, specified in the Qur'an as a way of redistributing wealth to poor and distressed Muslims. 'Islamicization neither undermined state finances nor helped the convert financially', according to Rizvi.

The third theory, which is by far the most popular one today, attributes conversion to a natural human desire to escape social oppression. As Dalits in post-Independence India converted to Buddhism to escape caste oppression, so those living under Muslim rule oppressed by the Hindu caste system are thought to have converted to Islam, with its message of social equality. But there are serious difficulties with this theory too, flattering as it may be to modern advocates of social justice. It is predicated on the concept of a monolithic Hindu social order, unchanging over time and equally oppressive in all parts of India, which is historically invalid. It assumes that Islam in pre-colonial times was linked with ideas of social equality, for which there is actually no evidence, as Eaton points out. Moreover, the geography of conversion to Islam is yet again opposed to the theory. The vast majority of Islamicization under the Delhi Sultanate and the Mughal empire took place not among Hindus in areas of historic Brahmin domination, such as the valley of the Ganges, but in areas that had never experienced the Hindu social order: among indigenous peoples in eastern Bengal, western Punjab, the Northwest Frontier and Baluchistan.

Just how complex was the question of conversion is shown by the life of the mystic poet Kabir, who is probably the best known of the many religious reformers who formed part of the Hindu *bhakti* movement, which flourished in the 14th–17th centuries. All of these reformers believed in the worship of a personal god through love, and in their vernacular language, rather than in the Sanskrit favoured by the Brahmins. Apart from Kabir, they include Sankaradeva from Assam, Nanak from Punjab, Chaitanya from Bengal, Meera Bai from Rajasthan, Tukaram from Maharashtra and Tyagaraja from Tamil Nadu. Nanak, the first of the ten Sikh gurus, founded Sikhism by combining elements from Hinduism and Islam into a monotheistic religion that rejected the caste system but in due course – under its tenth guru – adopted five distinctive outward forms of dress: long hair (to be covered by a turban) and an uncut beard, a comb, a short sword, a steel bangle and short trousers (for horse riding).

Kabir's dates are sometimes given as 1440–1518, but there is no certainty. Not even his family's religion is certain. Was he a Muslim, as his name suggests? Or perhaps a Hindu attracted to Islam? Tantalizing legends surround Kabir's birth in the region of Benares. In one version he is said to have been the illegitimate son of a Brahmin widow who, to avoid public shame, left her baby near a pond outside Benares, where he was found by a childless Muslim weaver and his wife, who adopted him; his name (which means 'Great' in Arabic) was given to him by a local judge.

In adult life Kabir became an ardent opponent of sectarianism, lambasting the religious beliefs and rituals of both Hindus and Muslims in bitter and sarcastic language that still has the power to offend. Here is a sample (translated by the modern poet Arvind Krishna Mehrotra):

If you say you're a Brahmin
Born of a mother who's a Brahmin,
Was there a special canal
Through which you were born?

And if you say you're a Turk
And your mother's a Turk,
Why weren't you circumcised
Before birth?

As for his own faith, Kabir declared:

114

Listen carefully,
Neither the *Vedas*
Nor the Qur'an
Will teach you this:
Put the bit in its mouth,
The saddle on its back,
Your foot in the stirrup,
And ride your wild runaway mind
All the way to heaven.

He also said:

I am not Hindu nor Muslim
Allah-Ram is the breath of my body!

When he died, Kabir's Hindu disciples wanted to cremate his body, while his Muslim disciples wished him to be buried. Today Kabir has two graves, one venerated by Muslims, the other by Hindus; and his reputation and poetry have been embraced as much, if not more, by Hindus (including Tagore) as by Muslims. For Hindus, Kabir seems to belong in the Vaishnavite tradition, that of devotees of Vishnu, while for Muslims, he is close to Sufism.

Kabir's vehemence against religious orthodoxy was presumably a response to the society of his age, observes Gail Omvedt in her study of Buddhism and Brahminism. 'Brahminism in alliance with kings, whether Muslim or "Hindu", was in firm control of [Kabir's] social world.' Certainly such conservatism was typical of both Delhi and Benares. They were barren places, artistically speaking. The aesthetic of the Delhi Sultanate was borrowed from the Middle East, as expressed in its mosques, fortifications and tombs, and was more forbidding than enchanting; the softening and enlivening influence of Indian art was yet to come. The Qutb Minar, the ruins

115

of Tughlaqabad and the Lodi tombs – perhaps the most striking survivals from the sultanate period in Delhi – are no match for the finest buildings of the Mughals.

But this picture was not so true away from the capital city, in the provinces of Bengal, the Deccan, Gujarat, Jaunpur, Kashmir and Malwa. The Delhi Sultanate reached its furthest extent in India in the 1330s, during the reign of Muhammad bin Tughlaq, and then started to fall apart. In 1336, two brothers whom the sultan is said to have captured and converted, renounced Islam and founded the Hindu kingdom of Vijayanagar, which over the next two centuries would become a great empire in what is now the southern state of Karnataka. Although Hindu in name, Vijayanagar was Hindu and Muslim in practice, its rulers even adopting the costume of the Delhi sultans as a norm of diplomatic dress. In 1338, Bengal became effectively independent of Delhi, followed by the Deccan in 1347 under Bahman Shah. During the next century, after Timur's sack of Delhi in 1398 that accelerated the sultanate's decline, all of the above provinces became either partly or entirely independent of the centre.

In such provincial capitals as Ahmedabad, Gaur, Hyderabad and Mandu, where Muslims were not in a majority, there was a much greater synthesis of Muslim and Hindu cultures in architecture than in Delhi. At Mandu, on a fortified hilltop with twenty-five miles of perimeter wall near Indore, in Madhya Pradesh, the Malwa sultans spent the century or so before they too fell to the Mughals, creating extraordinarily graceful and unorthodox architecture, both religious and secular – a foretaste of the best Mughal architecture. The domed tomb of the Malwa ruler Hoshang Shah, who ruled from 1405 to 1435, is the first building in India to have been entirely marble-clad. The beauty of its proportions moved the builder of the Taj Mahal, Shah Jahan, on a pilgrimage to Mandu in 1659, to 'show his reverence' in a Persian inscription beside the entrance door. The fanciful Jahaz Mahal or Ship Palace, 400-feet long, is a two-tiered edifice, with domed pavilions on its 'deck', and a sort of stone prow, which appears to float at anchor in an artificial lake if viewed from an appropriate angle, especially during the monsoons when the lake brims with water. Rupmati's Pavilion, built on a high point at the far edge of the fortress overlooking the Narmada River, is named after Rani Rupmati, a singer, a Hindu (possibly of Rajput origin) and the favourite queen of Baz Bahadur, Malwa's last sultan. Baz Bahadur and Rupmati are perhaps the Romeo and Juliet of India, celebrated in songs, poems and movies. Baz Bahadur was defeated in battle by the forces of the Mughal emperor Akbar in 1561 and forced to flee; Rani Rupmati was captured and committed suicide, apparently by swallowing ground diamonds.

SIX

The Mughal Empire

THE MUGHAL EMPIRE

The Mughals, for all the Medici-like aura that surrounds their name as India's most powerful and glamorous ruling dynasty, occupy an ambiguous position in modern India. In a nation that scarcely lacks for statues of public figures, since Independence not a single statue of a Mughal emperor has been erected in Agra, the former Mughal capital, as noted by the historian William Dalrymple. Nor has the Indian postal service produced any stamp with a portrait of a Mughal emperor, despite issuing stamps commemorating many comparatively obscure Indian leaders. Indeed, only four stamps from the decades since 1947 have referred directly to the Mughal rulers. One shows calligraphy by the last Mughal ruler, the accomplished Urdu poet Bahadur Shah Zafar, and was issued in 1975 on the bicentenary of his birth; another depicts the tomb of the emperor Akbar at Sikandra, near Agra; while the other two show the Taj Mahal at Agra: the tomb of Akbar's grandson, the emperor Shah Jahan, and his favourite queen, Mumtaz Mahal, which is often regarded as the greatest artistic achievement of the Mughals.

Such an absence of public depiction of the emperors during the three centuries or so of the Mughal empire, from its foundation by Babur in 1526 up to 1857, is easily explained. Orthodox Islam discourages portraiture: there are no portraits at all of the rulers of the Delhi Sultanate, for example – not even on their coins; the Mughal emperors were unorthodox in commissioning numerous miniature portrait paintings of themselves by their court artists. Nor is it surprising that the Mughal rulers were not publicly celebrated during the British Raj after 1857. Bahadur Shah Zafar, officially

known as the king of Delhi, was the titular leader of the disastrous uprising against British rule in 1857–58; the colonial authorities were therefore
hardly likely to celebrate Mughal rulers, however much they may have
wished to inherit the mantle of the Mughals as an aid to maintaining their
own power, by renovating Mughal monuments and using them as settings
for British imperial pomp and splendour. But the absence becomes harder
to comprehend in post-Independence India, especially at the time of the
centenary of the uprising in 1957, when Bahadur Shah Zafar might perhaps
have been expected to be hailed by Indians as an early freedom fighter
against colonialism.

Nehru, in *The Discovery of India*, expressed open admiration for the
Mughals, especially Akbar's reign as embodying some kind of Italian
Renaissance court. 'Round himself Akbar collected a brilliant group of men,
devoted to him and his ideals', wrote Nehru. 'It was in his reign that the cultural amalgamation of Hindu and Muslim in north India took a long step
forward. Akbar himself was certainly as popular with the Hindus as with the
Muslims. The Mughal dynasty became firmly established as India's own.'
But this somewhat romanticized feeling did not translate into official action
after 1947 and was, it seems, not widely shared by Nehru's contemporaries,
including Gandhi, and their descendants.

As Dalrymple remarks in *The Last Mughal*, his lively history of the
pivotal events of 1857–58:

The profoundly sophisticated, liberal and plural civilization championed by
Akbar, Dara Shikoh [eldest son of Shah Jahan] or the later Mughal emperors
has only a limited resonance for the urban middle class in modern India.
Many of these are now deeply ambivalent about the achievements of the
Mughals, even if they will still happily eat a Mughal meal, or flock to the
cinema to watch a Bollywood Mughal epic, or indeed head to the Red Fort [in
Delhi] to hear their prime minister give the annual Independence Day speech
from the battlements in front of the Lahore Gate.

Taking the long view of Mughal history, this attitude is comprehensible, however. For all its undoubted artistic achievements, especially in architecture and the visual arts, the Mughal empire was always a despotic and heavily militarized regime, even under Akbar – and even when compared with some of the militaristic regimes of the Delhi Sultanate. Secondly, the empire remained, in many ways, a foreign imposition on India, not least in its ruling cadre and its administrative language, Persian. Thirdly, the empire's state religion was of course Islam, though practised by its elite with widely varying degrees of orthodoxy.

On the whole, departures from Islamic orthodoxy – as seen in the building of the Taj Mahal, which despite being a tomb has the minarets appropriate to a mosque – would prove to be a strength for the empire. In matters of religion and politics, the Mughals were arguably stronger in India when their regime was inclusive of all faiths, as under Akbar in the second half of the 16th century, and weaker when they became more exclusively Islamic, as under Aurangzeb. It was, after all, Aurangzeb, the most orthodox of the Great Mughals, who weakened the empire by attempting to expand it to its greatest extent from the 1660s until his death in 1707, thereby creating the conditions for its decline and breakup during the first half of the 18th century.

The same is true, too, of the unorthodox way in which the emperors involved women in the running of the empire, whether as patrons of architecture and investors in business, or more directly in court politics during fratricidal succession struggles, and even as rulers in the case of Nur Jahan, the twentieth and favourite wife of Akbar's son Jehangir. In the memoirs and letters of the emperors are recorded Babur's Friday afternoon visits to his aunts, Akbar's devotion to his mother, Jehangir's admiration for Nur Jahan and Aurangzeb's respect for his sister, Jahanara, despite her opposition to his succession. It was Akbar's 80-year-old mother, along with one of his wives, who managed to patch up a feud between Akbar and Jehangir at the end of Akbar's life, prevent civil war between father and son, and ensure a peaceful succession.

Even from their unorthodox attitude to mood-enhancing drugs, which went against the tenets of the Qur'an, the Mughal emperors seem to have derived a certain strength. Many indulged seriously in alcohol and opium but managed to control their consumption, unlike some of their offspring who died from alcohol addiction, including two of Akbar's three sons. Babur, before a great battle with the Rajputs in 1527, ordered all of his gold and silver drinking goblets to be smashed and the metal given to the poor, and the supplies of wine in his camp to be destroyed. But a year or so later he wrote: 'Everybody regrets drinking and then takes the oath; but I have taken the oath and now regret it.' He soon returned to his old habits, much to the relief of his soldiers. Akbar, however, is on record as having tried the newly arrived intoxicant tobacco in a hookah, against the advice of his physician, on the grounds that 'we must not reject a thing that has been adopted by people of the world, merely because we cannot find it in our books; or how shall we progress?' – and then rejected the smoking habit, despite tobacco's popularity among the nobles of his court.

In many ways Babur, whose name means 'Tiger', set the tone for the entire dynasty, combining audacious conquest with intelligent hedonism. Born in Central Asia (now Uzbekistan) in 1483, the descendant of Timur on his father's side and of Genghis Khan on his mother's side, Babur was a swashbuckling adventurer and a distinguished military commander, determined to win for himself a kingdom worthy of his ancestry. His deepest desire was to retake his patrimony, Samarkand, but though he succeeded in doing so twice, the first time at the age of only 15, his army was unable to hold the city. Eventually, Babur captured Kabul and made it his base. From there he launched his first raid into northwest India in 1505. But it took another two decades before he made a direct attack on the Delhi Sultanate of Ibrahim Lodi, at the invitation of Lodi's opponent, the governor of the Punjab. In the decisive battle of Panipat in 1526, Babur defeated the Lodi army of 100,000 men supported by 1,000 elephants with a mere 12,000 men, by relying on a combination of the loyalty to him of his compact group, skilful manoeuvering by his cavalry, and the use of firearms and the new weapon of field artillery under the command of a Turkish officer (neither of which was available to the Lodi army).

Within this soldier-statesman, however, was a poet and a man of letters, 'of sensibility and taste and humour' (writes the historian Percival Spear), with a particular love of the Afghan hills and streams and of Persian gardens. The combination of soldier and artist is revealed in Babur's engaging memoirs, the *Baburnama*, written in his Turkic mother tongue, translated into Persian at the behest of Akbar, and then into English. In them Babur expresses a low opinion of the flat plains of Hindustan he had conquered, compared with the Persia and Afghanistan of his youth and early triumphs. He shows none of the curiosity about Indian life and thought to be found in his grandson Akbar, but rather eloquently expresses the Persian and Afghan orientation that would influence the Mughal elite from the beginning of the empire to its end in 1857. In Babur's words:

> Hindustan is a country that has few pleasures to recommend it. The people are not handsome. They have no idea of the charms of friendly society, of frankly mixing together, or of familiar intercourse. They have no genius, no comprehension of mind, no politeness of manner, no kindness or fellow-feeling, no ingenuity or mechanical invention in planning or executing their handicraft works, no skill or knowledge in design or architecture; they have no horses, no good flesh, no grapes or musk melons, no good fruits, no ice or cold water, no good food or bread in their bazaars, no baths or colleges, no candles, no torches, not a candlestick.

Although Babur died at Agra, in 1530, and was at first buried there, it is no surprise that his body was soon reburied in a tomb in Kabul, the place where he felt that he belonged.

Babur's son, Humayun, is normally regarded as the second Mughal emperor, who reigned from the death of Babur until 1556. Less well known is the fact that Humayun was emperor only in name for fifteen years; in fact, between 1540 and 1555, the fledgling Mughal empire ceased to exist. After a decade of fighting with the sultans of various provinces in the 1530s, in which he failed to introduce an effective administration, Humayun was chased out of Hindustan altogether after a battle with an Afghan leader who had risen to power in eastern India as the prime minister of the sultans of Bihar, Sher Khan. In place of Humayun, Sher Shah Suri, as Sher Khan now styled himself, reigned in Delhi until his death in 1545 in an accidental explosion of gunpowder. He proved to be an able ruler, who laid the foundations of systems of administration, revenue collection and justice on which Akbar would build. Sher Shah's most lasting achievement were four great roads across northern India (one of them a precursor of the modern Grand Trunk Road), lined with fruit trees and with 1,700 caravanserais placed at regular intervals. Humayun, by contrast, was forced into a wandering existence. He at first took refuge in the deserts of Sindh and Rajasthan, where he spent three years trying to raise support and produced his son Akbar, born at Umarkot in Sindh in 1542. The next year, he fled to Iran with a very small entourage and was welcomed by Shah Tahmasp, the Safavid ruler. After struggles with two of his brothers for control of eastern Afghanistan over the next decade, Humayun managed to return to power in Delhi, when his general, Bairam Khan, defeated the divided successors of Sher Shah in 1555. But he reigned again as Mughal emperor for only six months. In early 1556, it is said that Humayun was on the roof of his library in Delhi's Purana Qila (Old Fort) discussing with his astrologers when Venus was expected to rise, when he heard the call to prayer from a nearby mosque. Rising to go, he somehow caught his foot in his robe and fell, bashing his head on some stone stairs, and died two days later. 'Like his father, he both lost a kingdom, and gained one, and came from Kabul to do so', notes Francis Robinson in his history of the Mughal emperors.

Akbar was only 13 when his father died. Humayun had made Bairam Khan his son's formal guardian while Akbar was growing up in Afghanistan during his father's wilderness years. Bairam Khan immediately had Akbar formally crowned and then acted as his regent. In a second battle at Panipat, in late 1556, the general saved the newly restored empire by defeating a much larger Afghan force from the Suri dynasty. But in due course tensions grew between the regent and the youthful ruler. In 1560, they came to a head when Akbar successfully dismissed Bairam Khan, inviting him to proceed on pilgrimage to Mecca. Two years later, he was forced to discipline another general, his foster-brother Adham Khan, the conqueror of Malwa (including Mandu), who had murdered Akbar's newly appointed prime minister within the royal palace itself and may have intended to assassinate Akbar himself. Akbar personally struck Adham Khan on the head with a crushing blow from his fist and ordered that he be thrown from the terrace of the harem, twice, to ensure that his brains were spilled. Thus, aged 20, Akbar achieved a personal grip over the empire as it grew to cover most of the northern half of India, which would not slacken for the next four decades. He is, by universal consent, the greatest of the Great Mughals.

Part of Akbar's genius was undoubtedly his shrewd ability to understand and deal with people at all levels of society – perhaps born out of his insecure early years in Afghanistan, but certainly fed by his insatiable curiosity. He seems to have been equally at home with nobles and commoners, Muslims and Hindus, warriors and priests (including Jesuit Fathers from Goa), intellectuals and artists, the virtuous and the villainous. In one of the many intriguing stories told in the *Akbarnama*, Abu'l Fazl records a story he heard from the emperor himself of his attendance, aged 18 or 19, at a crowded local festival in Agra – incognito.

> He was engrossed in observing the various sorts and conditions of humanity present, when 'suddenly some ruffians recognized me and said so to one another. When I became aware of this, I without the least delay or hesitation rolled my eyes and squinted and so made a wonderful change in my appearance. In a way that they could not imagine I, as a spectator, was observing the

devices of Fate. When those people looked closely at me, they, on account of the change in my appearance, could not recognize me, and said so to one another: "These are not the eyes and features of the King." I quietly moved away from the scene and went to my palace.' While telling the story his Majesty showed us what he had done, and so made our wonder the greater. In truth, it was a very strange performance.

Akbar's most influential act of government policy was to institute an imperial civil service based on the concept of rank, or *mansab*, held by an officer, which came in thirty-three grades. In return for supplying a number of men and horses for military service – ranging from ten to 10,000 men – a *mansabdar* was granted the right to draw revenue from certain lands (known as a *jagir*) assigned to him. However, the *jagir* could not be held in the region where the officer was posted, and it was non-hereditary; moreover, the officer would be moved from one post to another during the course of his service; and upon his death, his property would be resumed by the state. Akbar's intention was to prevent the development of a landed aristocracy, and to limit the opportunities for corruption. But his *mansab-dari* system had the unintended effect of encouraging needless spending. 'Why not get the glory to be derived from ostentation and public works when you could pass nothing on to your family?' Spear observes. 'Thus the Mughal nobles were notable for their ostentation, their crowds of retainers with even more than average insolence of office, their works of piety in the shape of mosques, wells, and rest houses, of ease like their gardens and summerhouses, and of remembrance like their great domed tombs.'

The system was, however, open to both Hindus and Muslims, and deliberately included the Rajput warrior lineages, who were given high rank, despite a terrible military struggle between certain Rajput dynasties and the Mughal emperor in Rajasthan in the 1560s. At the same time, Akbar took Rajput princesses as wives, and arranged Rajput marriage alliances for his sons. This adroit policy towards the Rajputs helped to make the whole Hindu community accept the Mughal government as in some sense their own. In 1564, Akbar also lifted the imposition of the long-established *jizya* (poll tax) on non-Muslims. Even so, lists in the *Ain-i-Akbari*, the record of Akbar's fifty-year administration kept in Persian, show that the imperial service was dominated by foreigners. About 70 per cent of its personnel were from the northwest, and only 30 per cent from India, roughly half of the Indians being Muslim and half Hindu. This pattern persisted in the empire through the 17th century, and proved to be helpful to the Mughals' British colonial successors by accustoming Indians to administration by foreigners.

Akbar's curiosity about other religions is well known. Islam, on its own, did not satisfy him, as he made clear while hosting formal debates between Muslim theologians, to the consternation and anger of the orthodox. On one side of the great gate to the chief mosque in the extraordinary capital city, Fatehpur Sikri, which Akbar built near Agra in the 1570s, appears a Persian inscription that reads: 'Jesus Son of Mary (on whom be peace) said: The world is a bridge, pass over it, but build no houses on it.' In 1580, Akbar attracted Jesuits to his court and spent many months in colloquy with them; at times, he seemed to them to be on the point of converting to Christianity. Father Antonio Monserrate even accompanied the emperor and his army to Afghanistan and kept a detailed record of the campaign, 'though it is a wonder that he returned alive, for on the Khyber Pass he would certainly have been stoned to death for his denunciation of the Prophet before a crowd of angry Muslims, had not fear of Akbar restrained them', notes Laurence Binyon in his biography of Akbar. The emperor was also keenly interested in Zoroastrianism, Jainism and Hinduism. In 1582, he commissioned a Persian translation of *The Mahabharata*, in an abridged form, to be made with the help of learned Brahmins. This literal version was then polished by the poet Faizi, the brother of Abu'l Fazl, and completed in 1586 as the *Razmnama* (Book of Battles). Akbar ordered copies to be made for libraries so that knowledge of the work would spread among the nobility throughout the empire. Yet, in the end, it appears that no existing religion was sufficient for him, and this led to the creation of an eclectic cult based on his own person, known as the *Din Ilahi* (Divine Faith). The cult was, however, limited to his own circle and not promoted in the empire. In one of Akbar's remarks collected together at the end of the *Ain-i-Akbari* by Abu'l Fazl, he is quoted rather winningly as follows: 'The Indian sages say that for the garnering of good works, one should have death constantly in view, and, placing no reliance on youth and life, never comfort the self. But to me it seems that in the pursuit of virtue, the idea of death should not be thought of, so that without any hope or fear, one should practice virtue simply because it is good.'

However, not even Akbar could solve the problem of his succession – a problem that would dog every Mughal emperor after him. As with the Delhi Sultanate, vicious struggles between fathers, sons and brothers were common among the Mughals, given that the principle of primogeniture did not apply. In Akbar's case, since two of his three sons had predeceased him through alcoholism, the choice inevitably fell on his eldest son, Salim. He, however, now in his thirties, was so impatient to step into his father's shoes that he had coins struck in his name as emperor in 1602. Akbar sent his close friend Abu'l Fazl to intercede, and Salim had his father's trusted emissary murdered. Negotiations broke down altogether, as Akbar contemplated using the army against his son. But in 1604, Salim, now under pressure from his own son, was persuaded to come to court, where he was slapped in the face by his father and placed in the care of a doctor. The following year, on his deathbed, Akbar invested Salim as his successor. He titled himself Jehangir (World-Seizer).

Hardly surprisingly, Jehangir's own death in 1627 precipitated a succession crisis, too. The winner, Jehangir's third son Prince Khurram, on gaining the throne as Shah Jahan, immediately had six of his male relatives killed: his younger half-brother, the two sons of his deceased older brother and the three sons of his deceased uncle. Nur Jahan, Jehangir's powerful wife, was pensioned off; she retired from government to supervise the building of the late emperor's tomb in Lahore.

The most notorious succession struggle was that of Shah Jahan and his four sons, notably his eldest son Dara Shikoh and his third son Aurangzeb. Dara was his father's favourite and his designated successor. An intellectual and scholar, who had translated the *Upanishads* into Persian, and a patron of painting, music and dancing, he resembled his great-grandfather Akbar in his open-mindedness and wide-ranging religious interests. Aurangzeb, by contrast, was unloved by his father, with devastating results. A successful military commander and administrator, he was puritanical in personal behaviour and orthodox in religious matters. Aurangzeb disliked all that Dara represented, seeing him as a threat to Islam in India. In 1658, Aurangzeb seized the fort at Agra and imprisoned Shah Jahan there, within sight of the emperor's Taj Mahal. With the help of another brother, Aurangzeb then defeated Dara in battle near Agra, and declared himself emperor. Although Dara escaped, he was eventually handed over by a treacherous Afghan chieftain. Now Aurangzeb – supported by his sister Rawshanara but opposed by another sister Jahanara – had his elder brother killed for apostasy from Islam. Dara Shikoh's headless body was paraded through Delhi, and then buried in the tomb of Humayun. In a grisly revenge on his father, Aurangzeb is said to have had the severed head of Dara sent to the ageing Shah Jahan in his fortress prison inside a meat dish.

Like Akbar, Aurangzeb ruled for almost fifty years, during which he brought most of India at least nominally under Mughal control, and considerably increased the economic wealth of the empire. But this expansion came at a cost. Impressive and indomitable as he was, in most respects Aurangzeb's rule lacked the zest and flair of his great predecessor. Francis Robinson puts it well: 'once in power, all his passion was expressed through the business of ruling, which he embraced with an implacable and joyless sense of duty.' Many historians have seen this as the result of Aurangzeb's Islamic orthodoxy – for example, in his resented reimposition of the *jizya* abolished by Akbar, in 1679 – although religion was not always in evidence in his decisions. It is, however, indisputable that Aurangzeb succeeded in antagonizing a wide range of regional rulers by his, often brutal, military interventions: the Sikhs and the Jats in the Punjab, the Rathor Rajputs in Rajasthan, the Ahoms in Assam and, most of all, the Marathas in the Deccan, led by Shivaji until his death in 1680, and then by his son. Aurangzeb's obsessive focus on the Deccan during the second half of his rule, and his consequent absence from Agra and Delhi, combined with his ultimate failure to subdue the Marathas, despite campaigning relentlessly against them into his late eighties, prepared the way for the disintegration of the Mughal empire after his death, culminating in the sack of Delhi by the Persian invader, Nadir Shah, in 1739.

It is hard to disagree with Aurangzeb's own disillusioned and guilt-ridden assessment of himself, written to his son Prince Azam only a few days before he died:

> May peace be upon you and those who are near you. Old age arrived and . . . strength departed from the limbs. I came alone [into this world] and I go as a stranger [to the next world] . . . I was devoid of administrative [tact] and care for the welfare of the people. [My] dear life has been spent in vain. God is present in this world but I do not see Him. . . . The whole [royal] army is confused and confounded. . . . Though I have strong hope in the favours and mercy [of God], my actions do not allow me to think over [i.e. I am afraid on account of my actions] . . . Goodbye; goodbye; goodbye.

SEVEN

European Incursions and East India Companies

EUROPEAN INCURSIONS
AND EAST INDIA COMPANIES

~

Long before the Jesuits visited Akbar at the Mughal court in the 1580s, Europeans had made their way to India. The earliest to arrive – discounting Alexander of Macedon and his Greeks, who stopped not far beyond the Indus – were ancient Greek and Roman sailors and merchants, about whom little is known. Their reports of the mysterious lands of the East contributed to Ptolemy's map of the world in the 2nd century AD, and their yarns may have helped to spawn the fantastical tales of India in medieval European bestiaries.

The Indian elephant, for example, was said to have legs like pillars without knee joints, so that it could not get up if it fell over. Elephants therefore had to sleep standing up against trees; and so hunters were said to saw through trees half way in the hope that elephants would lean against these trees, fall down and become trapped.

Indubitably real, however, was the Greek and Roman maritime trade with India in spices and textiles in exchange for European gold. Roman coins excavated from peninsular India and Ceylon are so plentiful that the coins must have circulated at this period as Indian currency, although there is no evidence that European traders settled in the subcontinent. The first Europeans actually to live in India were Jews who settled on the Malabar coast. They probably arrived as early as the first century after the fall of Jerusalem in AD 70, given that a Roman merchant ship plying regularly between the Red Sea and Arabia, Malabar and Ceylon found a Jewish colony in Kodungallur (Cranganore) in the 2nd century. At any rate, a

Jewish community was established in Kodungallur by the 5th century, at the latest, when it received a grant of land and other rights from a local Indian ruler, recorded on a copper plate in an early Tamil script, which still exists.

The European colonialists who took over control of northern India from the Mughals in the mid-18th century were therefore relative late-comers from the West. The British arrived in India only in the early 17th century after the founding of the East India Company in London, with a royal charter from Queen Elizabeth dated 31 December 1600 granting the 'Governor and Company of Merchants of London trading into the East Indies' a national monopoly of trade in the East. Other nation-based East India Companies, founded by the Dutch, the Danes, the Portuguese and the French, were chartered in 1602, 1616, 1628 and 1664, respectively. Of these, the serious rival to the British was the Dutch East India Company, officially called the Vereenigde Oostindische Compagnie (VOC), which was particularly successful in Ceylon and south India, and of course in the Dutch East Indies and South Africa. By 1669, at the zenith of its success, the VOC had more than 150 merchant ships, 40 warships, 50,000 employees and a private army of 10,000 soldiers, and was the richest private company the world had ever known, paying a dividend of 40 per cent on the shareholder's original investment. Between its founding in 1602 and its liquidation at the end of the 18th century, the VOC operated 4,785 ships and carried more than 2.5 million tons of Asian trade goods, as compared with 2,690 ships operated by the British East India Company carrying one-fifth of the tonnage of its Dutch competitor.

But of course it was Portugal, not Holland or Britain, which was the earliest European nation to settle in and rule over any part of India. In 1498, Vasco da Gama sailed across the Indian Ocean from Malindi in east Africa to Calicut (Kozhikode) on the Malabar coast, in search of 'Christians and spices', as he said. In 1503, the Portuguese admiral, Afonso de Albuquerque, established the Portuguese empire in India by doing battle with the *zamorin* (ruler) of Calicut and building a fort at Cochin, which became the first Portuguese capital. On a second expedition, Albuquerque sailed further north and took Goa from the Muslim king of Bijapur in 1510, with some help from a small force of Malabari soldiers led by a Hindu privateer in the service of the Vijayanagar empire. Unsure of their victory after this conquest, the Portuguese lived on board their fleet anchored along the shore for ten years. Then they firmly established their rule on the west coast of India, known as the *Estado da India* (State of India), by trading with the world, building elaborate Catholic churches and colonial mansions in Goa, converting the local heathen, starting up the Inquisition and sending Jesuit emissaries to the courts of Akbar and Jehangir – as well as persecuting the Jews further down the coast, including the Jew Town at Cochin with its famous synagogue, which the Portuguese sacked when they occupied Cochin. In 1535, they acquired from the sultan of Gujarat the seven islands of Bombay – the name is probably derived from an Old Portuguese phrase – which were handed over to the British in 1661 as part of the dowry of Catherine of Braganza, daughter of the king of Portugal, when she married King Charles II. Portuguese rule in India lasted for some four and a half centuries until 1961, in which year Goa – along with two other Portuguese coastal enclaves further north on the coast of the Arabian Sea, Daman and Diu – was forcibly annexed by the Indian army at the behest of Nehru, bringing an end to the last European colonial possessions in India.

The Dutch explorer, Jan Huyghen van Linschoten, visiting Goa in 1583, noted that one could buy there the products of all Asia. Some of the church vestments were fine examples of local raised gold and silver embroidery, while a chasuble had all the qualities of Chinese porcelain in its style, motifs and composition, altar frontals were marked by Persian influence in their treatment of foliage, and capes displayed a Mughal flavour in their decorations of flower sprigs.

Portuguese global trade introduced into India an amazing variety of plants, vegetables and fruits from the Americas, Africa and the East Indies.

The chilli pepper – that apparently indigenous spice of Indian cuisine – came to India with the Portuguese from Pernambuco in Brazil. The cashew nut also came from Brazil, and the peanut from Africa. Tobacco arrived from the Americas via the Deccan at the Mughal court in Agra by the time of the Mughal emperor Akbar, as we know, and was denounced by Akbar's son Jehangir as a pernicious weed. The pineapple, brought from the Caribbean to Europe by Christopher Columbus, reached the dining table of the Mughal emperor via Portuguese merchants. The papaya came from the Spanish Indies 'by way of the Philippines or Luzon to Malacca and so to India', according to Linschoten. Cassava, the sweet potato, the mangosteen, the lichee, the sweet orange, medicinal drugs such as 'China root' (*Smilax glabra*) and decorative garden plants such as the 'marvel of Peru' (*Mirabilis jalopa*), were also introduced by the Portuguese. Their record of beneficial activity prompted the 17th-century French Protestant traveller, Jean-Baptiste Tavernier, who worked extensively in India as a diamond merchant, to remark that 'the Portuguese, wherever they came, make the place better for those that come after them'. So important was Portuguese as a language in India that throughout the 18th century the British East India Company required its ministers to learn it. Robert Clive, the founder of the Company's rule in Bengal, was fluent in Portuguese, though not in any Indian language. Portuguese was even used for some Protestant preaching in church in British Calcutta during the 1780s.

Portuguese rule in India was distinct from British rule in several important ways. From its beginnings around 1500, the Portuguese had modest territorial ambitions, regarding themselves as a primarily maritime power with only a small army, unlike the British. Secondly, the colonial authorities in Goa always ruled their Indian possessions in the name of the royal government in Lisbon, whereas the British ruled through the London-based court of directors of their East India Company, which was admittedly regulated with increasing firmness by the British Parliament after 1773 but not formally dissolved until the assumption of government in India by the British Crown after the uprising of 1857–58. British policy from the early decades of their rule was therefore dominated by the commercial considerations of a joint-stock company. Social reforms (for example, the abolition of *sati*), changes to Hindu and Muslim family law (for example, giving rights to women) and religious proselytization by Christians against idol worshippers, were discouraged on the grounds that they would upset Indians and therefore trade. Indeed, Christian missionaries were banned from British India until 1813, whereas the Inquisition operated in Goa from as early as 1560.

Perhaps most significant of all, the attitude to the colonized country in Portuguese Goa resembled that in the British dominions of America, Canada and South Africa rather than the one prevalent in the British Raj. The Portuguese in many cases regarded India, rather than Portugal, as their home, with generations born and brought up in Goa. By contrast the settlement of British men and women in India – though floated from time to time by influential Britons and even some Indians – was actively discouraged by the East India Company, for fear that it would lead to friction between British settlers and Indians. Those who did settle were looked down upon by those who did not; and if they married Indians, their offspring – originally known as Eurasians, but later called Anglo-Indians – were generally unwelcome in official circles. Instead of staying on, most of the British in India returned to Britain after completion of their service, unless they were unfortunate enough to succumb to disease like the linguist William Jones, mentioned earlier, who was a judge in Bengal; they also preferred, if feasible, to educate their children in Britain, not India. As a colonial governor of the Dutch East India Company, Anthony van Diemen, remarked in the first half of the 17th century, 'Most of the Portuguese in India look upon this region as their fatherland, and think no more about Portugal. They drive little or no trade thither, but content themselves with the port-to-port trade of Asia, just as if they were natives and had no other country.'

Nevertheless, Portuguese culture failed to spread in India, unlike British culture. Today, beyond Goa, it has almost completely vanished. 'The West, though mingling its Portuguese blood with the Indian, remained culturally alien and sterile', writes Percival Spear. Anyone visiting Panaji, the modern capital of Goa, India's smallest state, cannot fail to be struck by the impression that it is the only city in India that might almost be taken for a European city – not least in its orderliness and cleanliness.

At the heart of the *Estado da India*, there was a contradiction concerning assimilation between the colonizer and the colonized: although the Portuguese were less racially exclusive than the Indians (certainly as compared to the British), at the same time they were more religiously intolerant. The Inquisition in Goa brought to trial more than 16,000 persons, of whom fifty-seven were executed, during the two centuries up to its temporary abolition in 1774. The conversations about Christianity between the Jesuits from Goa and the Mughal emperor Akbar failed mainly for reasons of Catholic dogmatism, including disgust at Akbar's rejection of monogamy. In Goa itself, the Indians, for their part, while embracing Catholicism, generally continued to adhere to caste. When, in 2004, the British journalist Edward Luce, with his Indian wife, visited the home of a well-known Goan Catholic female author, Luce happened to ask her whether there was any Portuguese blood in her family. 'Oh no, that is out of the question,' she told him. 'Our family is Brahmin.' As for the Dalit Catholics in Goa, notes Luce, they have 'separate churches and separate cemeteries'.

The British East India Company made its first contact with India at Surat, an important commercial city and entrepôt on the coast of Gujarat, where its ships began to dock in 1608. It also despatched a Turkish-speaking emissary, Captain William Hawkins, to the court of the Great Mughal, where he was welcomed but granted no commercial rights. In 1611, it built its first Indian 'factory' (that is, a warehouse) on India's southeastern Coromandel coast at Masulipatnam (Machilipatnam), and a second factory at Surat in 1612. Then, again seeking a commercial treaty with the Mughal empire, the Company sent an ambassador, Sir Thomas Roe, to the Mughal court carrying a letter from the British king, James I, addressed to Jehangir. Landing at Surat, Roe proceeded to Ajmer, where Jehangir was holding his court. He attended at court from 1615 to 1618 and was a success, despite Jehangir's contempt for the presents that the ambassador brought from London, with the exception of some English paintings including portraits of the English royal family, which the emperor greatly admired. In 1617, Jehangir addressed the following letter to the British monarch via Roe, thanking James for his letter:

> Upon which assurance of your royal love I have given my general command to all the kingdoms and ports of my dominions to receive all the merchants of the English nation as the subjects of my friend; that in what place soever they choose to live, they may have free liberty without any restraint; and at what port soever they shall arrive, that neither Portugal nor any other shall dare to molest their quiet; and in what city soever they shall have residence, I have commanded all my governors and captains to give them freedom answerable to their own desires; to sell, buy, and to transport into their country at their pleasure.
>
> For confirmation of our love and friendship, I desire your Majesty to command your merchants to bring in their ships all sorts of rarities and rich goods fit for my palace; and that you be pleased to send me your royal letters by every opportunity, that I may rejoice in your health and prosperous affairs; that our friendship may be interchanged and eternal.

Jehangir's letter to James I was a reasonable start for the Company, especially as it openly mentioned protection from Portuguese commercial hostilities; but it was far from granting the favoured nation status that the court of directors in London had hoped for, and was in no sense a monopoly of Indian trade of the kind that the Company had been granted at home. In practice, the Company's 'factors' (merchants) would continue to be harassed in various ways by local officials in the ports and provincial capitals of the Mughal empire. What the Company was really seeking was an imperial decree to its sole advantage, known as a *firman*. The Mughal emperors, however, were in no pressing need of income from the British East India Company during the 17th century.

Even so, the Company's trade in and via India was permitted to expand, mainly in cotton, silk, indigo dye, saltpetre (the essential ingredient of gunpowder) and Chinese tea; the opium trade came later. In 1639, it founded a factory at Madras on the Coromandel coast, in territory outside Mughal control ruled by a governor of the Vijayanagar empire, and built Fort St George in 1644 to secure its trade. In 1668, it leased the islands of Bombay under a charter from the British Crown in exchange for a loan of £50,000 (with interest) to an impecunious Charles II and a yearly rent of £10, and fortified the Bombay Castle on the site of a manor house built by the Portuguese. In 1690, it established a settlement in Bengal at Calcutta, which was soon protected by Fort William. During the same period, the Dutch East India Company started factories on the Coromandel coast at Pulicat (1608), in Bengal at Chinsura (1656) and on the Malabar coast at Cochin (1669), as did the French East India Company south of Madras at Pondicherry (1674) and at Chandernagore in Bengal (1675). The forces required to defend these factories, consisting of Indian soldiers under European officers, were the nucleus of the national armies that would clash for control of India during the next century – in which wars Clive would first distinguish himself fighting against the French in the Carnatic region of southern India.

In the early 1670s, Bombay was attacked once by Dutch and twice by Siddi naval forces working for the Mughal emperor Aurangzeb in pursuit of his war against Shivaji and the Marathas. (Siddis were Indians of African ancestry.) In a further attack in 1689, Aurangzeb's target was the East India Company factory itself. This followed a period of tension between Company shipping and Mughal shipping using the port of Surat, leading to misjudged acts of piracy by the Company against Mughal shipping in the Arabian Sea. Aurangzeb retaliated with disastrous consequences for the British. Bombay was besieged from the sea, and when the garrison surrendered in early 1690, the Company had to accept the most humiliating peace terms. The envoys it sent to Aurangzeb had their hands bound and were obliged to prostrate themselves before the emperor, while agreeing to pay an indemnity of 150,000 rupees, to restore all captured Mughal ships and plundered goods in the harbour at Bombay, and to expel the British governor of Bombay from India. (He died before this could happen.) In return, the Mughal emperor graciously reinstated the Company's trading rights throughout the empire granted by his grandfather, Jehangir, in 1617.

Not until after the death of Aurangzeb in 1707 was the Company able to extract the *firman* it had long craved. It was granted in 1716 by the ineffectual emperor Farrukhsiyar, fully a century after the visits of Roe and Hawkins to Jehangir, following the failure of much bribery by a Company mission sent to Delhi, though only under duress. The Company had threatened to withdraw altogether from Surat and its other factories in Gujarat, entailing a serious loss of revenue to the Mughal treasury and the potential ruin of the empire's main port with the Arabian Sea. In exchange for a mere 3,000 rupees per year, the *firman* granted the Company duty-free trading rights in all of Bengal. However, its effect was less powerful than the British had hoped. By now, the Mughal emperor's writ did not run in the provinces, especially after the assassination of Farrukhsiyar in 1719. Taking advantage of the now obvious disintegration of Mughal imperial power, the governors (nawabs) of Bengal ignored the directive from Delhi and went on collecting customs duty from the East India Company. Farrukhsiyar's *firman* would, however, eventually prove useful in the hands of Clive, four decades later, when he wished to justify his overthrow of the nawab of Bengal, Siraj-ud-Daula, at the battle of Plassey in 1757.

Clive's pivotal victory at Plassey was secured by deceit, as is well known. Prior to the battle, he negotiated a pact, which was kept secret, with two of Siraj-ud-Daula's generals, who agreed to hold back their armies. Siraj-ud-Daula, learning of this only during the battle, had no choice but to flee, and was later assassinated. One of the generals, Mir Jafar, was now installed as nawab of Bengal, a puppet ruler supported by the forces of the Company. Three years later, after Clive had returned to England, the Company deposed Mir Jafar in favour of his son-in-law, Mir Qasim, but he too proved insufficiently generous to the Company's coffers, rebelled and fled to Oudh. Mir Jafar was reinstated as nawab.

In 1764, having defeated an alliance of troops led by Mir Qasim, the nawab of Oudh and the Mughal emperor Shah Alam II at the battle of Buxar in Bihar, the East India Company itself became the de facto ruler of Bengal. Clive now came back to India. In return for the Company's payment of a fixed annual revenue of 2.6 million rupees from Bengal to a destitute Shah Alam, the Company was granted in 1765 the *diwani* – the fiscal administration – of Bengal in a *firman* issued by the emperor sitting on his throne in Clive's tent at Benares, containing the following words:

> That whereas in consideration of the attachment and services of the high and mighty, the noblest of exalted nobles, the Chief of illustrious warriors, our faithful servants and well-wishers, worthy of all royal favours, the English Company, we have granted them the Dewannee of the provinces of Bengal, Bahar [Bihar], and Orissa . . . with an exemption from the payment of the Customs of the Dewannee, which used to be paid to the court. . . .

Technically, the Company was still some kind of vassal of Shah Alam, but this was merely a form of legal language to conceal the humiliating military and diplomatic reality. From now on, until 1857, the Mughal emperor would be a pensioner of the East India Company. As Clive himself remarked in his final private advice to the Company's directors in India before departing permanently for Britain in 1767: 'Nothing remains to him but the Name and Shadow of authority.' But Clive presciently warned his successors: 'This Name, however, this Shadow, it is indispensably necessary we should seem to venerate . . .', if British rule were to survive and take hold in India.

Clive is a controversial figure – a 'poacher turned gamekeeper' (says Spear) in his attitude to the Company's corruption – who was severely criticized in his own lifetime and committed suicide for unknown reasons in London in 1774 at the age of only 49. The year before his death, he famously told a parliamentary committee enquiring into the Company's takeover of Bengal and considering the official regulation of the East India Company: 'I walked through vaults which were thrown open to me alone, piled on either hand with gold and jewels! Mr Chairman, at this moment I stand astonished at my own moderation!' Yet it is indisputable that Clive enormously benefited from the takeover and its aftermath, to the tune of £400,000 – 'much the greatest fortune ever made by a [British] individual in India', according to the historian P. J. Marshall, who calculates that £1,250,000 were eventually distributed to British individuals from the Bengal treasury. In 1770, Bengal was struck by a terrible famine said to have taken ten million lives in a year, initiated by drought but aggravated by the Company's misgovernment. Undoubtedly, the early years of the Company in Bengal were 'chequered with guilt and shame', said Macaulay in Parliament in 1833 during the great debate on its further regulation, due to 'rapacious, imperious and corrupt' Company merchants, the so-called white nabobs (an Anglicized form of 'nawab'), inspired by Clive's example. When they returned to England from Bengal with their ill-gotten gains, the nabobs flaunted them before their shocked, and often envious, fellow countrymen.

The reform of the Company under the Regulating Act of 1773 began with the appointment of Warren Hastings as the first governor-general of India from 1774 to 1785. He deposed the Indian deputies who had hitherto collected revenue on the Company's behalf, and instituted a Board of Revenue in Calcutta and English collectors in the districts. By the time

Hastings left India, Bengal had been transformed from a revenue administration into a state. Reform gathered pace under the next governor-general, Lord Cornwallis. In 1793, he introduced the so-called Permanent Settlement of revenue due to the Company from large landlords (known as *zamindars*), in other words a permanently fixed amount of revenue rather than an annually varying sum, intended to encourage agricultural production and reduce exploitation of the tenant farmers. More successfully, Cornwallis divided the Company's service into commercial and political branches. From now on, a Company servant had to belong to one or the other branch. For a merchant, private trade was still permitted, but not for a government official, who had to be content with a large salary. Cornwallis also Europeanized the services, in the belief that corruption among Europeans could be controlled and even cured, unlike corruption among Indians. With the exception of one Indian judge in Benares, Ali Ibrahim Khan, regarded as incorruptible, all high Indian officials were dismissed and replaced by Europeans – a policy that would remain in force for more than a century, until 1909. The Cornwallis reforms of the late 1780s and 1790s marked the end of the dominance of trade in the Company's administration, the beginning of the Indian Civil Service ethos of the 19th century and the introduction of a racial aloofness into British rule that would characterize it until 1947.

Beyond Bengal, the Company was at war, first with the French and then with Indian rulers, for a century after the battle of Plassey, as it vastly expanded the territory that was either directly or indirectly under its control. Its armies consisted of small numbers of British officers commanding large numbers of Indian soldiers, supplemented by a smaller contingent of British soldiers. Their military superiority, at least to begin with, lay not in numbers and technology, as compared with the armies of the Mughal period, but rather in their 'rapidity and massing of firepower achieved through close formations of well-drilled men', notes Thomas Trautmann, although their Indian opponents soon learned the lesson and began training and drilling their troops with European officers, some of whom had served in the armies of the recently defeated Napoleon Bonaparte. In addition, the Company formed strategic alliances with Indian rulers against other Indian rulers, as it had with Mir Jafar in Bengal.

From 1767 to 1799, there were four Anglo-Mysore Wars in the south: the first and second against Hyder Ali, the sultan of Mysore, the third and fourth against his son, Tipu Sultan, who died defending his fortress at Seringapatam. Between 1775 and 1818, three Anglo-Maratha Wars occurred in central India, during the second of which Company troops captured Delhi in 1803 and with it the Mughal emperor, still Shah Alam II, who was found in the Red Fort seated under a tattered canopy, blind and decrepit, and left in peace by his British 'protectors'. The Ahom kingdom in Lower Assam, which Aurangzeb had attempted and failed to hold, was annexed in 1826, after the first Anglo-Burmese War, followed by Upper Assam in 1838. In the 1840s, after the death of the Sikh ruler Ranjit Singh in 1839, two Anglo-Sikh Wars ended in the annexation of Sindh and the Punjab. Next, under the governor-general Lord Dalhousie, the Company pursued a policy of political annexation of princely states with the threat of military force, culminating in the bloodless annexation of Oudh in 1856. By now, British rule covered almost the entire subcontinent, although one third of the landmass was left formally in the hands of princes, who controlled the internal affairs of their domains under the watchful eye of a British Resident, including the large states of Hyderabad, Kashmir, Rajputana (modern Rajasthan) and later Mysore.

The British empire in India, as it now was, would always rest ultimately on military force for its survival. However, it would prosper in the 19th century not by military means but through force of ideas. The advent of British rule was welcomed by large numbers of educated Indians, beginning in Bengal with figures such as the reformer Rammohun Roy and his friend, the entrepreneur Dwarkanath Tagore (grandfather of Rabindranath), who grasped not only the new opportunities for social improvement and personal enrichment but also the opening of India to the English language and to western education, literature, science and technology. The Mughal and nawabi rule of the very recent past seemed atavistic to these Indians. Realizing this, British officials and their advisers in Calcutta and London soon found themselves divided between those who wished to leave Indian society and religion alone – which was the original policy of the East India Company – and those who believed in intervention. The first group, known as Orientalists, supported the education of Indians in their own culture and in their own languages, including Sanskrit; the second, the Anglicists, favoured a broadly western-style education, chiefly in English.

In the 1780s, under Hastings, the Orientalists dominated. In 1784, for example, the Asiatic Society was founded by Jones with the aim of investigating and celebrating Indian, and more broadly Asian, culture. By the 1830s, however, the Anglicists had the upper hand, encouraged by both the evangelical Christians and the utilitarians in Britain – who included the historian James Mill and his philosopher son John Stuart Mill, both of them officials of the East India Company – although these two groups argued for the Anglicist policy from somewhat different points of view. Eventually, the Anglicists would form government policy, although the Orientalists would retain a degree of influence.

When Macaulay, the son of an evangelical social reformer and former colonial governor in Africa, arrived in India in 1834 as the first law member of the governor-general's council, he immediately embraced the Anglicist cause. After being introduced to the former Wadiyar raja of Mysore, who had been placed on the throne by the Company as a child after its defeat of Tipu Sultan in 1799 and then deposed by the British for maladministration in 1831, Macaulay felt contemptuous. The raja's palace was a 'mixture of splendour and shabbiness which characterizes the native courts', he wrote to his sister in England. Its private drawing room full of English furniture, proudly displayed to him by the raja, was not unlike that of 'a rich, vulgar, Cockney cheesemonger', and its household gods included 'a fat man with a paunch like Daniel Lambert's [the fattest man in England], an elephant's head and trunk, a dozen hands, and a serpent's tail' – Macaulay's inaugural encounter with Ganesh. But instead of blaming the raja for his failure to measure up to English standards, Macaulay severely censured the former governor-general, Lord Wellesley, for his original policy towards the raja. 'To give a person immense power, to place him in the midst of the strongest temptations, to neglect his education, and then to degrade him from his high station because he had not been found equal to the duties of it, seems to me to be a most absurd and cruel policy'. Instead of having allowed the young raja to grow up as a confused Hindu, without good tuition, the British should have educated him as 'an accomplished English gentleman'.

Yet perhaps, in his heart, Macaulay was not entirely convinced by his Anglicist prescription for successful British rule in India. He himself had agreed to leave London and take a post in the empire for strictly pecuniary, rather than any missionary, reasons; his explicit intention was to save enough money in Calcutta in order to be able to retire to England as a gentleman scholar. Macaulay continued his family letter with a frank warning: 'We are strangers [here]. We are one in two or three thousand to the natives. The highest classes whom we have deprived of their power would do anything to throw off our yoke. A serious check in any part of India would raise half the country against us.' Two decades later, in 1857, this part of Macaulay's analysis would prove to be formidably accurate.

THE 'JEWEL IN THE CROWN'

To English Royalists of the 17th century, the Great Rebellion was the name for what modern historians call the English Civil War. Likewise, the watershed events of 1857–59 that terminated the East India Company and ushered in the rule of the British Crown with India as its brightest imperial jewel – beginning with the mutiny of eighty-five sepoys at Meerut and ending in the British deportation from Delhi of the former Mughal emperor, Bahadur Shah Zafar – have undergone various name changes over the course of a century and a half.

To the British of the Raj, the events were known either as the Sepoy Mutiny or as the Indian Mutiny, or often simply as the Mutiny – the term favoured even by Edward Thompson in his revisionist tract, *The Other Side of the Medal*. To others, however, they had a wider significance. Karl Marx, commenting at the time in articles for an American newspaper, was the first westerner to refer to the struggle as a 'national revolt'. Half a century later, the Indian revolutionary and Hindu nationalist Veer Savarkar published his *History of the War of Indian Independence* in Marathi, followed by an English translation printed outside India in 1909, which was promptly banned as seditious by the Indian government and remained proscribed until the end of the Raj in 1947, after which it was reprinted in India. Nehru, in *The Discovery of India*, more or less endorsed Savarkar's nomenclature for what happened in 1857, claiming that: 'It was much more than a military mutiny and it spread rapidly and assumed the character of a popular rebellion and a war of Indian independence.' Savarkar's term was also borrowed in 1959 when Marx's 1850s newspaper articles appeared in Moscow under the title, *The First Indian War of Independence*. But the historian Surendra Nath Sen, in his influential study *Eighteen Fifty-Seven*, published in 1957 by the Indian government, was somewhat more cautious:

> Outside Oudh and Shahabad [in Bihar] there is no evidence of that general sympathy which would invest the Mutiny with the dignity of a national war. At the same time it would be wrong to dismiss it as a mere military uprising. The Mutiny became a revolt and assumed a political character when the mutineers of Meerut placed themselves under the king of Delhi [Bahadur Shah Zafar] and a section of the landed aristocracy and civil population declared in his favour. What began as a fight for religion ended as a war of independence for there is not the slightest doubt that the rebels wanted to get rid of the alien government and restore the old order of which the king of Delhi was the rightful representative.

Today, most historians avoid 'National' and 'War of Independence', and use 'Mutiny', 'Rebellion', 'Revolt' or 'Uprising', for example Rosie Llewellyn-Jones in *The Great Uprising in India, 1857–58: Untold Stories, Indian and British*. 'I would prefer to call it the 1857 Uprising', notes Andrew Ward in *Our Bones Are Scattered: The Cawnpore Massacres and the Indian Mutiny of 1857*. 'But whether in India, the United Kingdom, or the United States, whenever I sit down with historians to talk about 1857, no matter how fastidious we try to be, by the end of the evening we are all talking about the Mutiny.' William Dalrymple, too, favours 'Uprising', but sidesteps the issue with his title *The Last Mughal: The Fall of a Dynasty, Delhi, 1857*.

The first and foremost difficulty for 20th-century Indian nationalists wishing to claim the Mutiny as a forerunner of the national freedom movement was that the violent unrest of 1857–58 barely touched most of India. It was restricted to Delhi, the United Provinces (Uttar Pradesh) – most famously Meerut, Lucknow and Cawnpore (Kanpur) – and parts of central India and Bihar: areas that included the major recruiting grounds of the sepoys, most of whom came from Oudh in the United Provinces. In the east, the sepoys stationed in Bengal at Berhampore and Barrackpore became agitated, but were soon neutralized by British troops redeployed from China and the Persian Gulf. In the northwest, the Punjab had recently been settled after the Anglo-Sikh Wars. In the west and south, the Bombay and Madras armies both remained loyal to the British.

Secondly, it was a backward-looking uprising, which aimed to reinstate the *ancien régime* of the Mughals and to preserve the dominance of the higher castes in the countryside. It was 'essentially . . . a feudal outburst,' wrote Nehru (who was himself from Allahabad in the United Provinces), 'headed by feudal chiefs and their followers', notably the landed gentry (*talukdars*) of Oudh. The *talukdars* were disaffected from the British in 1857 because they had recently, after the Company's annexation of Oudh the previous year, been deprived of their undocumented ancestral lands by a British land settlement in favour of their tenant farmers; yet the tenants, rather than being grateful to the British for their new property rights, sympathized more with their masters, to whom they were bound by ties of tribal kinship and feudal allegiance. Hence the fact that the uprising held little or no resonance for educated Indians in the major cities of British colonial origin, such as Bombay, Calcutta and Madras.

Lastly, the uprising failed not because it lacked courageous soldiers and sufficient weapons and military training but chiefly because of its dearth of unified leadership – unlike its British opponents. Bahadur Shah Zafar was 81 years old in May 1857 and a poet entirely without military experience, incapable of active leadership even if he had desired it. The uprising's other leaders were far from inspiring figures, with two notable exceptions, the Maratha leader Tatya Tope and Lakshmibai, the rani of Jhansi (in the United Provinces), who are widely regarded as heroes in India. 'The leaders of the revolt could never agree. They were mutually jealous and continually intrigued against one another. They seemed to have little regard for the effects of such disagreement on the common cause. In fact, these personal jealousies and intrigues were largely responsible for the Indian defeat', admitted the former freedom fighter Maulana Azad, by then minister of education in Nehru's government, in his substantial foreword to Sen's *Eighteen Fifty-Seven*.

Perhaps the only ray of encouragement for 20th-century nationalists was the absence in the uprising of communal antipathy between Hindus and Muslims, as witness the surprising fact that Hindu sepoys, who formed the great majority in the Company's army, rallied voluntarily to the cause of a Muslim figurehead. On the other hand, this Hindu–Muslim alliance may have arisen as much out of mutual antipathy to the British army authorities on account of their insensitivity to both Hinduism and Islam as out of mutual regard for each other. The interaction between the Hindu sepoys and Bahadur Shah Zafar's court in the Red Fort at Delhi was continually vexed. Azad's claim that there was not even 'a single instance when there was a clash or conflict on a communal basis' among the rebels in 1857–59 is historically inaccurate. Still less convincing is his statement – surely influenced by nationalist propaganda – that 'before the days of British rule, there was no such thing as the Hindu–Muslim problem in India.'

The proximate cause of the Mutiny was undoubtedly the army's offence to the religion of both the Hindu sepoys (most of whom were of high caste) and the Muslim sepoys arising from the enforced introduction in early 1857 of the notorious Enfield rifle cartridges covered in grease, probably containing beef or pork fat, which the sepoys were ordered to bite in order to release the gunpowder. The underlying cause, however, was the growing social gap between Indians and British, starting from the Cornwallis administrative reforms of the 1790s. As Dalrymple nicely observes, the wills of Company civil servants show a steep decline in the number of them that mention Indian wives and consorts (*bibis*), from one out of three wills in 1780–85 to one out of four in 1805–10 to one out of six in 1830 to practically none by the middle of the century. In the 1780s, young Englishmen joined the Company before their 16th birthday and were generally unmarried on arrival in India; by the 1850s, they arrived in their mid-twenties, often with an English wife in tow.

In the Company's army, Indians outnumbered British by a ratio of about nine to one in 1857. Moreover, sepoys and sahibs – their British officers – were no longer living on terms of intimacy, according to a unique memoir, *From Sepoy to Subedar*, written by a sepoy who remained loyal during the Mutiny (unlike his son, who became a rebel), published a decade or so after the events. Speaking of the Company's army in the early years of the century, Subedar Sitaram Pandey recalled:

> In those days the sahibs could speak our language much better than they do now, and they mixed more with us. Although officers today have to pass the language examination, and have to read books, they do not understand our language . . . The only language they learn is that of the lower orders, which they pick up from their servants, and which is unsuitable to be used in polite conversation. The sahibs often used to give nautches [performances by professional Indian dancing-girls] for the regiment, and they attended all the men's games. They also took us with them when they went out hunting . . . Nowadays they seldom attend nautches because their padre sahibs have told them it is wrong. . . . I know that many officers nowadays only speak to their men when obliged to do so, and they show that the business is irksome and try to get rid of the sepoys as quickly as possible. One sahib told us that he never knew what to say to us. The sahibs always knew what to say, and how to say it, when I was a young soldier.

This apartheid – in which many British, including the younger army officers, now openly referred to Indians with contempt as 'niggers' – unquestionably grew in the late Victorian decades after the Mutiny, along with an increasing confidence among the British in their imperial mission. But it was far from being a product of the events of 1857, as is often assumed. One has only to read Macaulay's writings in India to appreciate its existence and development during the 1830s. The change in attitude began in the early decades of the century and was encouraged by the widespread success of British-officered armies against native rulers, in which serving sepoys acquiesced, and by the evangelical Christian movement, which was contemptuous of Indian religions. The Mutiny was not its point of origin, only its ugliest expression – despite many acts of Indian and British heroism and kindnesses shown by individual Indians to fugitive Britons during this terrible period.

In late September 1857, after the British-led forces had captured Delhi through a bloody assault, the governor-general, Lord Canning, wrote disgustedly of a 'violent rancour of a very large proportion of the English Community against every native Indian of every class', in a letter to Queen Victoria. 'There is a rabid and indiscriminate vindictiveness abroad, even amongst many who ought to set a better example, which it is impossible to contemplate without something like a feeling of shame for one's fellow countrymen', he noted. 'Not one man in ten seems to think that the hanging and shooting of 40 or 50,000 Mutineers beside other rebels, can be otherwise than practicable and right . . .'

The mutineers and their supporters had committed some appalling atrocities, headed by Nana Sahib's ordering of the cold-blooded massacre at Cawnpore of just over 200 European women and children, most of whose bodies were stuffed into a well. But the British retribution, when it came, was out of proportion to their tribulations. It had a racist tinge, as Canning had feared, and was often lynch law, judging from the frank letters and reports written at the time by British soldiers and civilians on the spot. One example will suffice, from an anonymous letter about the British sack of Delhi published in the *Bombay Telegraph* in September 1857:

All the city people found within the walls when our troops entered were bayonetted on the spot; and the number was considerable, as you may suppose, when I tell you that in some houses forty and fifty persons were hiding. These were not mutineers, but residents of the city, who trusted to our well-known mild rule for pardon. I am glad to say they were disappointed.

For some months in 1857–58, Delhi was a ghost city inhabited chiefly by corpses. It would take a long time to recover. 'By God, Delhi is no more a city, but a camp, a cantonment', lamented the Urdu poet Ghalib, one of a handful of survivors from the Mughal court, in 1861. 'No Fort, no city, no bazaars, no watercourses . . .'.

Memoirs of the British participants in the Mutiny, written later, tend to be more reticent. 'Many men whose names will never be forgotten in India seem to have kept absolute silence on the deeds which made them memorable there; you can meet their sons today, and find that they know nothing of what happened', remarked Thompson in 1925. The number of Indians killed in the suppression of the Mutiny cannot be quantified for lack of documentary evidence, almost all of which comes from the British side. Thompson offers no estimate, neither does Sen. Ward estimates 'thousands', Dalrymple 'tens if not hundreds of thousands', a recent Indian writer, Amaresh Misra, 'almost ten million people over ten years beginning in 1857', which seems unlikely. What is certain is that very little of the indiscriminate British slaughter was admitted in print by the earlier British historians of the Raj, and none of it was (or is) taught in British school history, only the heroism of the British side. In a three-volume *History of the Indian Mutiny* running to over 1,500 pages, published in 1904–12, the Indian administrator and historian Sir George Forrest, son of an army captain who had won a Victoria Cross at the siege of Delhi for preventing the British powder magazine from falling into the hands of the mutineers, made not a single reference to any British atrocities, not even glancingly. 'Justice was done, mercy shown to all who were not guilty of deliberate murder, the land cleansed of blood', runs the final sentence of Forrest's enormous history. 'One might throw the lists open to the literature of the whole world, and still not find a more superb example of smug effrontery', comments Thompson.

On 1 November 1858, repression officially gave way to concilia-tion. Queen Victoria's proclamation, read out at every station in India, announced that the East India Company was no more and the British gov-ernment would now rule India directly; that the existing treaties between the Company and native princes would be honoured; that there would be no further annexations of territory; that there would be a general amnesty for all rebels except those who had taken part in the murder of Europeans; and that religious toleration would be observed and ancient customs would be respected. The celebrated war correspondent William Howard Russell, who had reported the Mutiny for *The Times* in London, attended the ceremony in Allahabad at which Canning himself read out the royal proclamation from a platform. Russell was 'greatly amused' to overhear a British sergeant who was on duty at the foot of the platform staircase loudly instructing one of his men, 'I am going away for a moment; do you stay here and take care that no *nigger* goes up.'

Not officially announced was a drastic reorganization of the army in India, to ensure that no further rebellion would be possible. By 1863, the number of Indian troops had been reduced from over 200,000 to 140,000, and the number of European troops had increased to 65,000; from now on, the ratio of Indians to British would be maintained at about five to two. Artillery training for Indian troops was abandoned. Many regiments were disbanded. New and extant regiments were deployed around India in such a way as to avoid concentrating together soldiers hailing from any one region; while the rapid expansion during the 1860s and 1870s of the railway system, opened in 1853, made the movement of troops much easier than it had been in 1857. Recruitment moved away from its former areas in the United Provinces and Bihar to the Punjab and the hill regions; many of the new recruits were Sikhs and Gurkhas, whom the British came to see as 'martial peoples'. Both groups had fought enthusiastically for the British side in Delhi, the Sikhs being keen to avenge their historic oppression by several Mughal emperors. In addition, large areas of Mughal Delhi were levelled for defensive purposes, including 80 per cent of the Red Fort, part of which was replaced by a hideous British barracks – a 'fearful piece of vandalism . . . of the most splendid palace in the world', noted the architectural historian James Fergusson in 1876, which still shocks the informed visitor to Delhi.

The government's policy to support princely rule, however archaic this was and almost regardless of the idiosyncrasies of individual princes, and to avoid confrontation with Hinduism and Islam, was, in effect, a conciliatory gesture towards the conservative demands of the 1857 rebels and a repudiation of the Anglicizing policy followed since the 1830s. In fact, it was a regression to the policy of non-interference in religions, customs and traditions of the early days of the East India Company in Bengal. For example, Canning, now transformed from a governor-general into a viceroy, quickly restored the confiscated lands of the *talukdars* of Oudh – some of whom had supported the rebels – in order to win their loyalty. In addition, the *talukdars* were granted judicial and financial powers without precedent, thereby reinforcing the feudal order. And when, at the same time, the government of Bombay declared that all government-funded schools must admit students without regard to religion or caste, it then backed away in the face of a threatened upper-caste boycott, which ensured the continued exclusion from government education of any untouchable students. After the promulgation of the Indian Penal Code (drafted by Macaulay) in 1861, which involved little practical change, social legislation was abandoned until 1929, the date of an Age of Consent Act aimed at preventing child marriages, which the government did little to enforce.

Overall, the post-Mutiny policy marked the beginning of 'an extreme unwillingness to interfere with religious and caste questions', noted Edward Thompson and G. T. Garratt in their still remarkably balanced 1934 study, *Rise and Fulfilment of British Rule in India*. 'The Englishman's duty was to keep the peace, maintain law and order, bring India some of Europe's material blessings, but not to worry about the Indian's family life or private morals.' Ironically, the policy's introduction coincided with the government's founding, in 1857, of colonial India's first universities, in Bombay, Calcutta and Madras, in which the language of instruction was English and the modern educational curriculum ran diametrically opposite to the post-Mutiny policy. Eventually, these two government policies – the politically conservative one and the educationally progressive one – were bound to come into unresolvable conflict.

One further important legacy of the Mutiny has been mentioned already. It stimulated racial arrogance among the British, with a concomitant bitterness among Indians. The official failure to condemn British post-Mutiny excesses, while highlighting Indian excesses – not least with memorials to the British dead in Cawnpore, Lucknow and Delhi – rankled with Indians for decades. 'There is no memorial for the Indians who died', noted Nehru in 1945. Racial discrimination became elevated into a form of loyalty to the Raj and institutionalized in the civil service and the army through their opposition to promoting Indians to positions of responsibility, notwithstanding individual British officers who disagreed with it. The Indian Civil Service appointed its first Indian (Satyendranath Tagore, elder brother of Rabindranath) in 1863 and its next Indians in 1869, yet by 1911 – the year of the Delhi Durbar for King George V and the zenith of the Raj – a mere 6 per cent of ICS officers were Indians; in the Indian Army, there were no commissioned Indian officers until after the First World War. For all his genuine Anglophilia, the Harrow-educated Nehru wrote bluntly of the period from the Mutiny onwards that: 'The future historians of England will have to consider how far England's decline from her proud eminence was due to her imperialism and racialism, which corrupted her public life and made her forget the lessons of her own history and literature.'

The introduction of western liberal ideas and culture through education in English, coupled with the stinging wound to Indian pride inflicted by British imperialism and racialism, gave birth to a variety of religious and social reform movements initiated by Indians, not by the British, during the second half of the 19th century, prior to the emergence of the nationalist movement.

In Bengal, there was the monotheistic Brahmo Samaj (Society of Brahma), inaugurated by Rammohun Roy in 1828 as the Brahma Sabha and led by Debendranath Tagore, the son of Dwarkanath and the father of Rabindranath, until his death in 1905, and also by Keshab Chandra Sen. Drawing its membership mainly from high-caste intellectual Hindus exposed to western learning and Christianity, the Brahmo Samaj firmly opposed idol worship and, less firmly, the practice of caste, while considering Brahmos still to be Hindus. Later on came the Ramakrishna Mission, taking its teachings from the unlettered mystic Ramakrishna Paramahamsa and led by the Calcutta University-educated Narendranath Datta, who adopted the name Swami Vivekananda. Having travelled in the United States to great acclaim in 1893, Vivekananda vigorously preached a Vedantic philosophy based on the *Upanishads* to America and Europe, while encouraging Indians to reform Hindu social practices, before his premature death in 1902.

In the Punjab, there was the Arya Samaj, founded in 1875 by Dayananda Saraswati, a Hindu ascetic unversed in English but well versed in Sanskrit. His motto was 'back to the *Vedas*' and to a society free of caste, idol worship, multiple gods, temples and elaborate rituals. Everything worth knowing, even the most recent western technology such as the railways, was said to be alluded to in the *Vedas*. Anti-Christian, the Arya Samaj aimed to convert Indians from other religions to Hinduism. It spread overseas at the turn of the century to the many colonies where Hindus had settled, such as Fiji and Trinidad.

In Maharashtra, unlike in Bengal, social reform was generally considered more important than religious reform, so the reform movements operated within Hinduism. Among the best known was the Satyasodhak Samaj (Society of Truthseekers), founded in 1873 by the low-caste Jyotirao

Phule to fight oppression by the Brahmins. Besides writing a great deal, Phule started girls' schools, schools for untouchables and a foundling home for widows' children. His work marks the beginning of the anti-Brahmin political movement in Maharashtra, and heralds the 20th-century Maharashtrian movement for the emancipation of the untouchables led by Ambedkar.

Finally, Indian Muslims, aware of their increasing political, social and economic disadvantage after the disappearance of Mughal culture in the Mutiny, started the Aligarh movement to encourage Muslim exposure to modern ideas. In 1875, Sir Syed Ahmed Khan, a scholar and jurist who had been close to both the Mughal court and the East India Company, founded the Mohammedan Anglo-Oriental College in Aligarh on the model of an English public school (later renamed the Aligarh Muslim University); its primary aim was to expose Muslim students to instruction in English and science. 'Reason alone is a sufficient guide' was his favourite statement. A decade later, he started the annual Mohammedan Educational Conference, which would provide the seedbed for the All-India Muslim League, founded in 1906 after his death. (His grandson, Syed Ross Masood, formed a close friendship with E. M. Forster, who dedicated his novel *A Passage to India* to Masood.)

The Brahmo Samaj was the most influential of these early movements among Hindus, judging by its spread within the major cities of India and its stimulation of other movements, including the Arya Samaj. The writer Nirad C. Chaudhuri, who was born in East Bengal in 1897, was not a Brahmo, but imbibed Brahmo values as a child. In Chaudhuri's view, under Brahmo and related reforming influences, the Hindu middle class in the period 1860–1910 showed 'greater probity in public and private affairs, attained greater happiness in family and personal life, saw greater fulfill-ment of cultural aspirations, and put forth greater creativeness' than at any time in recent centuries. A Bengali of the next generation, Satyajit Ray, whose family were prominent Brahmos, though he himself was not, also admired the period. Brahmos of the late 19th century, said Ray, were 'very powerful figures, very demanding figures with lots of social fervour in them: the willingness, the ability and the eagerness to do good to society, to change society for the better.' All this was true, at least in Bengal; and yet Brahmoism failed to inspire the vast majority of Indians. Ultimately more concerned with intellectual and religious matters than with social reform and political freedom, Brahmoism declined and gave way to explicitly political movements, including Marxism, some of whose leading members were Brahmos.

The most important of these was the Indian National Congress, which met for the first time in 1885, in Bombay; after 1920, under the leadership of Gandhi, it would lead the Indian freedom movement. Its first president was an Anglophile Indian barrister, W. C. Bonerjee, but its founder – and the general secretary during its first decade – was a British civil servant, Allan Octavian Hume, with an anti-establishment streak and a passion for Indian ornithology. During the Mutiny, Hume saw active service at the head of an irregular force of Indian troops recruited by himself, for which he was decorated by the government; but his subsequent criticism of British repression and his zealous promotion of Indian agricultural reform irritated his superiors. 'An unsafe, impulsive, insubordinate officer' by his own admission, Hume took early retirement from the Indian Civil Service in 1882. His founding of the Congress arose directly from the viceroy Lord Ripon's controversial Ilbert Bill of 1883, which sought to give Indian judges some jurisdiction over Europeans. Appalled by the European community's attacks on the bill, reminiscent of the racist language used in the Mutiny, Hume issued an appeal to Indian graduates of Calcutta University to organize themselves for national reform. As a firm believer in constitutional methods, Hume was convinced that the councils of the Raj needed to hear advice and criticism from a group of informed Indian leaders.

For many years, the Indians in the Congress were more moderate than Hume. In fact, until 1916 the Congress was barely more than a talking club for the westernized elite of Bombay, Calcutta and Madras, not a real political party with local branches, a regular membership and an annual subscription. It had a small impact on the government, which introduced at its own stately pace a degree of elected representation for Indians in the Indian Councils Act of 1909 (the Morley-Minto reforms), including contentious reserved seats for Muslims at the insistence of the Muslim League. 'The pre-Gandhian Congress . . . remained always little more than an annual conference, organized by a small "inner circle" of leaders maintaining contact through private correspondence', notes the historian Sumit Sarkar. When Rabindranath Tagore attended early Congress meetings he criticized how much time went on hospitality and chatter, instead of constructive work. In his novel *The Home and the World*, written in 1915–16, a patriotic leader of the Swadeshi (Our Country) movement in Bengal brazenly declares: 'When I was attached to the Congress party I never hesitated to dilute 10 per cent of truth with 90 per cent of untruth.'

In the meantime, some Indians took to extremism. It began in Maharashtra under the direction of Bal Gangadhar Tilak with the murder of two British officers in 1897, then started in Bengal and later spread to the Punjab. The non-violent Swadeshi movement – provoked by Lord Curzon's viceregal decision to partition the large province of Bengal in 1905 without consulting any of its inhabitants, whether Hindu or Muslim, soon dissipated itself in Hindu–Muslim riots and terrorist attacks on government officials. In 1909, an India Office official was assassinated in London by an Indian working under the direction of Savarkar, who was convicted and sentenced to life imprisonment for the crime. In 1912, a bomb was thrown into the howdah of the viceroy's elephant during a ceremonial procession in Delhi to celebrate the move of India's capital from Calcutta to Delhi. Lord Hardinge, though wounded, escaped, along with his wife, but the mahout was killed. During most of the First World War, a Punjabi terrorist movement based in California, the Ghadar party, conspired against the Indian government with German government assistance; it even targeted Tagore for assassination on his visit to San Francisco in 1916. At a sensational Hindu–German Conspiracy Trial in San Francisco in early 1918, one of the Indian Ghadar defendants shot dead another defendant in open court, and was himself shot dead by a US marshal firing across the room over the heads of the attorneys.

Inevitably, Indian terrorism provoked British repression. In March 1919, the Indian government passed the Rowlatt Act, indefinitely extending the 'emergency measures' that had been in force during the First World War to control public unrest and extirpate conspiracy, which included arrest without warrant and indefinite detention without trial. There were immediate public protests. In the Punjab, the response was particularly turbulent. At Amritsar, a mob murdered five British men, beat up a British female missionary and left her for dead, and ransacked and burned many buildings before the arrival of troops. On 13 April, Gurkhas under British command fired without warning for between ten and fifteen minutes on an unarmed public protest meeting of some 20,000 people in an area of open ground enclosed by high walls known as the Jallianwala Bagh. They killed at least 480 people, but almost certainly many more, and wounded several thousand, who were left overnight without medical treatment because of a curfew.

This was the most brutal government repression since the Mutiny in 1857, and, as in that fateful time, the action received immediate and vocal support from the majority of Britons, in Britain as well as in India, with more discreet support from Indian vested interests. But after a critical public enquiry, in a British parliamentary debate the following year even Winston Churchill, then secretary of state for war and no friend to Indian political freedom, called the mass shooting 'without precedent or parallel in the modern history of the British empire. It is an event of an entirely different order from any of those tragical occurrences which take place when troops are brought into collision with the civil population. It is an extraordinary event, a monstrous event, an event which stands in singular and sinister isolation.' Although Churchill saw no comparison with the repression of the Mutiny, his condemnation of the Amritsar massacre was unreserved.

After Amritsar, it was clear to both the British and the Indian elites that the British empire in India was entering its final phase. Neither the moderate constitutional approach of the Congress, nor the violent strategy of the extremists, nor the repression of Indian political aspirations by military force, seemed to have any realistic prospect of long-term success. The stage was set for a new technique of political agitation: the non-cooperation movement led by an Indian-born, London-trained lawyer, who had cut his political teeth as an activist against colonialism in South Africa over two decades, before returning to India for good in 1915 – Mohandas Karamchand Gandhi.

END OF EMPIRE

Among the influential British who became openly opposed to imperialism in India in the wake of the Amritsar massacre in April 1919 was the author, editor and political activist Leonard Woolf. In the first decade of the century he had spent more than six years as a notably effective, at times even ruthless, colonial officer in Ceylon before resigning in 1911 and returning to England, where he married Virginia Stephen and became a founding figure of the Bloomsbury Group. By the 1920s, Woolf was regularly encouraging Labour politicians in Britain to meet Indian demands for self-government. Looking back over the disappearance of the British empire in the subcontinent during his lifetime, in his autobiography written in the 1960s, he observed:

> I have no doubt that if British governments had been prepared to grant in 1900 what they refused in 1900 but granted in 1920; or to grant in 1920 what they refused in 1920 but granted in 1940; or to grant in 1940 what they refused in 1940 but granted in 1947 – then nine-tenths of the misery, hatred, and violence, the imprisonings and terrorism, the murders, flogging, shootings, assassinations, even the racial massacres would have been avoided; the transference of power might well have been accomplished peacefully, even possibly without Partition.

The first Indian to make a public protest against the Amritsar massacre was not Gandhi or any other leader of the Indian National Congress, but rather Rabindranath Tagore. Unable to persuade the politicians in Calcutta to hold a meeting against the Punjab repression because they feared government reprisal under the Rowlatt Act, at the end of May 1919 Tagore reluctantly wrote a personal letter to the viceroy, Lord Chelmsford. 'The accounts of the insults and sufferings undergone by our brothers in the Punjab have trickled through the gagged silence, reaching every corner of India, and the universal agony of indignation roused in the hearts of our people has been ignored by our rulers – possibly congratulating themselves for imparting what they imagine as salutary lessons . . .'. Tagore then asked to be relieved of the knighthood conferred upon him in 1915 by Chelmsford's more liberal predecessor, Lord Hardinge. 'The time has come when badges of honour make our shame glaring in the incongruous context of humiliation, and I for my part wish to stand, shorn of all special distinctions, by the side of those of my countrymen who for their so-called insignificance are liable to suffer a degradation not fit for human beings.'

Tagore's letter was published in the Indian press in early June 1919 and widely read within India, though largely ignored in the London press. But this public gesture of non-cooperation with the government did not catch the imagination of Indians. Probably it was made too soon, long before the government's judge-led public enquiry into the massacre known as the Hunter Commission, the parliamentary debate in the House of Commons in July 1920 and Gandhi's launch of the non-cooperation movement in 1921. For whatever reason, not one Indian political leader, including those from Bengal, openly welcomed Tagore's gesture – not even Gandhi.

During the 1920s and 1930s, Tagore, while admiring Gandhi enough to lead the way in calling him 'Mahatma' (Great Soul), would be Gandhi's most even-handed and intelligent critic, in return for which Gandhi would call Tagore 'Gurudev' (Spiritual Teacher). When Tagore died in 1941, Nehru, again languishing in jail, noted in his diary:

Gandhi and Tagore. Two types entirely different from each other, and yet both of them typical of India, both in the long line of India's great men. How

171

rich and extravagant is India to produce two such men in a generation – just to show what she can do even in her present distress and lowly state. . . . There are many of course who may be abler than them or greater geniuses in their own line. Einstein is great. There may be greater poets than Tagore, greater writers . . . It is not so much because of any single virtue but because of the *tout ensemble*, that I felt that among the world's great men today Gandhi and Tagore were supreme as human beings. What good fortune for me to have come into close contact with them.

Many others since Nehru have been intrigued by the comparison between Gandhi and Tagore, including three remarkably different Nobel prize-winners: Aung San Suu Kyi, Amartya Sen and the brilliant scientist Subrahmanyan Chandrasekhar, who said in 1995: 'Tagore was intellectually more perceptive than Gandhi.' A recent biographer of Gandhi, Kathryn Tidrick, remarks that: 'Had Gandhi not lived, Tagore would be remembered as the quintessential Indian of the first part of the 20th century.' So it is worth taking time to understand their major points of disagreement over non-cooperation, before turning to the more familiar landmarks of the Indian independence struggle. Indeed, the issues that Gandhi and Tagore debated would continue to resonate in India well after political independence in 1947.

In March 1921, Tagore, then lecturing in the United States (where Gandhi never went), fired the first salvo in a letter published in a Calcutta magazine:

Non-cooperation appear[s] to me to be the progeny of the union of rejection from one party and dejection from the other party and therefore though I tried to shed upon it my best smile, I long hesitated to welcome it to my heart . . . It is like the exclamation of a malcontent dog to its neglectful master: I was willing to guard your door and beautifully wag my tail at you, if you had provided me with the remnant of your dinner, but as you never cared to do so, I go to join my own species.

Gandhi responded in June:

> In my humble opinion, rejection is as much an ideal as the acceptance of a thing. It is as necessary to reject untruth as it is to accept truth. All religions teach that two opposite forces act upon us and that the human endeavour consists in a series of eternal rejections and acceptances . . . *Neti* [not this] was the best description the authors of the *Upanishads* were able to find for Brahman [God].
>
> I therefore think that the Poet [i.e., Tagore] has been unnecessarily alarmed at the negative aspect of Non-cooperation. We had lost the power of saying "no" to the Government. This deliberate refusal to cooperate is like the necessary weeding process that a cultivator has to resort to before he sows. Weeding is as necessary to agriculture as sowing.

Although Gandhi was probably not aware of it, he was here following in the footsteps of the Buddha. The first historical example of non-cooperation comes from the Buddhist literature, noted the Buddhist monk and scholar Walpola Rahula. It occurs shortly before the Buddha's death, when he asks his disciples after he is gone to boycott a violent monk, Channa – his former charioteer – who has persistently refused to follow his teachings. 'Don't talk to Channa; don't advise him; don't associate with him; if he talks to you, don't answer him; completely boycott him and avoid him.' In this case non-cooperation succeeded: Channa in due course admitted his fault, promised to follow the Buddha's teachings and became a good man.

In early September 1921, Gandhi came in person to Calcutta in the hope of recruiting Tagore for the political movement. They met at Tagore's ancestral house behind closed doors, and their momentous conversation was not reported at the time; but soon afterwards Tagore reconstructed it for the benefit of his friend, the agricultural economist Leonard Elmhirst (later co-founder of the Dartington Hall Trust), who published it only in the 1970s, long after the passions of the time had cooled.

'Gurudev, you were yourself a leader and promoter of the Swadeshi movement some twenty years ago', said Gandhi. 'You always wanted Indians to stand on their own feet as Indians and not to be poor copies of westerners. My "Swaraj" [Home Rule] movement today is the natural off-spring of your own "Swadeshi". Join me now and fight with me for Swaraj.'

'Gandhiji, the whole world is suffering today from the cult of a selfish and short-sighted nationalism. India has all down her history offered hospitality to the invader of whatever nation, creed or colour. I have come to believe that, as Indians, we not only have much to learn from the West but that we also have something to contribute. We dare not therefore shut the West out.' Western ideas and achievements would help Indians to learn how to collaborate among themselves, Tagore implied.

'Gurudev, I have already achieved Hindu–Muslim unity.' Here Gandhi was referring to his controversial support for Indian Muslims in the Khilafat movement, a violent pan-Islamist organization, which had become embroiled in serious anti-British and anti-Hindu rioting in 1921. Tagore dissented: 'When the British either walk out, or are driven out, what, Gandhiji, will happen then? Will Hindu and Muslim then lie down peacefully together? You know they will not!'

'But, Gurudev, my whole programme for the winning of Swaraj is based on the principle of non-violence. That is why, as a poet, who believes in peace, you can feel free to ally yourself with this peaceful movement and work for it.'

'Come and look over the edge of my veranda, Gandhiji, look down there and see what your so-called non-violent followers are up to.' The non-cooperators had stolen pieces of foreign-made cloth from the nearby bazaar and lit a bonfire with them in the courtyard of Tagore's house. 'You can see for yourself. There they are howling around it like a lot of demented dervishes. Is that non-violence, Gandhiji? We Indians are, as you well know, a very emotional people. Do you think you can hold our violent emotions under firm control with your non-violent principles? No! You know you can't. Only when the children of our different religions, communities and castes have been schooled together can you hope to overcome the violent feelings which exist today.'

So Gandhi appealed to Tagore – who had opened his school at Santiniketan in 1901, followed by an international university, Visva-Bharati, in 1921 – to support his own new programme of national education. 'Hundreds of young teachers and students are now, at my suggestion, leaving the government schools and colleges. They are enlisting in my scheme.'

'Yes, but, Gandhiji, I notice that you first pick out the brightest of the young men and enlist them in your political organization. The less bright you allow to open schools that can offer only a travesty of education.' These new schools, Tagore said, had too limited an objective. 'This is why I am inviting scholars [to Santiniketan] from all over the world to come and help and at the same time to learn something from the creative aspects of our own culture.' The first of these visitors, a highly distinguished Indologist from Paris, was about to arrive in Santiniketan.

Tagore went on to accuse Gandhi of manipulating the people with symbols instead of substance. 'But Indians by nature have always been worshippers of symbols, of images', Gandhi countered. When talking of economic wrongs, Gandhi said, it was legitimate to refer to foreign-made cloth as 'impure'. Only a word such as this would induce Indians to sacrifice their foreign-made cloth and burn it. (A decade later, in his inspired Salt March to the coast, Gandhi would turn the collection of untaxed sea salt, in defiance of a British government monopoly on salt, into another resonant symbol of political protest. He would also deploy symbolism in his condemnation of orthodox Hindu practices such as animal sacrifice and untouchability.)

'Well,' said Gandhi, 'I can see my request for your help is almost hopeless. If you can do nothing else for me, at least you can put these Bengali *bhadralok* [gentlemen] to shame by getting them to do something practical.

Gurudev, you can spin. Why not get all your students to sit down around you and spin.' They both laughed, since Tagore was well known for being a thoroughly unmechanical person. 'Poems I can spin, Gandhiji, songs and plays I can spin, but of your precious cotton what a mess I would make!'

Spinning and the spinning wheel, the *charka*, would become a focus of irreconcilable disagreement between Gandhi and Tagore. Gandhi, as is well known, was generally agin machines, which he early on equated with 'sin' and 'evil' in his 1909 nationalist tract, *Hind Swaraj*, though not without giving machinery careful thought and to some extent softening his opposition over time. He opposed the bicycle, mainly on the grounds that the cost of buying such a luxury would get Indians into debt. He employed typists in his legal practice in South Africa, learned how to type and then abandoned the typewriter back in India, disliking it as 'a cover for indifference and laziness', he claimed, preferring to handwrite his voluminous letters and articles. He opposed the rice mill, firstly because it would deprive very poor women of their income from pounding rice, secondly because pounding was good exercise and thirdly because milling removed the vitamin thiamine in the pericarp of the rice grain, causing the tragic disease beriberi. But he much favoured the spinning wheel and also the treadle sewing machine, notably those made by the Singer company – 'one of the few useful things ever invented', he said. This was not only because the *charka* provided employment and clothing – hand-woven *khadi* – for poor, unemployed Indians but also because he firmly believed that spinning encouraged self-rule, both of the individual and the political kind. Tagore, though generally in favour of science and modern technology (as he made clear in his conversations with Albert Einstein), as firmly detested the notion that to be a true Indian one must regularly spin. He termed Gandhi's spinning decree 'the cult of the *charka*'.

After their meeting Tagore published a powerful essay, 'The call of truth'. Gandhi replied equally powerfully with 'The great sentinel' – his name for Tagore. The rising Nehru read both essays in 1921 and found himself agreeing more with Gandhi. 'But the more I have read what Tagore wrote then, the more I have appreciated it and felt in tune with it', he wrote on Tagore's birth centenary in 1961, when he was prime minister. Their exchange, in Nehru's view, represented 'two aspects of the truth, neither of which could be ignored.'

The first phase of non-cooperation ended in February 1922, when a crowd of Congress and Khilafat volunteers, after being fired on by police, set fire to a police station at Chauri Chaura in the United Provinces; twenty-two policemen inside were either hacked to death as they fled or forced back into the flames, to the cries of 'Mahatma Gandhi *ki jai*!' ('Victory to Mahatma Gandhi!'). Gandhi called off the movement – but not immediately, as is often stated, only after several days of difficult deliberation with himself and others. Satan had tempted him to carry on with the campaign, he confessed later, by arguing that withdrawal would be 'cowardly'.

Throughout his career in India, Gandhi was acutely aware of India's potential for violence. In 1918, writing to an English clergyman friend, C. F. Andrews, who claimed that Indians had in the past repudiated 'blood-lust', Gandhi frankly disagreed. 'Is this historically true? I see no sign of it in *The Mahabharata* or *The Ramayana*,' he noted, or in the ancient law code of Manu, which 'prescribes no such renunciation that you impute to the race'. As for the period of Muslim domination in India, 'The Hindus were not less eager than the Mahomedans to fight. They were simply disorganized, physically weakened and torn by internal dissensions.' Buddhism was banished from India with 'unspeakable cruelty', he claimed, if the legends were true. Even among the Jains – among whom Gandhi had grown up in Gujarat – the doctrine of non-violence had failed. 'They have a superstitious horror of blood[shed], but they have as little regard for the life of the enemy as an European.' He concluded soberly: 'All then that can be said of India is that individuals have made serious attempts, with greater success than elsewhere, to popularize the doctrine. But there is no warrant for the belief that it has taken deep root among the people.'

However, this view of Indian violence does not account for Gandhi's delay in suspending non-cooperation in 1922. Not only had he expected violence in the struggle, he could even welcome it – provided that it was the violence of others bravely borne by the non-cooperators. As the historian Faisal Devji writes in *The Impossible Indian: Gandhi and the Temptation of Violence*, 'if Gandhi was horrified by the violence exercised from time to time by his followers, he longed to provoke it from those who had to be opposed by their non-violence.' Hence, Gandhi's recommendation of non-violent non-cooperation to the British in the face of a Nazi invasion of Britain in 1940. And also his surprising decision to volunteer as a recruiting sergeant for the Raj in the final year of the First World War (at the time he wrote to Andrews). After traipsing through Indian villages in 1918 with a notable lack of success in recruiting farmers for the European trenches, Gandhi expressed his disgust 'that not one man has yet objected because he would not kill. They object because they fear to die. This unnatural fear of death is ruining the nation.' He made other comparable statements on the difference between killing and dying, and implied many times that India's political independence would come violently. As far back as *Hind Swaraj*, he wrote that if Indians should begin to fight after a British withdrawal, 'there can be no advantage in suppressing an eruption: it must have its vent. If therefore, before we can remain at peace, we must fight among ourselves, it is better that we do so.' In 1930, he observed: 'I would far rather be witness to Hindus and Mussulmans doing one another to death than that I should daily witness our gilded slavery.' In April 1947, before the Partition was officially agreed, he told the last viceroy, Lord Mountbatten, that 'the only alternatives were a continuation of British rule to keep law and order or an Indian bloodbath. The bloodbath must be faced and accepted.'

What neither Gandhi nor any other leader of the Congress in the 1920s anticipated is that the Hindu–Muslim problem would be solved not only by bloodshed but also by the division of the subcontinent into two nations. Although Sir Syed Ahmad Khan had supported the idea of a separate Muslim nation in the late 19th century, which was reiterated by the poet and philosopher Sir Muhammad Iqbal in 1930, the political possibility of Pakistan would catch hold only after 1937, as a result of the stand-off between the British, the Congress and the Muslim League, led by Mohammed Ali Jinnah. With the outbreak of the Second World War in 1939, 'There would seem to have been rivalry as to which side should make the most mistakes', notes a wry Percival Spear. Who was most responsible for Partition – the British government, the Indian National Congress or the All-India Muslim League – and whether the split could have been avoided in favour of a unitary, federal India, or rendered less violent given more time for the handover of power, are still very controversial issues for historians, made more so by the ongoing conflict between India and Pakistan since 1947.

Jinnah was born in Karachi to a merchant family with no particular interest in religion, and trained as a lawyer in 1890s London, where he was influenced by English liberalism. He then returned to India to practise as the sole Muslim barrister in Bombay, and entered politics, first in the Congress in 1904 and then, after the Morley-Minto reforms of 1909, as an elected representative on the Imperial Legislative Council for the reserved Muslim seat of Bombay. In 1913, he became the leader of the Muslim League and continued in this role until 1947. His dual involvement with the Congress and the League in these early days was dedicated to persuading both bodies to work in harmony for reforms of the viceroy's legislative councils. At the Congress and League annual meetings in Lucknow in 1916, Jinnah engineered a pact regarding the percentage of reserved seats for Muslims in each council. He became the acknowledged leader of Indian politics in the 1917–18 negotiations for the next round of reforms by the British enshrined in the Government of India Act of 1919. Indeed, he epitomized the Anglophile elite who ran the pre-Gandhi Congress. But now his relations with both the British and the Congress came under severe strain. Jinnah was opposed to the government's repression in the Punjab, and also opposed to Gandhi's alliance with the Khilafat movement, which he regarded as an endorsement of Muslim religious fanaticism. In 1919, he resigned from the Imperial Legislative Council in protest at the passing of the Rowlatt Act, and in 1920 he resigned his positions in the Congress, after being humiliatingly shouted down by delegates to the annual Congress meeting when he argued against the non-cooperation movement and in favour of constitutional politics.

'The fact is – as Jinnah seems dimly to have perceived – that with Gandhi's decision not to cooperate with the British and to launch a campaign of civil disobedience the seeds of separation were being sown', comments a British civil servant in the Punjab during the years leading up to the Partition, Penderel Moon, in his famous memoir *Divide and Quit*. 'Civil disobedience involved an appeal to the masses, and an appeal to the masses by an organization headed and symbolized by Gandhi was necessarily an emotional, semi-religious appeal to the Hindu masses and not to the Muslims; for Gandhi with all his fads and fastings, his goat's milk, mud baths, days of silence and fetish of non-violence was pre-eminently a Hindu.'

The gap between Jinnah and Gandhi from the beginning of their relationship right up to the Partition – despite the fact that both were London-trained lawyers – was unbridgeable: in education, politics, culture, religion, tastes and personal habits, symbolized by the polar opposition in their dress. A classic photograph of the two leaders at their failed talks on the issue of Pakistan in Bombay in 1944 shows a wizened Gandhi clad in a dhoti and shawl and holding a wooden staff like a Hindu mendicant, gesturing open-handedly towards Jinnah, who stands quite stiffly in an impeccably creased three-piece Savile Row suit with a cigarette in his hand. When Gandhi was assassinated in 1948, Jinnah chose to describe him as 'one of the greatest men produced by the Hindu community'.

The Congress's Nehru Report on constitutional reform, produced under the presidency of Motilal Nehru in 1928 as a riposte to the all-British Simon Commission, was deeply unsatisfactory to Jinnah and the Muslim

League. The report rejected the idea of reserved electorates for any community or weightage for minorities, which had been agreed in the Lucknow pact of 1916. And it proposed that the provinces of India should give up certain residuary powers, such as defence, to the central government, which the Muslim League knew would inevitably be dominated by the Congress after the departure of the British.

But it was really the failure of the Muslim League in the 1937 provincial elections – the first to be held under the 1935 Government of India Act – that proved to be the parting of ways between Congress and the League. Despite the retention by the British government of separate electorates for Muslims (and some other minorities, including untouchables), the Muslim League won only 21 per cent of the reserved Muslim seats, while the Congress formed governments in six out of eleven provinces. In 1940, meeting at Lahore, the League officially committed itself to a demand for 'separate and sovereign Muslim states . . . in which the Muslims are numerically in a majority, as in the north-western and eastern zones of India' – in other words the areas that became West and East Pakistan in August 1947. When after this announcement Maulana Azad, then president of the Congress, proposed talks with Jinnah, Jinnah rejected the overture outright in a telegram: 'Can't you realize you are made a Muslim show-boy Congress President? . . . The Congress is a Hindu body. If you have self-respect resign at once.'

The simultaneous resignation of the six Congress provincial ministries in protest at the viceroy's lack of consultation of Congress in declaring war against Germany in 1939 weakened the Congress's negotiating position with both the British and the Muslim League. For the British, especially an intransigently imperialist Churchill, the League was now a useful tool in the battle to retain India. Gandhi's declaration of the violent Quit India movement in August 1942, which immediately incurred the prolonged imprisonment of the Congress leadership (except for the Bengali leader Subhash Chandra Bose, who had escaped India in 1941 in order to pursue the path of armed resistance), played into the hands of the Muslim

League, leaving it to drum up popular support without interference from the Congress. In the 1945–46 general elections, the Muslim League polled 87 per cent of the Muslim vote and won all thirty of the Muslim seats in the central legislative assembly, and 75 per cent of the Muslim vote in the provincial assemblies, securing 439 out of the 494 Muslim seats. Jinnah's time had arrived. After the breakdown of complicated negotiations between the British, the Congress and the League, Jinnah went all out for the creation of Pakistan by calling for direct action on the streets on 16 August 1946. The resultant communal riots in Bengal and Bihar over several months – especially in Calcutta, where 5,000 people, mostly Muslims, were killed in four days – pressurized the British government, now led by Labour, into declaring in February 1947 that the British would leave India by June 1948, and the Congress, led by Nehru, into at last accepting the inevitability of Partition. When Mountbatten arrived in Delhi in late March, his almost insuperable task was to work out how to achieve the division of the subcontinent in a way that would satisfy both Congress and the Muslim League.

Why did the British rush the process, so that India became independent in August 1947, ten months ahead of the British government's timetable? Opinion among historians is divided. Some, including Moon, take the view that a longer period for the transfer of power would have precipitated a civil war between Hindus, Sikhs and Muslims. Others think that Mountbatten's haste encouraged the violence that did break out, and blame the British for cynicism. According to the historian Mushirul Hasan, 'The British, having read the writing on the wall, had no desire or motivation to effect a *peaceful* transfer of power.' The answer depends to a great extent on how the historian interprets the centuries of Hindu–Muslim relations in the subcontinent.

By 3 June, the Mountbatten plan was agreed by both parties: it entailed a 'mutilated and moth-eaten Pakistan', Jinnah admitted, consisting of the Muslim-majority districts of West Punjab and East Bengal; and it was resisted by Gandhi up to the moment of its announcement. In mid-July, the British Parliament ratified the plan and declared that Independence for India and Pakistan would come into effect on 15 August. In the meantime, with the agreement of Jinnah and Nehru, a British lawyer, Sir Cyril Radcliffe, frantically got to work defining the boundaries of the nations-to-be, while Mountbatten, assisted by an Indian civil servant, V. P. Menon, flattered and coerced hundreds of Indian princes into relinquishing states they had ruled since the days of the East India Company. On 14 August, Jinnah presided over a ceremony in Karachi to declare Independence for Pakistan, while in Delhi, near midnight on the same day, Nehru spoke eloquently to the Indian Constituent Assembly of the end of the British Raj and India's long-awaited 'tryst with destiny'.

But it is perhaps the private words of Radcliffe in a letter to his stepson in England, written on 13 August, that offer 'the true imperial epitaph' (as Sunil Khilnani aptly remarks in *The Idea of India*):

> I thought you would like to get a letter from India with a crown on the envelope. After tomorrow evening nobody will ever again be allowed to use such stationery and after 150 years British rule will be over in India – Down comes the Union Jack on Friday morning and up goes – for the moment I rather forget what, but it has a spinning wheel or a spider's web in the middle. I am going to see Mountbatten sworn in as the first Governor-General of the Indian Union at the Viceroy's House in the morning and then I station myself firmly on the Delhi airport until an aeroplane from England comes along. Nobody in India will love me for the award about the Punjab and Bengal and there will be roughly eighty million people with a grievance who will begin looking for me. I do not want them to find me. I have worked and travelled and sweated – oh I have sweated the whole time.

On 17 August 1947, Radcliffe flew out of Delhi accompanied by the secretary to the boundary commission. Before the plane took off, the pilot searched it for bombs.

That same day, the Radcliffe award was announced by Mountbatten. For the next three months, much of the Punjab was enveloped in civil war on either side of the new boundaries between India and West Pakistan. In Bengal, there was relatively little slaughter – mainly because of the courageous personal presence of Gandhi – but almost as much displacement of people. Estimates of the total number of deaths vary hugely, from 200,000 to as many as three million. Estimates of the refugee population are more precise. Between 1946 and 1951, about six million Muslims migrated to Pakistan, as against nearly nine million Hindus and Sikhs moving in the opposition direction – four million of whom migrated to India from what became East Pakistan, and five million from West Pakistan. (Among the latter was a 14-year-old Sikh, Manmohan Singh, who would become prime minister of India half a century on.) The end of the British empire in India caused one of the largest forced migrations in the history of the world.

TEN

The World's Largest Democracy

'As the years pass, British rule in India comes to seem as remote as the Battle of Agincourt', remarked the journalist and broadcaster Malcolm Muggeridge as the mid-1960s began to swing in London, with a touch of satirical exaggeration. Muggeridge, who had been a young teacher in India in the 1920s, died in 1990; and within a decade there were almost no British survivors of the colonial period. But while life under the Raj had finally just about receded into history – in India as well as in Britain – its legacy, which pervaded the subcontinent in the decades after 1947, continued to influence Indians in ways that were both diverse and profound, for better and worse. (The same is true of Pakistanis, but that is a subject for another book.)

At the political level, against the expectations of many non-Indians in its early decades, the Republic of India has of course preserved and developed the system of parliamentary democracy implanted on Indian soil in the 1930s by the Raj. It is now the largest democratic system in the world, governing half of the global population that lives in a democracy, in stark opposition to China, which went for Communism at almost the same time as India went for democracy. It has also defended India's colonially demarcated borders – in the eastern Himalayas, in Kashmir and in Bengal – through wars fought with China in 1962 and with Pakistan in 1947, 1965, 1971 and 1999, which led to the creation of Bangladesh in 1971.

At the level of official administration, India has benefited enormously from the unifying effect and usefulness of the English language, introduced in the 1830s into the civil service and law courts in place of the Persian language of the Mughal empire. In 1947, it also took over, almost intact, 'the entire colonial state apparatus, with its laws, conventions, ubiquitous rules [and] faith in the impartiality of the few good men that comprised the state,' writes Pratap Bhanu Mehta in *The Burden of Democracy*. In fact, without the Indian Civil Service – trained by the British but staffed largely by Indians at Independence – it is doubtful whether India would have survived as a nation in the traumatic period following the Partition.

At the educational and cultural level, there is still much appreciation in India for the heritage of English literature, liberal attitudes and rational thinking – not to speak of sportsmanship and cricket – that formed the outlook of a generation of Indian political leaders, especially Nehru. This legacy helped to prevent independent India from yielding to military coups and dictatorship (unlike Pakistan), apart from the hiccup of Indira Gandhi's emergency rule in 1975–77. It also stimulated the work of some of the most original Indian artists and scientists, such as the novelist R. K. Narayan, the film director Satyajit Ray, the nuclear scientist Homi Bhabha and the experimental physicist Chandrasekhara Venkata Raman. On the front jacket of a recent biography of Macaulay, subtitled 'Pioneer of India's Modernization', the Indian publisher makes the reasonable claim: 'If you're an Indian reading this book in English, it's probably because of Thomas Macaulay.' The book's author, Zareer Masani (who comes from a family of distinguished Parsis), himself writes: 'Whatever one thinks of Macaulay's personal prejudices, and he had many, his institutional legacies, I would argue, are the glue that still holds independent India together as a multilingual, democratic, federal state with English as its lingua franca.'

Although the political and administrative influence of colonialism receives more attention from both Indian and foreign historians, for obvious reasons, the cultural influence is perhaps more interesting, because it is unique to India rather than being shared with other post-colonial nations of the former British empire. Consider, for example, the astonishing life of the early 20th-century Tamil mathematician Srinivasa Ramanujan, who has long been regarded as one of the great mathematicians of all time. Beyond the world of mathematics, Ramanujan's life has inspired in Britain and the United States an excellent television documentary, *Letters from an Indian Clerk*, made for his birth centenary in 1987, a major biography, *The Man Who Knew Infinity*, an award-winning theatre production and a novel, as well as a 'Google doodle' on the internet search engine to celebrate Ramanujan's 125th birth anniversary in 2012.

In barest outline, Ramanujan, born in 1887 to poor parents, was an impoverished, devout, Brahmin clerk working at the Madras Port Trust, self-taught in mathematics and without a university degree, who claimed that his mathematics was guided by a Hindu goddess, Namagiri. Ramanujan was inclined to say: 'An equation for me has no meaning, unless it represents a thought of God.' Out of desperation at the dearth of appreciation of his theorems by university-trained mathematicians in India, in 1913 Ramanujan mailed some of the theorems, without proofs, to a leading mathematician (and confirmed atheist), G. H. Hardy, based at Cambridge University. Despite their unfamiliar and highly improbable source, the formulae were so transcendently original that Hardy dragged a reluctant Ramanujan from obscurity in India to Trinity College, Cambridge, where he collaborated extensively with him, published many joint papers in journals, and demonstrated that Ramanujan was a mathematical genius. In 1918, Ramanujan was elected the first Indian fellow of Trinity College and of the modern Royal Society. (The very first, a Parsi shipbuilder, was elected in 1841, before the reform of the Royal Society.) But, having fallen mysteriously ill – possibly with tuberculosis – and attempted suicide on the London Underground, Ramanujan then returned to India to recuperate, still producing major new theorems on his sickbed, and died tragically in 1920 at the age of just 32.

After his death, a dazzled Hardy wrote of Ramanujan:

The limitations of his knowledge were as startling as its profundity . . . His ideas as to what constituted a mathematical proof were of the most shadowy description. All his results, new and old, right or wrong, had been arrived at by a process of mingled argument, intuition, and induction, of which he was entirely unable to give any coherent account.

Ramanujan's American biographer Robert Kanigel writes in his masterly study that: 'Ramanujan's life was like the Bible, or Shakespeare – a rich find of data, lush with ambiguity, that holds up a mirror to ourselves or our age.' Kanigel gives four fascinating examples. First, the colonial education system flunked Ramanujan out of college in his teens – but a few individuals in India sensed his brilliance and rescued him from near-starvation by getting him a job as a clerk. Second, Hardy recognized Ramanujan's genius from his 1913 letter – but drove him so hard in Cambridge that he may have hastened his Indian protégé's death. (Ramanujan, characteristically, had predicted his death before the age of 35, from his horoscope.) Third, had Ramanujan received Cambridge-style mathematical training in his early life he might have reached still greater heights – but possibly, instead, such training might have stifled his originality. Lastly, Hardy, as an atheist, was convinced that religion had nothing to do with Ramanujan's intellectual power – but it is at least plausible that Hindu India's longstanding mystical attraction to the concept of the infinite was a vital source of Ramanujan's creativity. 'Was Ramanujan's life a tragedy of unfulfilled promise? Or did his five years in Cambridge redeem it?' asks Kanigel. 'In each case, the evidence [leaves] ample room to see it either way.' Ramanujan's contemporary in age, Nehru – for whom the development of science and technology in the service of industrialization was a national priority – was understandably divided in his response. In his *Discovery of India*, published on the threshold of Independence, Nehru chose to derive a political message from Ramanujan's story:

> Ramanujan's brief life and death are symbolic of conditions in India. Of our millions how few get any education at all, how many live on the verge of starvation; of even those who get some education how many have nothing to look forward to but a clerkship in some office on a pay that is usually far less than the unemployment dole in England. If life opened its gates to them and offered them food and healthy conditions of living and education and opportunities of growth, how many among these millions would be eminent scientists, educationists, technicians, industrialists, writers, and artists, helping to build a new India and a new world?

Ramanujan may have been a very unusual case who succeeded by a lucky chance against the colonial odds. Yet he was not entirely alone in colonial Indian mathematics and science. Despite little support for pure research from the government pre-1947, several scientists from Bengal and Tamil Nadu, educated and working in India, made internationally recognized contributions to science. In the 1890s, the experimental physicist Jagadish Chandra Bose became the first modern Indian scientist to receive western acclaim, including a fellowship of the Royal Society in 1920, for work that contributed to the development of wireless telegraphy and radio. (One of Bose's inventions was used by Guglielmo Marconi without attribution, after Bose had refused to take out a patent.) In the 1920s, Meghnad Saha was a remarkable astrophysicist nominated for a Nobel prize, who in 1938 founded the important National Planning Committee of the Congress with Nehru as chairman. Also in the 1920s, the theoretical physicist Satyendranath Bose, with the collaboration of Einstein, gave his name to Bose-Einstein statistics and the boson, a class of subatomic particles, which includes the photon. The experimental physicist C. V. Raman conducted pioneering research on the scattering of light, and was awarded India's first Nobel prize in science in 1930. Before 1947, ten Indian scientists (if we include the mathematician Ramanujan) had been elected fellows of the Royal Society.

Since Independence, however, Indian science has been notable more for its lack of originality. Post-colonial India has failed to fulfil the scientific promise shown by its exceptional scientists in the first half of the 20th century. Indian-born scientists have continued to make discoveries – as witness the Nobel prizes for the biochemist Hargobind Khorana (1968), the astrophysicist Subrahmanyan Chandrasekhar (1983) and the molecular biologist Venkatraman Ramakrishnan (2009) – but their research was in each case conducted outside India, mainly in the United States and the United Kingdom. (Moreover, Chandrasekhar's Nobel prize was for work done in the 1930s.)

This failure has occurred despite the huge expansion of Indian science post-1947 as a result of the money and staff poured into scientific higher education and research by the Indian government under Nehru, such as the foundation of the Indian Institutes of Technology, conceived by a British-Indian government committee in 1946 and launched in the late 1950s; of the burgeoning of India's nuclear and space programmes; and of the boom in Indian business, especially its computing and software industry, since the early 1990s. Although Indian laboratories for some years after Independence continued to be underfunded compared to western and Japanese laboratories, in the past few decades India's leading institutions, such as the Tata Institute for Fundamental Research in Mumbai and Pune and the Indian Institute of Science in Bangalore (also founded by the Tata company), have caught up with their foreign equivalents in terms of financial support, if not in achievement. A senior professor at the Indian Institute of Science, the chemist Gautam Desiraju, who did his doctoral training in the United States but returned to India permanently in the late 1970s, lamented in the science journal *Nature* in 2012:

At the glitzy level, we have had no Nobel prize winner since C. V. Raman, no highly Shanghai-ranked university, no miracle drug for a tropical disease and no sequencing of the rice genome. At the industrial level, there have been no breakthroughs to rival the telephone, the transistor or Teflon. At the organizational level, we do not have a postdoctoral system worth the name, and our undergraduate teaching is in a shambles. We figure occasionally in the best journals, yet we tolerate plagiarism, misconduct and nepotism. And yet, the innate abilities and talents of India are palpable. Why is it that this country has not been able to harness its strengths into deliverables?

The principal reason for the lacklustre performance in creative research appears to be the Indian government's bureaucratic dominance of Indian universities and even the best national laboratories and research institutes since 1947. Thus, the vice-chancellors and directors of these institutions are always appointed not by the faculty of the institution in question but by government committees sitting in New Delhi ('conclaves of old men', says Desiraju), which are inevitably caught up more in politics than in promoting education and science. Secondly, these research institutions are not involved in undergraduate teaching, while the universities, which do teach undergraduates, are generally not involved in research. As a result, 'the majority of higher education institutions in the country are currently dysfunctional', observes the Indian-American economist Pranab Bardhan.

To this bureaucracy is added the deadening effect of caste politics. This has intensified in India since 1947, with the introduction of caste-based reservation of jobs under India's new constitution in 1950, drafted by the untouchable leader Ambedkar, who became India's first law minister, and government attempts to implement further reservation recommended by the Mandal Commission in 1980, creating violent protests and suicides among the upper castes. By the mid-1990s, the administration of the caste-reservation programme had developed into 'a massive, inefficient and highly dispiriting apparatus', in which the most sought-after benefits were jobs in the bureaucracy of the programme itself, note Oliver Mendelsohn and Marika Vicziany in their study, *The Untouchables*. 'No serious observer now imagines that the scheme is anything so grand as a way of overcoming the overall subordination of the untouchables.' In a nationwide poll of 15,000 Indians by the Delhi-based Centre for the Study of Developing Societies in 2006, 74 per cent of respondents – and 56 per cent of graduates – said they did not approve of intercaste marriages. 'In India you do not cast your vote; you vote your caste', a Congress politician remarked pithily in 1995. Although this observation is true more of the villages than of the towns, caste is definitely more important than socio-economic status in deciding how Indians vote, as shown by the long-running political success of the caste-based Bahujan Samaj party in Uttar Pradesh, which virtually annihilated the state's Congress party in the 1990s.

Caste politics certainly affected Indian science before 1947; indeed scientists who were Brahmins dominated the first Hindu nationalist group, the Rashtriya Swayamsevak Sangh (National Patriotic Organization), founded by a physician in 1925, which is the parent of the BJP. Although many of the most original of Indian scientists have been Brahmins (including three of the four Nobel laureates, Raman, Chandrasekhar and Ramakrishnan), some were not, notably Saha, who was the son of a low-caste grocer from East Bengal, for which he suffered considerable discrimination that helped to motivate his interest in nationalist politics. At any rate, casteism is anathema to the practice of outstanding science because it encourages the perpetuation of social hierarchies and discourages the questioning approach to knowledge integral to science. Desiraju is hard-hitting in his criticism of this crucial handicap on Indian science:

> Our cultural value system, backed by Hindu scriptural authority, has created a strongly feudal mindset among Indians. Centuries of servitude, right up until 1947, have made the average Indian docile, obedient and sycophantic.

'Behave yourself and be rewarded', is the pragmatic mantra. I believe this feudal-colonial mentality has had far-reaching and debilitating consequences for research.

In many ways, the history of Indian science since Independence reflects the contradictory history of India as a whole in this period. The expansion of Indian higher education has produced many more graduates than existed in the colonial period; but the overall standard of intellectual life has if anything declined because of an entrenched cultural conformism, which takes the political form of Hindu nationalism. The authority of central government, inherited from the Raj, has led to some remarkable techno-logical successes based on western models; but it has stifled individuality and originality in Indian society. The increasingly populist nature of Indian democracy, expressed in the fragmentation and decline of the Congress and the rise of the Hindu nationalist and caste-based parties in the 1989 general election and after, has provided more opportunities for worthwhile achievement by the many, especially in the middle class; but this has come at the expense of the excellence achieved by the few under the undemocratic and inegalitarian colonial regime. Ramanujan's triumph over adversity in the 1910s appears, alas, to have been more like a one-off success than the harbinger of Indian eminence of which Nehru dreamed in 1946.

To what extent was Nehru himself responsible for these contradic-tions? For example, he did more than anyone in post-Independence India to develop a higher education system that might conceivably have recognized the potential of a future Ramanujan – and yet he signally failed to improve the government-funded school education system that flunked Ramanujan in the first decade of the century. At the time of Nehru's death in 1964, literacy had risen from 12 per cent of India's population in 1947 to only 30 per cent, while primary and secondary school education was still firmly divided into an inferior public system and a superior private one: a split that the government's Kothari Commission roundly condemned in 1966 as 'increasing social segregation and perpetuating and widening grade distinctions'. Of course, the inertia of the bureaucracy was partly to blame for this lack of educational progress: in 2011, India still had a literacy rate, at 74 per cent, that was well below the world's average, 84 per cent, and the world's largest population of illiterates, along with a public system of school education that was generally regarded as dismal ('absolutely dismal', noted Amartya Sen in 2013). Universal, free and compulsory education for all children between the ages of 6 and 14, though stated as a directive policy in the 1950 constitution, has yet to be achieved. That said, it is undoubtedly the case that India's first prime minister showed curiously little enthusiasm for creating a system of mass education, despite his enormous political authority in the 1950s.

If Mahatma Gandhi was in some sense the founding father of the Indian nation, Nehru – with some help from India's first home affairs minister, Vallabhbhai Patel, and its first law minister, Ambedkar – was its builder. Nehru served as prime minister for seventeen years from 1947 until 1964; his daughter, Indira Gandhi, and his grandson, Rajiv Gandhi, served as prime minister for a further twenty years, between 1966 and 1989 (with a gap in 1977–80 after the Emergency); Rajiv's widow, Sonia Gandhi, became president of the Congress in 1998, turned down the prime ministership after the general election of 2004, but retained considerable control over the direction of the government. Hence Nehru – and the political dynasty he founded, whether intentionally or not – has unquestionably exerted more influence on modern India than any other single politician since Gandhi. A discussion of Indian history since 1947 must entail an assessment of Nehru's life, work and legacy.

Today, Nehru tends to be regarded more as a nationalist and socialist intellectual than as a statesman, because of his vaunted but ineffective non-aligned foreign policy and his mishandling of India's dispute with China over Tibet and the status of the Dalai Lama, which escalated into a brief war disastrous for his reputation. But it should not be forgotten that Nehru had personal courage and popular appeal on a level comparable with that of his mentor Gandhi. During the Partition riots Nehru, like Gandhi, went into the thick of the violence. On one occasion in Delhi in 1947, according to an elderly witness interviewed by Patrick French in his history of Partition, *Liberty or Death*, Nehru climbed on a wall and stopped a communal riot by telling the rioters: 'I want to be the prime minister of a country where Hindus, Muslims, Sikhs and Christians can live in harmony. Did we get our freedom so that you could kill each other?' In India's first general election, held in 1951–52, which had an electorate spread over more than a million square miles, Nehru travelled 25,000 miles by air, car, train and boat. 'He addressed 300 mass meetings and myriad wayside ones. He spoke to about twenty million people directly, while an equal number merely had his *darshan*, eagerly flanking the roads to see him as his car whizzed past', writes Ramachandra Guha, who quotes an anonymous Congress booklet, no doubt gilded but nevertheless evocative of a politically more innocent time:

> [At] almost every place, city, town, village or wayside halt, people had waited overnight to welcome the nation's leader. Schools and shops closed: milk-maids and cowherds had taken a holiday; the kisan [farmer] and his helpmate took a temporary respite from their dawn-to-dusk programme of hard work in field and home. In Nehru's name, stocks of soda and lemonade sold out; even water became scarce . . . Special trains were run from out-of-the-way places to carry people to Nehru's meetings, enthusiasts travelling not only on foot-boards but also on top of carriages. Scores of people fainted in milling crowds.

The result was an overwhelming majority for the Congress in the lower house of Parliament (the Lok Sabha): 74.4 per cent of the seats under the first-past-the-post system. Nonetheless, twenty-eight Congress ministers failed to win a seat, and more than half of the electorate, 55 per cent, voted for non-Congress candidates. In fact, at the height of Congress's success – between Independence and India's defeat of Pakistan in the Bangladesh war in 1971 – over the course of five general elections Congress's average share of the vote remained 45 per cent; it never once won a majority of the votes.

Moreover, in the state elections of 1951–52, the party did less well, winning 68.6 per cent of the seats with 42.4 per cent of the vote. This pattern, too, would be repeated in later polls, creating standoffs between the Congress and opposition parties in the states that the central government increasingly resolved by recourse to coercive powers inherited from colonial times: 'heirlooms of the Raj, eagerly appropriated by Congress', in the wry phrase of historian Perry Anderson. These powers had been retained in Article 356 of the Constitution with the approval of Nehru and Patel and delegated to the president, who usually followed the advice of the prime minister. President's Rule was first used at the request of Nehru in 1951, in the Punjab, to remove the chief minister, and notoriously in 1959, in Kerala, when the Communist state government was dismissed by the president despite its enjoying a majority in the state legislature. Up to 1964, President's Rule was invoked nine times, but over the next three decades over ninety times – for example, during the Communist-led Naxalite movement in West Bengal in the early 1970s, the Assam agitation against illegal migrants in the 1980s and the Sikh agitation for Khalistan in the Punjab that led to the assassination of Indira Gandhi in 1984 – until in 1994 a Supreme Court judgment reduced the abuse. Since 1994, the power has been invoked less than twenty times, most notably to deal with Jammu and Kashmir, which fell under President's Rule in 1990–96, 2002 and 2008–09. 'The representative institutions of Indian democracy were thus from the start anchored in a system of electoral distortion, and armour-plated with an ample repertoire of legal repression', notes Anderson. Even so, Nehru was much more sparing in his use of such repression than most of his successors.

He also handled with considerable skill the vital matter of the reorganization of the states, including the patchwork of princely states, inherited from the Raj. Although he was not sympathetic to the linguistic division of India (which has twenty-two official languages, including Hindi but excluding English), Nehru was compelled to accept the need for some new linguistic states by a violent agitation among Telugu-speakers for a Telugu-speaking state in the northern portion of the Madras state; this new state was inaugurated in 1953 as Andhra state. In response to further linguistic agitations, especially from Marathi-speakers in Bombay and Punjabi-speakers, including the Sikhs, Nehru set up a commission that led to the States Reorganization Act in 1956, which defused some of the tension in Bombay state and the Punjab, and further expanded Andhra state into Andhra Pradesh by adding to it the Telugu-speaking areas of the former Hyderabad princely state, including the city of Hyderabad. In 1960, however, after further agitation Bombay state had to be split into Marathi-speaking Maharashtra and Gujarati-speaking Gujarat. Then in 1966, soon after Nehru's death, following years of protest by Sikh organizations, the Punjab was split into two new states: Punjab for Punjabi-speakers, and Haryana for Hindi-speakers, with the newly completed city of Chandigarh on the border between the two states as a union territory acting as the capital for both states; the remaining Pahari-speaking areas were given to the hill state now known as Himachal Pradesh, with its capital at Shimla.

Other new states were created less on linguistic and more on ethnic and political lines, often after years of armed regional rebellion. The first was Nagaland in the north-east of India, carved in 1963 from the state of Assam. It was followed by more north-eastern states, Arunachal Pradesh, Manipur, Meghalaya, Mizoram and Tripura, in the 1970s and 1980s. In 2000, Chhattisgarh, Jharkhand and Uttarakhand were created out of Madhya Pradesh, Bihar and Uttar Pradesh, respectively, in the first two instances as a result of the longstanding demands of tribal peoples, generally now known as *adivasis* (aboriginals). In 2013, Telangana was created out of the northern part of Andhra Pradesh, including Hyderabad. Today, there are twenty-nine Indian states and seven union territories (including Delhi): more than the eight major and five minor provinces of British India, yet far fewer than the 565 princely states existing in 1947.

However, Nehru's greatest success lay not in holding fair elections and holding together the Indian Union, but in his social legislation, which reformed Hindu personal law. The British had abolished *sati* and introduced the Indian Penal Code (drafted by Macaulay) to cover criminal law, but they had made no attempt to introduce a common civil code to replace the religiously sanctioned laws of India's many different communities, governing such matters as marriage, divorce, alimony and inheritance. Nehru, backed by Ambedkar – both of whom were lawyers trained in the British tradition – was determined to do this. But both men quickly realized that there was little support for a common code among the large Muslim minority. Muslim personal law was therefore left alone by Nehru, and remains unreformed – despite an abortive attempt in the mid-1980s by the government of Rajiv Gandhi, who backed off for fear of losing Muslim votes. Nehru and Ambedkar concentrated instead on a common, secular code for Hindus, Sikhs, Christians and other religious communities. Their intention was to replace a Hindu personal law still largely based on the ancient laws of Manu – in which caste mattered more than the individual, the 'joint' family was the norm, the marriage of children was arranged by their parents, the man was master of the woman – with a more individualist and liberal view of human rights. Unsurprisingly, Nehru had a bruising fight on his hands to enact the legislation, not least with a socially conservative president, Rajendra Prasad, which lasted for nearly ten years after Independence. At one point, Nehru referred Parliament ironically to the fidelity of women stressed in *The Ramayana* and *The Mahabharata*, in order to remind its (mainly male) members of the hypocrisy endemic in the Hindu personal law. 'It is only the women who have to behave like Sita and Savitri; the men may behave as they like.' In the end, the legislation had to be split up. In 1955, the Hindu Marriage Act was passed, followed by three more acts in 1956, covering succession, guardianship, adoption and alimony. Finally, though, women acquired equal rights with men in regard to the succession to and holding of property; monogamy was put on a legal basis; and divorce entailed the payment of alimony.

Nehru's greatest failure was his economic policy, which has come to dominate his reputation since the liberalization of the Indian economy in the 1990s. This is somewhat unfair, given the meagre and uncompetitive industrial base on which he had to build in 1947; the fact that Indian industrialization postdated democracy (unlike in most European countries); and that Nehru's successors were more blameworthy than him until the 1990s – not least in the way that they turned a blind eye to bribery at the highest levels of politics. However, Nehru himself cannot be acquitted of setting a bad economic example, with his heavy, government-directed emphasis on bureaucrats and planning committees (led by the physicist and statistician Prasanta Mahalanobis), rather than businessmen and companies, as the primary source of major investment decisions. His overweening faith in science and technology, such as large dams, was also ill-informed, though commonly shared at this time of widespread belief in scientific progress. Nehru stated that: 'It is science alone that can solve the problem of hunger and poverty, of insanitation and illiteracy, of superstition and of deadening custom and tradition, of vast resources running to waste, of a rich country inhabited by starving people . . .'. Rhetoric such as this led him, and subsequent Indian leaders, to waste precious resources on nuclear power, which is yet to prove itself economic in India and is 'very unlikely' to do so, according to the physicist and environmentalist M. V. Ramana, in his ironically entitled book on nuclear energy in India, *The Power of Promise*.

The legacy of Nehruvian central planning, compounded by two decades of economic stagnation and growing corruption under Indira Gandhi and the coalition governments of 1977–80, created an insidious 'licence-inspector-quota raj', in which government ministers and bureaucrats in New Delhi with control over an array of industrial licences had the power to make or break business decisions, often in exchange for large bribes. In one of several absurdities cited by the analyst Shankar Aiyyar, a Small-Scale Industries licence issued in Delhi capped production of video-cassettes by a business at a quota of 20,000 per year, as against a manufacturing capacity for the imported cassette-making machine of 20,000 per week. In order to keep the machine running at full capacity throughout the year, the owner of the machine was therefore compelled to register the same business fifty-two times under different names, even though the address for the manufacturing unit remained identical. 'In my thirty years in active business,' writes Gurcharan Das—the former executive turned student of *The Mahabharata* mentioned earlier—in his book *India Grows at Night*, 'I hardly met a single official who really understood my business, yet he had the power to ruin it.'

Some of these crippling restrictions were lifted in the mid-1980s by the Congress government of Rajiv Gandhi, which abolished licensing in thirty industries and encouraged the use of information technology. But after 1987, with the revelation of the Bofors corruption scandal over arms sales involving alleged kickbacks to key defence officials and politicians at the very top of the Congress government, the reform process stalled and Rajiv Gandhi lost power in the elections of 1989. By the summer of 1991, India found itself on the edge of bankruptcy as a result of the collision of three international events: the disappearance of India's trade with the Soviet Union after the latter's collapse in 1990–91; the loss of remittances from hundreds of thousands of Indian workers in Kuwait following the invasion by Saddam Hussein in 1990; and a spike in the price of oil because of the Gulf War that more than doubled the monthly bill for India's petroleum imports from $280 million to $671 million. In order to secure a massive rescue loan from the International Monetary Fund, the Indian government under Prime Minister Narasimha Rao and his finance minister, Manmohan Singh, was left with no alternative but to agree to dismantle most of the licence-inspector-quota raj that had grown up since 1947. Economic liberalization got underway the following year, producing dramatic growth against a background of unprecedented political turmoil: six prime ministers and five governments during the 1990s. With it began a new, and still developing, phase in India's contradictory history.

POSTSCRIPT

An American economist has predicted that in the next century
India will be an economic superpower. I don't want India to be
an economic superpower. I want India to be a happy country.
(Industrialist J. R. D. Tata, 1992)

Contemporary India pulsates with newly created wealth, energy and
optimism. It also teems with historic poverty, violence and distress. The
economic reforms of 1991 led to the growth of a large and unprecedented
middle class: between a fifth and a third of the country by income, as
compared with less than 2 per cent at Independence. Yet between 1995
and 2012 nearly 285,000 Indian farmers (according to conservative official
figures) committed suicide, in despair at their indebtedness created by the
drive towards corporate farming: 'the largest sustained wave of such deaths
recorded in history', notes the journalist P. Sainath. And 50 per cent of
Indian households have to resort to open defecation for lack of a household toilet, according to the national census of 2011. Extreme polarization
defines India today and demands attention, whether from politicians, business people and economists, writers and artists, or simply the concerned
Indian citizen. In almost every country in the world – but possibly most of
all in India – the disparity between haves and have-nots increased during
the two decades on either side of the new millennium, including the financial crash of 2008. So did the extent and scale of corruption, despite the
disappearance of most of the 'licence raj'.

In mid-1991, at the same time that the Indian government was facing financial bankruptcy, the 70-year-old Satyajit Ray gave a press interview in which he commented trenchantly on corruption. 'Looking around me I feel that the old values of personal integrity, loyalty, liberalism, rationalism and fair play are all completely gone,' said Ray. 'People accept corruption as a way of life, as a method of getting along, as a necessary evil. In accepting material comforts you grow numb with placid acceptance. Maybe you resist in the beginning. But the internal and external pressures crowd to a point where you learn to overlook the moral decline they spell.' This was no off-the-cuff remark; Ray's last three films, including his 1989 adaptation of Henrik Ibsen's play, *An Enemy of the People*, updated to contemporary Bengal, had been explicit meditations on corruption. In fact, the subject had preoccupied his films ever since the making of his sinister tragi-comedy, *The Middle Man*, in 1975, in protest against Indira Gandhi's Emergency, with its devastating vignette of a shady Congress politician that somehow eluded the censors in Delhi.

Two decades after Ray's death in 1992, corruption was a word on the lips of every Indian. Since the unresolved Bofors scandal of the late 1980s, there had been a catalogue of financial misbehaviour at the top of government, the military and business. 'Moral failure pervaded our public life and hung over it like Delhi's smog', wrote Gurcharan Das in *The Difficulty of Being Good*, published in 2009, soon after its author was shocked by the public revelation of the largest fraud in Indian corporate history, perpetrated by the founder of an internationally respected Indian software company, Satyam Computer Services. Das listed a variety of less extreme examples:

One out of five members of the Indian parliament elected in 2004 had criminal charges against him. A survey by a Harvard professor found that one out of every four teachers in government primary schools is absent and one out of four is simply not teaching. A World Bank study found that two out of five doctors do not show up at state primary health centres and that 69 per cent of their medicines are stolen. A cycle rickshaw driver in Kanpur routinely pays a fifth of his daily earnings in bribes to the police. A farmer cannot hope to get a clear title to his land without bribing a revenue official and that too after a humiliating ordeal of countless visits to the revenue office.

In his book *Public Money Private Agenda*, published in 2013, the journalist A. Surya Prakash catalogues how government largesse provided under the Members of Parliament Local Area Development Scheme, established in 1993 to give MPs power to help their constituents directly, has been regularly diverted from financing public facilities, such as community halls and computers for schools, into private and commercial facilities, such as premises for local lawyers' associations and shopping complexes, not to mention untraceable 'assets'. 'Parliamentarians fail to realize that the credibility of Parliament remains intact only when privileges and ethics are seen as two sides of the same coin', writes Prakash. Instead, 'their hackles are raised when people demand that the concept of accountability ought to keep pace with the burgeoning privileges of MPs.'

In response to rising public pressure, peaking in the national anti-corruption movement of 2011–12 led by Anna Hazare, action was taken by a reluctant central government to punish the most flagrant malfeasance. However, the cancer seemed too deeply rooted in the Indian body politic to be removed without systemic reforms. Public-interest litigation filed in 1999 by professors at one of the Indian Institutes of Management calling themselves the Association for Democratic Reforms, backed by India's Supreme Court, intending to compel political parties to reveal election candidates' criminal convictions and cases pending against them, was resisted by twenty-one political parties. It was eventually implemented, yet, after the 2009 elections, more than a quarter of the elected MPs had criminal records, including pending charges of murder. Moreover many, perhaps most, educated Indians appeared to accept corruption as a corollary of becoming personally richer. Even Das – pursuing his faith in the free market advocated in *India Unbound* – had earlier welcomed the idea that economic growth required that 'people shamelessly follow their self-interest in the bazaar rather than lofty moral principles', although he now admitted to having second thoughts.

For sure, official corruption has been a fact of life in all societies in certain periods, not least in the 'rotten boroughs' of early 19th-century Britain before the reform of the House of Commons in 1832. In India, it was rife in Mughal Delhi in the period after the death of Aurangzeb in 1707, and in mid-18th-century Bengal under the East India Company nabobs before the reforms of Hastings and Cornwallis. It must have flourished, too, in the Mauryan empire, judging from the blunt advice on controlling official corruption in Kautilya's *Arthashastra*, which includes the recommendation that corrupt officials be publicly smeared with cow dung and ashes. But also true is that such corruption was stamped on during the British Raj and frowned on in the nationalist movement under Gandhi and Nehru. Of all the pungent criticisms levelled against these two extraordinary Indian leaders, no one has accused them of feathering their own nests by accepting bribes. The rot started after Nehru, as is generally agreed, with Indira Gandhi, her sons Sanjay and Rajiv, and their successors.

If this is not discouraging enough – as well as potentially damaging for the future growth of the Indian economy – India's once-creative intellectual life also seems in danger of atrophy. Scientific research lacks originality, as already discussed. In commerce, Indian technology companies have invested too little in research and development, notes Dinesh Sharma in his recent history of India's IT industry, *The Long Revolution*. One highly successful IT entrepreneur, Nandan Nilekani, regrets that 'lack of innovation seems to be the default mindset' in his *Imagining India: Ideas for the New Century*. The offices of India's IT companies in Bangalore, Hyderabad, Gurgaon and elsewhere may look 'like twinkling towers of innovation', an American sociologist, Shehzad Nadeem, writes in his well-researched study, *Dead Ringers:*

How Outsourcing is Changing the Way Indians Understand Themselves, but in reality, says Nadeem, 'like plastic fruit, they are imitations'. A former director-general of the Council of Scientific and Industrial Research in New Delhi, Raghunath Anant Mashelkar, agrees with this criticism: 'Historically India has not done well in science-led innovation but now it can't remain a nation of imitators.'

India in the early 21st century has no lack of competent academics, commentators and journalists, not to speak of successful writers and artists, as well as a core of well-trained and altruistic professionals in, for example, health care. However, it sorely needs original thinkers, independent of the government, approaching the calibre of its pre-Independence reformers, writers and scientists, such as Gandhi, Tagore, Raman and Ramanujan, not to speak of such historical religious figures as Kabir and of course the Buddha.

Gurcharan Das is probably the best of the current Indian public intellectuals, with a pan-Indian – even international – audience beyond their particular discipline. But he was educated and trained largely outside India, in the United States, where professional immigrants from India such as Amartya Sen have been able to make a considerable national impact; and Das is one of a group small enough to be counted on the fingers of two hands. V. S. Naipaul's hopeful prediction in an essay for the magazine *India Today* on the 50th anniversary of Independence in 1997, that 'in another ten years, India will probably be one of the world's most intellectually gifted countries', has not been fulfilled. More accurate, one fears, is the homegrown analysis of Markandey Katju, chairman of the Press Council of India and a former Indian Supreme Court judge. In 2012, Katju deplored the fact that the large majority of his fellow countrymen – he controversially claimed '90 per cent' – prefer to vote on the basis of caste rather than merit, to believe in astrology, to turn cricket into a 'religion' and to idolize 'Bollywood' stars, rather than attempt to improve democracy and society by rational and scientific thinking. 'I want to see Indians prosper, I want poverty and unemployment abolished, I want the standard of living of the

80 per cent poor Indians' – those who live on less than about $2.50 per day, according to the World Bank – 'to rise so that they get decent lives', said Katju. 'But this is possible [only] when their minds are rid of casteism, communalism and superstition'.

The infection of current Indian culture by 'Bollywood' films tends to confirm Katju's scathing judgement. Once upon a time, beginning in the 1950s – the era of the actor-directors Guru Dutt and Raj Kapoor – Hindi films were watchable enough as entertainment, with some talented acting, witty dialogues and lovely songs (though almost always unimaginatively directed); they were something of a guilty pleasure for artistically discerning Indians, as I recall during the 1970s. But now most of the films are just vehicles for the display of consumerism and raunchiness. Yet, so commercially successful is the film industry that even academics and serious writers have been seduced into lauding its output. It takes one of the industry's own to speak the truth. In 2009, the Urdu poet, scriptwriter and hugely successful songwriter, Javed Akhtar, remarked of current Hindi films: 'In a way, they mirror the fact that we are not ready to stop and think. Everybody is in a hurry and is looking for instant gratification without caring for those around them. We are making films that sell this lifestyle to a small, affluent, multiplex-going audience that doesn't bother about the small town and rural population.' By contrast, said Akhtar, Satyajit Ray's films 'depicted a compassion, a sensitivity that is sadly missing not just from films, but from our lives as well.' They famously lack villains: 'Ray's characters only had negative shades. They were people trapped in their own thinking and beliefs. While Hindi films had ferocious villains who only evoked hatred, you actually felt sad for Ray's negative characters. Such was the sensitivity of the man.' Akhtar concluded by suggesting: 'We need to take a long, hard look at ourselves. Or else, we shall continue to feel incomplete and fail to appreciate the subtlety that Ray's films depicted.'

Needless to say, I couldn't agree more. Culture matters as much as politics and economics. Only a great civilization with a long train of achievement could have given birth to the films of Satyajit Ray. So I would add my own, objective, suggestion to Akhtar's subjective one. Indians need to become curious to study India's history more critically, in particular its dynastic tendency, as a way of understanding their present and future. *The Mahabharata* may be an important guide to history, as Gandhi believed; but so is Gibbon's *Decline and Fall*. Otherwise – to recall the aphorism of a western philosopher about failing to remember the past – India risks condemning itself to repeating its past mistakes.

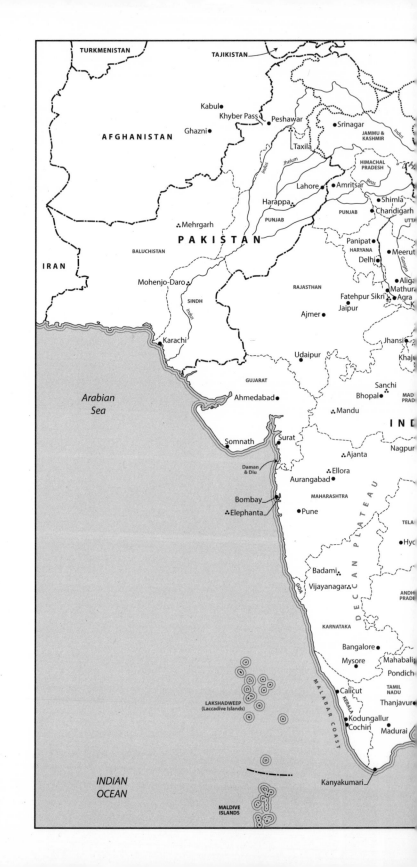

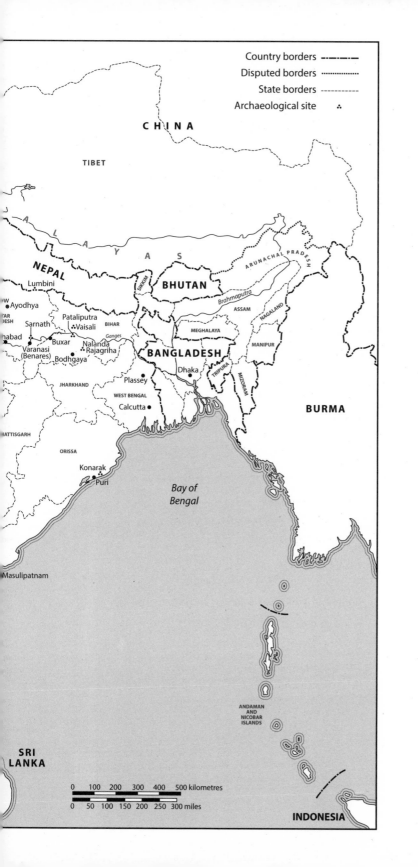

Country borders ·—·—·—
Disputed borders ··········
State borders ———————
Archaeological site ⚬

CHINA

TIBET

H
I
M
A
L
A
Y
A
S

NEPAL

Lumbini

Ayodhya

Pataliputra
BIHAR   Vaisali
Sarnath

SIKKIM

BHUTAN

ARUNACHAL PRADESH

Brahmaputra

ASSAM

NAGALAND

MEGHALAYA

MANIPUR

TAR
DESH

habad   Buxar   Nalanda
Varanasi   Rajagriha
(Benares) Bodhgaya

Ganges

BANGLADESH

Dhaka

TRIPURA

MIZORAM

JHARKHAND

Plassey

WEST BENGAL

Calcutta

BURMA

HATTISGARH

ORISSA

Konarak
Puri

Bay of
Bengal

Masulipatnam

ANDAMAN
AND
NICOBAR
ISLANDS

SRI
LANKA

0   100   200   300   400   500 kilometres

0   50 100 150 200 250 300 miles

INDONESIA

CHRONOLOGY

BC

c. 7000	Village habitation at Mehrgarh (Baluchistan)
c. 2600–1900	Indus Valley civilization
second mill.	Migration of Aryans into northwest India
c. 1500–1200	Composition of *Rigveda*
c. 1200–500	Composition of later *Vedas*, *Samhitas*, *Brahmanas* and *Upanishads*
c. 950	Mahabharata War
? 563–483	Life of Siddhartha Gautama, founder of Buddhism
sixth/fifth cent.	Life of Vardhamana the Mahavira, founder of Jainism
c. 543–321	Magadhan empire
326	Alexander the Great invades Punjab
c. 321–298	Reign of Chandragupta Maurya
fourth cent.	Composition of Kautilya's *Arthashastra*
c. 300	Composition of *Ramayana* begins
c. 269–232	Reign of Asoka; inscriptions in Brahmi and Kharoshti
c. 200	Cave paintings begin at Ajanta
c. 187	End of Mauryan empire
second cent.	Shunga dynasty in north India
late second cent.	Monsoon wind permits Greeks to sail across Indian Ocean

AD

first cent.	Bharata Natyam dance form emerges in Tamil Nadu
first cent.	Buddhism reaches Southeast Asia and China
first cent.	Roman maritime trade with India begins
78	Saka era begins
first–second cent.	Jews settle at Kodungallur
c. 200	*Ramayana* reaches its present form
c. 300–888	Pallava dynasty in south India
320–*c.* 335	Reign of Chandra Gupta I
c. 400	*Mahabharata* reaches its present form
early fifth cent.	Faxian visits India
fifth cent.	Nalanda University founded
sixth cent.	Buddhism becomes influential in Japan
c. 500	Second wave of Huna invasions
c. 550	End of Gupta empire
c. 550–757	First Chalukya dynasty in Deccan
606–47	Reign of Harsha
629–45	Xuanzang visits India
c. 630–970	Eastern Chalukya dynasty in Deccan
712	Arabs occupy Sindh
c. 750–950	Gurjara-Pratihara dynasties in Ganges basin
757–973	Rashtrakuta dynasty in Deccan
c. 760–1142	Pala dynasty in Bengal, Bihar and Assam
c. 850–1267	Chola dynasty in south India
10th–12th cent.	Odissi dance form emerges in Orissa
c. 916–1203	Chandella dynasty in central India
973–*c.* 1189	Second Chalukya dynasty in Deccan
973–1048	Life of al-Biruni
1001	Mahmud of Ghazni begins raids on India
1026	Destruction of Somnath Temple
1192	Second battle of Tarain

c. 1190s	Destruction of Nalanda University
c. 1200	'Arabic' numerals, invented in India, reach Europe
1206–1526	Delhi Sultanate
1228–1826	Ahom dynasty in Assam
1325–51	Reign of Muhammad bin Tughlaq
1336–1565	Vijayanagar empire
1398	Timur sacks Delhi
1401–1562	Malwa Sultanate
? 1440–1518	Life of Kabir
15th–16th cent.	Sattriya dance form emerges in Assam
1498	Vasco da Gama reaches India
16th cent.	Mohinyattam, Kathak and Kuchipudi dance forms emerge in Kerala, north India and Andhra Pradesh, respectively
1526–1858	Mughal empire
1556–1605	Reign of Akbar
1600	East India Company founded (London)
1627–1658	Reign of Shah Jahan
1632–1640s	Taj Mahal built
17th cent.	Kathakali dance form emerges in Kerala
1680	Death of Shivaji
1707	Death of Aurangzeb
1739	Nadir Shah sacks Delhi
1757	Battle of Plassey
18th cent.	Manipuri dance form emerges in Manipur
1764	Battle of Buxar
1765	East India Company granted fiscal administration of eastern India
1770	Famine in Bengal
1774–85	Governor-generalship of Warren Hastings
1784	Asiatic Society of Bengal founded

1786	Indo-European language family announced by William Jones
1793	Permanent Settlement of Bengal and reform of civil service
1799	Death of Tipu Sultan
1828	Brahma Sabha (later Brahmo Samaj) founded by Rammohun Roy
1830s	English replaces Persian in government administration/ education
1857–58	Sepoy Mutiny and Indian Uprising
1858	British Crown replaces East India Company as ruler of India
1885	Indian National Congress founded
1905	Partition of Bengal; Swadeshi movement in Bengal
1906	All-India Muslim League founded
1909	Indian Councils Act (Morley-Minto Reforms)
1912	Capital of India moved from Calcutta to Delhi
1913	Rabindranath Tagore awarded Nobel Prize in Literature
1914–18	First World War
1918	Srinivasa Ramanujan awarded fellowship of Royal Society
1919	Amritsar massacre
1921	Non-cooperation movement launched by Mahatma Gandhi
1930	Chandrasekhar Venkata Raman awarded Nobel Prize in Physics
1935	Government of India Act
1937	First democratic elections, won by Indian National Congress
1939–45	Second World War
1940	Pakistan resolution by All-India Muslim League

1942	Quit India movement launched by Gandhi
1943	Famine in Bengal
1947	Independence of India and Partition into India and Pakistan
1947–64	Prime ministership of Jawaharlal Nehru
1948	Gandhi assassinated
1956	States Reorganization Act
1962	Indo-China War
1968	Hargobind Khorana awarded Nobel Prize in Physiology or Medicine
1971	Bangladesh War
1975–77	Emergency declared by Indira Gandhi
1983	Subrahmanyan Chandrasekhar awarded Nobel Prize in Physics
1984	Indira Gandhi assassinated
1991	Rajiv Gandhi assassinated
1991	Liberalization of Indian economy leads to rapid growth
1992	Satyajit Ray receives Academy Award for Lifetime Achievement
1992	Destruction of Babri Masjid, Ayodhya
1998	Bharatiya Janata Party elected to lead national coalition government
1998	Amartya Sen awarded Nobel Prize in Economics
2009	Venkatraman Ramakrishnan awarded Nobel Prize in Chemistry

With a vast subcontinent and more than four millennia to cover, plus some of the imperial history of the Islamic world and the colonial history of modern Europe, it is difficult to know where to begin in recommending reading about the history of India. This brief survey covers the sources of every major quotation in the book, while also mentioning some important unquoted sources and giving some references to subjects omitted from the main text for lack of space. Much as I would like to have included a few books and articles in Indian languages, I have stuck to English, given that there are more than twenty official languages in India, of which I myself read only one (Bengali); and that rustily. I have also omitted references to the internet – invaluable as it is for research – purely for lack of space, as is customary with short histories.

Before coming to the individual chapters, something should be said about histories of India as a whole. The sole, up-to-date, short history in print is Thomas R. Trautmann's 250-page *India: Brief History of a Civilization* (New York, 2011), an introductory textbook for American students that stresses the pre-colonial over the colonial period and naturally avoids expressing many personal opinions. Other one-volume textbooks by professional academics are considerably longer, for example, Hermann Kulke and Dietmar Rothermund's *A History of India* (fifth edition, London, 2010). None, it must be said, is an enjoyable read. By contrast, the writer and historian John Keay's 600-page *India: A History* (London, 2000) is aimed at a non-academic readership, well researched and enjoyably written, with plenty of opinion but not always factually accurate, especially on the modern period. Otherwise, general histories come in more than one volume, written by more than one expert. The best known, rightly so, is *The Wonder That Was India*, vol. 1 by A. L. Basham (third revised edition, London, 1967), covering the period up to the coming of Islam, and vol. 2 by S. A. A. Rizvi (London, 1987), taking the story up to 1700; to which must be added *Early India: from the Origins to AD 1300* by Romila Thapar (London, 2002) and *A History of India*, volume 2, by Percival Spear (revised edition, London, 1978), covering from the Mughal empire to the post-Independence period. Also still valuable are some of the scholarly essays in Basham's edited collection, *A Cultural History of India* (Oxford, 1975), and the well-illustrated Time-Life *Cultural Atlas of India* (Amsterdam, 1995) by Gordon Johnson (general editor of the *New Cambridge History of India*) with contributions from others. Another highly illustrated book, Manosi Lahiri's *Mapping India* (New Delhi, 2012), shows maps of India through the ages, beginning with Ptolemy's. Some of the above books are long in the tooth, especially Spear's book and Basham's two books, the older of which was influenced by the first flush of Indian independence. Even so, no academic or general writer has yet managed to beat Basham's *Wonder* for its range, its depth, its readability and the quality of its many translations from Indian languages.

Introduction

I begin with two classics: Jawaharlal Nehru's *The Discovery of India* (London, 1946) and Nirad C. Chaudhuri's *The Autobiography of an Unknown Indian* (London, 1951). Both books are intellectually flawed but beautifully written. B. R. Ambedkar's *The Untouchables: Who Were They?: And Why They Became Untouchables* (New Delhi, 1948) is also historically important, and powerfully argued, as is the Marxist D. D. Kosambi's *The Culture and Civilisation of Ancient India in Historical Outline* (London, 1965). All my quotations from Mahatma Gandhi may be found in the comprehensive volumes of the *Collected Works of Mahatma Gandhi*, published by the Indian government since 1958.

Most of Satyajit Ray's English writings on Indian and world cinema and culture, dating from 1948–91, can be found in his two collections, *Our Films Their Films* (New Delhi, 1976) and *Deep Focus: Reflections on Cinema* (New Delhi, 2012). Ray's English screenplay of *The Chess Players* appears in *The Chess Players and Other Screenplays*, edited by me (London, 1989). My biography of Ray is *Satyajit Ray: The Inner Eye* (second edition, London, 2004).

Amartya Sen's academic writings are extensive. The most readable of those about India are collected in *The Argumentative Indian: Writings on Indian History, Culture and Identity* (London, 2005). Sen's magazine article on Indian growth, 'Putting Growth in its Place' (*Outlook*, 14 November 2011), was written with his collaborator Jean Drèze, with whom he wrote *An Uncertain Glory: India and Its Contradictions* (London, 2013). Ramachandra Guha's critical review of Sen's 2005 collection, 'Arguments with Sen' (*Economic and Political Weekly*, 40 (2005), pp. 4420–25), was followed by Sen's response, 'Our Past and Our Present' (*Economic and Political Weekly*, 41 (2006), pp. 4877–86). Guha's thorough and impressive history of India since 1947, *India after Gandhi: The History of the World's Largest Democracy* (London, 2007), is essentially a political and economic, rather than a cultural, study.

Selecting the most significant from the outpouring of books about the 'new' India is inevitably invidious, nor can I claim to have read all of them. But I can vouch for the intelligence and readability of the following books (in date order of publication): V. S. Naipaul's *India: A Million Mutinies Now* (London, 1990), which should be compared with Naipaul's more personal first book on India, *An Area of Darkness* (London, 1964); Sunil Khilnani's *The Idea of India* (London, 1997; revised edition, 2003); Gurcharan Das's *India Unbound: From Independence to the Global Information Age* (New Delhi, 2000); Pratap Bhanu Mehta's *The Burden of Democracy* (New Delhi,

2003); Edward Luce's *In Spite of the Gods: The Strange Rise of Modern India* (London, 2006; second edition, 2011); Pranab Bardhan's *Awakening Giants, Feet of Clay: Assessing the Economic Rise of China and India* (Princeton, 2010); Patrick French's *India: A Portrait* (London, 2011); Katherine Boo's *Behind the Beautiful Forevers: Life, Death and Hope in a Mumbai Slum* (London, 2012); Aman Sethi's *A Free Man: A True Story of Life and Death in Delhi* (London, 2012); and Shankkar Aiyar's *Accidental India: A History of the Nation's Passage through Crisis and Change* (New Delhi, 2012). Also of interest, though less well written, is A. P. J. Abdul Kalam's *Turning Points: A Journey through Challenges* (New Delhi, 2012), given that its scientist author served as a notable president of India.

I have omitted from the book recent English-language fiction about India, because there are so many writers and none of them is absolutely outstanding, at the literary level of R. K. Narayan (or Naipaul). Interesting are: Aravind Adiga, Amit Chaudhuri, Anita Desai, Amitav Ghosh, Rohinton Mistry, Arundhati Roy and Salman Rushdie. Also omitted, with regret, are visual artists such as M. F. Husain, Bhupen Khakhar, K. G. Subramanyan, Abanindranath and Gaganendranath Tagore and Ravi Varma, though I have made an exception for my favourite modern Indian artist, Benode Bihari Mukherjee. See *Benodebehari Mukherjee (1904–1980): Centenary Retrospective* (New Delhi, 2006), the catalogue of a National Gallery of Modern Art exhibition curated by the painter Gulammohammed Sheikh and R. Siva Kumar.

1 The Indus Valley Civilization
Accessible, well-illustrated studies of the Indus Valley civilization include: Michael Jansen, Máire Mulloy and Günter Urban's *Forgotten Cities on the Indus: Early Civilization in Pakistan from the 8th to the 2nd Millennium BC* (Mainz, 1991); Jonathan Mark Kenoyer's *Ancient Cities of the Indus Valley Civilization* (Karachi, 1998); and Jane R. McIntosh's *A Peaceful Realm: The Rise and Fall of the Indus Civilization* (Oxford, 2002).

The leading study of the Indus script is Asko Parpola's erudite *Deciphering the Indus Script* (Cambridge, 1994), but for a brief introduction see the relevant chapter in my *Lost Languages: The Enigma of the World's Undeciphered Scripts* (revised edition, London, 2009). Gregory L. Possehl's *Indus Age: The Writing System* (Philadelphia, 1996) discusses in detail, often entertainingly, the many attempts to decipher the script since the 1920s. A recent attempt by N. Jha and N. S. Rajaram published in *The Deciphered Indus Script: Methodology, Readings, Interpretations* (New Delhi, 2000) is criticized by Michael Witzel and Steve Farmer in 'Horseplay in Harappa' (*Frontline*, 13 October 2000).

Nayanjot Lahiri's *Finding Forgotten Cities: How the Indus Civilization Was Discovered* (New Delhi, 2005) is a well-written history. Sudeshna Guha's edited collection, *The Marshall Albums: Photography and Archaeology* (Ahmedabad, 2010), is a lavishly illustrated study of the work of Sir John Marshall, though it devotes relatively little space to the Indus Valley.

2 Vedas, Aryans and the Origins of Hinduism

The best-known modern version of the *Vedas* is *The Rig Veda: An Anthology*, translated by Wendy Doniger (London, 1981). *The Upanishads*, translated by Juan Mascaró (London, 1965), is one of several currently available translations. Rabindranath Tagore's comment on the *Upanishads* appears in *Selected Letters of Rabindranath Tagore*, edited by Krishna Dutta and Andrew Robinson (Cambridge, 1997).

Thomas R. Trautmann's *Aryans and British India* (Berkeley, 1997) is the most readable introduction to the tangled debate about the Indo-Aryans, especially when read alongside Trautmann's edited collection, *The Aryan Debate* (New Delhi, 2005), which includes S. P. Gupta's 'The Indus-Saraswati Civilization: Beginnings and Developments'. The most comprehensive discussion is, however, Edwin Bryant's *The Quest for the Origins of Vedic Culture: The Indo-Aryan Migration Debate* (New York, 2001). A fierce critic of the Indo-Aryan theory as racist is the archaeologist

Dilip K. Chakrabarti in his book, *The Oxford Companion to Indian Archaeology: The Archaeological Foundations of Ancient India, Stone Age to AD 13th Century* (New Delhi, 2006).

Enjoyable biographies of William Jones, Friedrich Max Müller and Rammohun Roy are, respectively: Michael J. Franklin's *Orientalist Jones: Sir William Jones, Poet, Lawyer, and Linguist, 1746–1794* (Oxford, 2011), supplemented by Alexander Murray's edited collection, *Sir William Jones 1746–1794: A Commemoration* (Oxford, 1998); Nirad C. Chaudhuri's *Scholar Extraordinary: The Life of Friedrich Max Müller* (London, 1974); and Amiya P. Sen's *Rammohun Roy: A Critical Biography* (New Delhi, 2012).

3 Buddha, Alexander and Asoka

There are dozens of recent introductions to the life and thought of the Buddha. I recommend: Karen Armstrong's *Buddha* (London, 2000); Paul Williams with Anthony Tribe and Alexander Wynne's *Buddhist Thought* (second edition, London, 2012); Pankaj Mishra's *An End to Suffering: The Buddha in the World* (London, 2004); and *The Dhammapada: The Sayings of the Buddha*, translated by Thomas Byrom (London, 2002). Also of interest, though hard going, is Thomas McEvilley's *The Shape of Ancient Thought: Comparative Studies in Indian and Greek Philosophies* (New York, 2002), on how Buddhism may have reached the classical world; and Donald S. Lopez Jr's *From Stone to Flesh: A Short History of the Buddha* (Chicago, 2013), on how East and West understood the Buddha prior to the 19th century. The much-disputed dating of the Buddha is discussed by Richard Gombrich in Heinz Bechert's edited collection, *The Dating of the Historical Buddha*, vol. 2 (Göttingen, 1992). Criticism of this book, mainly by Indian scholars, appears in A. K. Narain's edited collection, *The Date of the Historical Sakyamuni Buddha* (New Delhi, 2003).

Buddhism's disappearance in India and its modern revival are the subject of Gail Omvedt's *Buddhism in India: Challenging Brahmanism and Caste* (New Delhi, 2003) and Trevor Ling's *Buddhist Revival in*

India: Aspects of the Sociology of Buddhism (Basingstoke, 1980). The story of the European scholars responsible for Buddhism's rediscovery is told in Charles Allen's *The Buddha and the Sahibs: The Men Who Discovered India's Lost Religion* (London, 2002); and the Ajanta cave paintings (now almost hidden in darkness for visitors) are wonderfully displayed in the photographer Benoy K. Behl's *The Ajanta Caves: Ancient Paintings of Buddhist India* (London, 1998). On the Mahabodhi Temple, see Alan Trevithick's *The Revival of Buddhist Pilgrimage at Bodh Gaya (1811–1949): Anagarika Dharmapala and the Mahabodhi Temple* (New Delhi, 2006) and David Geary, Matthew R. Sayers and Abhishek Singh Amar's edited collection, *Cross-disciplinary Perspectives on a Contested Buddhist Site: Bodh Gaya Jataka* (London, 2012). Rabindranath Tagore's comment on the Buddha appears in his 'Buddhadeva' (*Visva-Bharati Quarterly*, winter 1956/57, pp. 169–76).

An excellent recent biography of Alexander is Paul Cartledge's *Alexander the Great: The Hunt for a New Past* (London, 2004). On the later Greek influence in northwestern India, see A. K. Narain's *The Indo-Greeks* (revised edition, New Delhi, 2003). Charles Allen's *Ashoka: The Search for India's Lost Emperor* (London, 2012) is a well-constructed history that does not skimp on difficult scholarly issues. The attorney Bruce Rich promotes Asoka (and Kautilya) for the modern world in *To Uphold the World: A Call for a New Global Ethic from Ancient India* (Boston, 2010), without being entirely convincing.

4 Hindu Dynasties

There are no accessible studies focusing on the Hindu dynasties, so it is best to read the general histories of Romila Thapar and A. L. Basham. Brief introductions to the ideas behind classical Hinduism include K. M. Sen's venerable *Hinduism* (London, 2005, with a foreword by Sen's grandson, Amartya Sen) and Sue Hamilton's *Indian Philosophy: A Very Short Introduction* (Oxford, 2001), as well as A. L. Dallapiccola's *Hindu Myths*

(London, 2003). I also recommend Richard Lannoy's *The Speaking Tree: A Study of Indian Culture and Society* (London, 1971).

The novelist R. K. Narayan's 'shortened modern prose versions' of the Indian epics are: *The Ramayana* (London, 1972) and *The Mahabharata* (London, 1978). There is a translation by the Sanskrit scholar John D. Smith, *The Mahabharata: An Abridged Translation* (London, 2009). Rudyard Kipling's comment on *The Mahabharata* appears in *Kipling's India: Uncollected Sketches 1884–88*, edited by Thomas Pinney (Basingstoke, 1986). Gurcharan Das stimulatingly relates *The Mahabharata* to modern Indian concerns in *The Difficulty of Being Good: On the Subtle Art of Dharma* (New York, 2009). Many classics of Sanskrit literature are available in the translations of the Oxford series World's Classics and the series Penguin Classics.

On Hindu aesthetics, T. Richard Blurton's *Hindu Art* (London, 2002) is a good introduction. George Michell's *The Penguin Guide to the Monuments of India*, vol. 1 (London, 1989), covering Buddhist, Jain and Hindu structures, is intended as a guidebook but in addition serves as an excellent source of reliable information, based on the author's thorough research on the spot. There are also numerous large-format, highly illustrated studies intended for both scholars and coffee tables, such as A. L. Dallapiccola's edited collection, *Krishna: The Divine Lover* (London, 1982) and Christopher Tadgell's *The History of Architecture in India* (London, 1990). On India's relationship with Southeast Asia, there is a dearth of writing; Paul Wheatley's 'India Beyond the Ganges: Desultory Reflections on the Origins of Civilization in Southeast Asia' (*Journal of Asian Studies*, 42:1 (1982), pp. 13–28) is good.

5 The Coming of Islam

Francis Robinson's highly illustrated reference book, *The Mughal Emperors: and the Islamic Dynasties of India, Iran and Central Asia* (London, 2007), has the virtue of seamlessly combining the Islamic world, beginning with the Mongols in Iran, and the later world of Indian Islam. S. A. A. Rizvi's essays on medieval Indian Islam in A. L. Basham's *A Cultural History of India* are also helpful. The archaeologist and sailor Brian Fagan's *Beyond the Blue Horizon: How the Earliest Mariners Unlocked the Secrets of the Oceans* (London, 2012) has a chapter on the maritime history of the Arabs in the Indian Ocean.

The translation of al-Biruni by Edward C. Sachau, *Alberuni's India* (London, 1888; abridged edition by Ainslie Embree, New York, 1971), is a crucial contemporary source on the Muslim conquests. Sita Ram Goel's edited collection, *Hindu Temples: What Happened to Them*, vols 1 and 2 (New Delhi, 1993–98), makes an impassioned Hindu nationalist case for the severity of Muslim iconoclasm. More measured assessments appear in Richard M. Eaton's brief *Temple Desecration and Muslim States in Medieval India* (New Delhi, 2004) and in Eaton's edited collection, *India's Islamic Traditions, 711–1750* (New Delhi, 2003), in which his introduction discusses theories of conversion to Islam. Romila Thapar investigates Muslim iconoclasm at Somnath in depth in *Somanatha: The Many Voices of a History* (New Delhi, 2004). Some evidence for the destruction of Nalanda appears in C. Mani's edited collection, *The Heritage of Nalanda* (New Delhi, 2008). On the Vijayanagar empire, the leading modern authorities are John M. Fritz and George Michell. Among their several books, an excellent illustrated introduction is *Hampi Vijayanagara* (revised edition, London, 2011).

A well-known early edition of Kabir in English is *One Hundred Poems of Kabir*, translated by Rabindranath Tagore with the assistance of Evelyn Underhill (London, 1915). More reliable editions include a translation by Charlotte Vaudeville, *Kabir* (Oxford, 1974), and another by the poet Arvind Krishna Mehrotra, *Songs of Kabir* (New York, 2011).

6 The Mughal Empire

Bamber Gascoigne's beautifully illustrated, but also seriously researched, history of the Mughal empire, *The Great Moghuls* (London, 1971), has worn well. There are of course many illustrated books on Mughal art and culture, such as the Victoria & Albert Museum's *The Indian Heritage: Court Life and Arts under Mughal Rule* (London, 1982). An up-to-date cultural study, based on an exhibition taken from the manuscript collections of the British Library, is J. P. Losty and Malini Roy's *Mughal India: Art, Culture and Empire* (London, 2012).

Philip Davies's *The Penguin Guide to the Monuments of India*, vol. 2 (London, 1989) covers Islamic and Rajput buildings, including those of the Mughals, and is a useful reference source. On the Taj Mahal, the definitive book is Ebba Koch's *The Complete Taj Mahal: and the Riverfront Gardens of Agra* (London, 2006), while Giles Tillotson's *Taj Mahal* (London, 2008) is a briefer history, which also explores the cultural significance of the Taj to the world.

Among books about individual Mughal emperors, the foremost is probably the memoirs of Babur. The original translation is *Memoirs of Zehir-Ed-Din Muhammed Babur, Emperor of Hindustan* by John Leyden and William Erskine (revised edition, Oxford, 1921), from which I quote. There is also a 1921 translation by Annette Susannah Beveridge, *Babur Nama* (abridged edition by Dilip Hiro, London, 2007), and an illustrated large-format edition translated by Wheeler M. Thackston, *The Baburnama: Memoirs of Babur, Prince and Emperor* (New York, 1996). The art historian and poet Laurence Binyon's brief biography, *Akbar* (London, 1932), is still worth reading, while Shireen Moosvi's collection, *Episodes in the Life of Akbar: Contemporary Records and Reminiscences* (New Delhi, 1994), captures the diverse facets of Akbar's personality vividly. William Dalrymple's *The Last Mughal: The Fall of a Dynasty, Delhi, 1857* (London, 2006) portrays the last Mughal ruler, his court in Delhi and his downfall.

7 European Incursions and East India Companies
India's trading history is covered in Tirthankar Roy's *India in the World Economy: from Antiquity to the Present* (Cambridge, 2012). Dick Whitaker's

'Conjunctures and Conjectures: Kerala and Roman Trade' (*South Asian Studies*, 25 (2009), pp. 1–9) contains informed speculations on the earliest period. James Chiriyankandath's 'Nationalism, Religion and Community: A. B. Salem, the Politics of Identity and the Disappearance of Cochin Jewry' (*Journal of Global History*, 3 (2008), pp. 21–42) is good on the Jewish community. On the Portuguese empire, J. B. Harrison's essay in A. L. Basham's *A Cultural History of India* is an excellent introduction; Heta Pandit's edited collection, *In and Around Old Goa* (Mumbai, 2004) is also useful, with good illustrations. The most complete history of Assam, at least for the Ahom and colonial period, is probably still Edward Gait's *A History of Assam* (second edition, Calcutta, 1926).

On the origins and development of the British trading empire, a general history is John Keay's *The Honourable Company: A History of the English East India Company* (London, 1991). The period is also covered in an excellent and well-illustrated exhibition catalogue edited by C. A. Bayly, *The Raj: India and the British 1600–1947* (London, 1990); in studies of Robert Clive and the Company in Bengal, such as Nirad C. Chaudhuri's *Clive of India: A Political and Psychological Essay* (London, 1975) and P. J. Marshall's *East Indian Fortunes: The British in Bengal in the Eighteenth Century* (Oxford, 1976); and in Gillian Tindall's *City of Gold: The Biography of Bombay* (London, 1982).

On the controversy between the Orientalists and the Anglicists, see Lynn Zastoupil and Martin Moir's edited collection, *The Great Indian Education Debate: Documents Relating to the Orientalist-Anglicist Controversy, 1781–1843* (London, 1999). It also features in Jon E. Wilson's *The Domination of Strangers: Modern Governance in Eastern India, 1780–1835* (Basingstoke, 2008); in Rosane Rocher and Ludo Rocher's biography of the founder of the Royal Asiatic Society, *The Making of Western Indology: Henry Thomas Colebrooke and the East India Company* (London, 2012); and in Blair B. Kling's *Partner in Empire: Dwarkanath Tagore and the Age of Enterprise in Eastern India* (Berkeley, 1976).

8 The 'Jewel in the Crown'
Life in the Indian Army before the 1857 Mutiny is described in James Lunt's
edition of Sita Ram Pandey's *From Sepoy to Subedar* (London, 1970) and
in Rudrangshu Mukherjee's brief account, *Mangal Pandey: Brave Martyr or
Accidental Hero?* (New Delhi, 2005). Although there is some doubt about
the authenticity of Pandey's manuscript, most military historians accept it
as genuine.

William Howard Russell's *My Diary in India, in the Year 1858–9*,
2 vols (London, 1860) is a vital eye-witness account of the last stage of the
Mutiny and its aftermath. Modern historical accounts include: Surendra
Nath Sen's *Eighteen Fifty-Seven* (New Delhi, 1957); Christopher Hibbert's
The Great Mutiny: India 1857 (London, 1978); Rudrangshu Mukherjee's
Avadh in Revolt, 1857–1858: A Study of Popular Resistance (New Delhi,
1984); Andrew Ward's *Our Bones Are Scattered: The Cawnpore Massacres
and the Indian Mutiny of 1857* (London, 1996); Rosie Llewellyn-Jones's *The
Great Uprising, 1857–58: Untold Stories, Indian and British* (Woodbridge,
2007); and Amaresh Misra's *War of Civilizations: India AD 1857* (New
Delhi, 2007). The British demolition of part of the Red Fort in Delhi is
criticized in James Fergusson's *History of Indian and Eastern Architecture*
(London, 1876). On the Indian Civil Service, see David Gilmour's *The
Ruling Caste: Imperial Lives in the Victorian Raj* (London, 2005).

Some 19th-century Indian reform movements are discussed in
Ramachandra Guha's edited collection, *Makers of Modern India* (Cambridge,
MA, 2011), which includes essays by Sir Syed Ahmed Khan, Jyotirao Phule
and Bal Gangadhar Tilak. The Brahmo Samaj is covered in David Kopf's
The Brahmo Samaj and the Shaping of the Modern Indian Mind (Princeton,
1979). Sumit Sarkar's *The Swadeshi Movement in Bengal 1903–1908*
(Calcutta, 1973) is the standard history of the Swadeshi movement.

On the Amritsar massacre, Winston Churchill's humane parliamentary speech in 1920 appears in his *India: Speeches and an Introduction*
(London, 1931), which may be compared with his later contempt for

Indian lives, described in Madhusree Mukerjee's *Churchill's Secret War: The British Empire and the Ravaging of India during World War II* (New York, 2010). Recent studies of Amritsar include Nick Lloyd's *The Amritsar Massacre: The Untold Story of One Fateful Day* (London, 2011) and Nigel Collett's biography, *The Butcher of Amritsar: General Reginald Dyer* (London, 2005).

9 End of Empire

The conversation in 1921 between Mahatma Gandhi and Rabindranath Tagore appears in Leonard K. Elmhirst, *Poet and Plowman* (Calcutta, 1975). For a detailed discussion of their relationship, see Krishna Dutta and Andrew Robinson's biography, *Rabindranath Tagore: The Myriad-Minded Man* (revised edition, London, 2007), and also Sabyasachi Bhattacharya's edited collection, *The Mahatma and the Poet: Letters and Debates between Gandhi and Tagore, 1915–1941* (New Delhi, 1997). Gandhi's early views on machines are found in his *Hind Swaraj and Other Writings* (Cambridge, 1997), edited by Anthony J. Parel; all of his views are discussed in David Arnold's *Everyday Technology: Machines and the Making of India's Modernity* (Chicago, 2013).

There is of course no end to books on Gandhi. Two recent biographies of interest are his grandson Rajmohan Gandhi's *Mohandas: A True Story of a Man, His People and an Empire* (New Delhi, 2006) and especially Kathryn Tidrick's *Gandhi: A Political and Spiritual Life* (London, 2006). Faisal Devji's *The Impossible Indian: Gandhi and the Temptation of Violence* (London, 2012) grapples with Gandhi's attitude to violence. Arthur Herman considers *Gandhi and Churchill: The Epic Rivalry That Destroyed an Empire and Forged Our Age* (London, 2008).

The best introduction to the Partition of India is *The Partition Omnibus* (New Delhi, 2002), with an introduction by Mushirul Hasan, which includes the full texts of two books by two civil servants present at the Partition: Penderel Moon's *Divide and Quit* (London, 1964) and

G. D. Khosla's *Stern Reckoning: A Survey of the Events Leading Up To and Following the Partition of India* (New Delhi, 1950). Other eye-witness accounts appear in Patrick French's *Liberty or Death: India's Journey to Independence and Division* (London, 1997) and in Nirad C. Chaudhuri's *Thy Hand, Great Anarch!: India 1921–1952* (London, 1987). Cyril Radcliffe's letter is quoted from Edmund Heward's biography, *The Great and the Good: A Life of Lord Radcliffe* (Chichester, 1994). The effect of Partition on the Indian princes is discussed in my book, *Maharaja* (London, 1988).

Leonard Woolf's verdict on the British-Indian empire is from his memoir, *Downhill All The Way: An Autobiography of the Years 1919–1939* (London, 1967). For an Indian view, see the historian Tapan Raychaudhuri's memoir, *The World in Our Time* (Delhi, 2011). More objective verdicts appear in Lawrence James's *Raj: The Making and Unmaking of British India* (London, 1997), Piers Brendon's *The Decline and Fall of the British Empire, 1781–1997* (London, 2007) and John Darwin's *Unfinished Empire: The Global Expansion of Britain* (London, 2012).

10 The World's Largest Democracy
Zareer Masani's *Macaulay: Pioneer of India's Modernization* (Noida, 2012) makes a thought-provoking case. The importance of English in India emerges fascinatingly from Henry Yule and A. C. Burnell's dictionary-cum-glossary-cum-encyclopedia, *Hobson-Jobson* (London, 1886; recent editions, Sittingbourne, 1994, with a 'historical perspective' by Nirad C. Chaudhuri, and Oxford, 2013, edited by Kate Teltscher).

Srinivasa Ramanujan comes alive in Robert Kanigel's *The Man Who Knew Infinity: A Life of the Genius Ramanujan* (New York, 1991). On the history of Indian mathematics before Ramanujan, see Kim Plofker's *Mathematics in India* (Princeton, 2009). The current state of Indian science is described in Gautam S. Desiraju's 'Bold Strategies for Indian Science' (*Nature*, 484 (2012), pp. 159–60). Its troubled development during the 20th century occupies Abha Sur's *Dispersed Radiance: Caste, Gender, and*

Modern Science in India (New Delhi, 2011) and also Jahnavi Phalkey's 'Not only Smashing Atoms: Meghnad Saha and Nuclear Physics in Calcutta, 1938–48' in Uma Das Gupta's edited collection, *Science and Modern India: An Institutional History, c. 1784–1947* (New Delhi, 2011). On modern caste politics in general, see Oliver Mendelsohn and Marika Vicziany's *The Untouchables: Subordination, Poverty and the State in Modern India* (Cambridge, 1998).

The most substantial biography of Jawaharlal Nehru is Sarvepalli Gopal's *Jawaharlal Nehru: A Biography*, 3 vols (London, 1975–84), but there are many other more recent biographies. Katherine Frank's *Indira: The Life of Indira Nehru Gandhi* (London, 2001) is probably the best biography of Indira Gandhi. Perry Anderson's *The Indian Ideology* (Gurgaon, 2012) is highly critical of Nehru and the Nehru-Gandhi dynasty – too dismissive of Nehru, but nevertheless worth reading.

On the current Indian economy, among many recent books I recommend: a provocative collection of essays, *The Elephant Paradigm: India Wrestles with Change* (New Delhi, 2002), and *India Grows at Night: A Liberal Case for a Strong State* (New Delhi, 2012), by Gurcharan Das, a former businessman with philosophical training; William Nanda Bissell's *Making India Work* (New Delhi, 2009), an ethical plan for development by a successful Indian businessman; sociologist Shehzad Nadeem's *Dead Ringers: How Outsourcing is Changing the Way Indians Understand Themselves* (Princeton, 2011); journalist Dinesh Sharma's detailed history *The Long Revolution: The Birth and Growth of India's IT Industry* (New Delhi, 2009); M. V. Ramana's *The Power of Promise: Examining Nuclear Energy in India* (New Delhi, 2012), a scientist's highly informed, independent and balanced assessment of the reasons for the failure of India's nuclear power industry; and Aseem Shrivastava and Ashish Kothari's disturbing study of corporate power, *Churning the Earth: The Making of Global India* (New Delhi, 2012), by an economist and an ecologist.

Postscript

Satyajit Ray's 1991 interview (with Gowri Ramnarayan) is quoted in my *Satyajit Ray: A Vision of Cinema* (London, 2005, with photographs by Nemai Ghosh). Extracts from Javed Akhtar's memorial lecture on Satyajit Ray appear in my *The Apu Trilogy: Satyajit Ray and the Making of an Epic* (London, 2011), and more fully in the *Times of India*, 4 May 2009. V. S. Naipaul's comment appears in 'A Million Mutinies' (*India Today*, 18 August 1997). Markandey Katju's remarks are from the *Indian Express*, 9 April 2012. Significant studies of corruption are: A. Surya Prakash's *Public Money Private Agenda: The Use and Abuse of MPLADS* (New Delhi, 2013) and Arvind Kejriwal's *Swaraj* (New Delhi, 2012), written by a former inland revenue official turned social activist and politician.

ACKNOWLEDGMENTS

Unlike some of my earlier books on Indian subjects, this book is chiefly a work of synthesis. The many historians on whose work I have drawn are duly acknowledged in the main text and in Further Reading. I thank Jamie Camplin of Thames & Hudson, who first commissioned me to write on India in the 1980s, for keeping faith with my writing over a quarter of a century. I also thank the book's editor, Julia MacKenzie, for some perceptive suggestions, and Maria Ranauro for her picture research.

LIST OF ILLUSTRATIONS

Frontispiece Girl seated beside a street shrine in Rajasthan, 1950s. Photo Richard Lannoy

pp. 28–29 Left: 'Unicorn' seal, 2500–2000 BC, excavated at Mohenjo-daro. National Museum of India, New Delhi. Photo Art Archive/DeA Picture Library/G. Nimatallah; Right: 'Proto-Shiva' seal, 2500–2000 BC. Photo Erja Lahdenperä for *Corpus of Indus Seals and Inscriptions* 1 (1987), M-304 A, courtesy Archaeological Survey of India and Asko Parpola

pp. 46–47 Vishnu as Matsya killing the demon Shankhasura and rescuing the four *Vedas*. Pahari School, *c*. 1760. Gouache painting on paper, 16.4 × 25.4 cm (6½ × 10 in.), British Museum, London

pp. 62–63 Excavation photo of the discovery of Asoka's lion capital at Sarnath, 1905. Museum of Archaeology and Anthropology, University of Cambridge, image no. P.44599.ORT

pp. 82–83 Thomas and William Daniell, *Sculptured Rocks, at Mavalipuram [Mahabalipuram], on the Coast of Coromandel*, October 1792 or February 1793, plate 1, *Oriental Scenery, V: Antiquities of India*, 1799. Coloured aquatint, British Library, London

pp. 100–101 Qutb Minar, Delhi, *c*. 1880. Photo Universal Images Group/SuperStock

pp. 118–19 Attributed to Bhawani Das, The rulers of the Mughal dynasty with their ancestor Timur (centre), *c*. 1707–12. First, second and third from far left: Aurangzeb, Jehangir and Humayun; first, second and third from far right: Shah Jahan, Akbar and Babur. Opaque watercolour and gold on paper, 25.8 × 34.2 cm (10⅛ × 13½ in.), The Nasser D. Khalili Collection of Islamic Art, MS 874. Photo Nour Foundation, London

pp. 132–33 Attributed to Chokha, A processional scene depicting Captain (later Colonel) James Tod riding an elephant. Udaipur, 1817. Opaque watercolour on thin cardboard, 25.2 × 40.5 cm (9⅞ × 16 in.), Victoria & Albert Museum, London

pp. 150–51 Reception for King George V and Queen Mary at the Gateway of India, Bombay, December 1911, on their arrival in India for the Coronation Durbar in Delhi. Photographed by Myers Brothers

pp. 168–69 Jawaharlal Nehru and Mahatma Gandhi, 1946. Photo Universal History Archive/Getty Images

pp. 186–87 Film still from *Aparajito*, the second part of the Apu Trilogy directed by Satyajit Ray, 1956, showing Apu in Benares

INDEX

INDEX

da Gama, Vasco 135
Dalai Lama (14th) 69, 197
Dalhousie, Lord (governor-general) 146
Dalits 12, 67, 84, 95–6, 113, 139, 160,
 163, 175, 181, 194
Dalrymple, William 120, 121, 153, 155,
 158
Daman 136
dance 13
Dara Shikoh (Mughal prince) 121, 130
Darius I 79
Darius III 75
Das, Gurcharan 86, 203, 205, 207, 208
Datta, Narendranath *see* Vivekananda,
 Swami
Deccan 98, 110, 116, 131, 137
Delhi 8, 66, 77, 104, 105, 110–1,
 115–16, 125, 130, 131, 142, 146,
 153, 155, 157–8, 160, 161, 165, 182,
 183, 198
Delhi Durbar (1911) 161
Delhi Sultanate 103, 110, 111, 112, 113,
 115–16, 120, 122, 123, 129
Demetrius I 93
democracy 10, 16, 24, 25, 188, 196, 199,
 202, 206, 208
Desiraju, Gautam 193–4, 195–6
Devji, Faisal 178
dhamma see *dharma*
Dharamsala 67
dharma 37, 66, 79–80
Dharma Sabha 49
Dharmapala, Anagarika 68
Dharmasvamin 67, 105
Diemen, Anthony van 138
Din Ilahi 129
Diu 136
diwani 143
Doniger, Wendy 51, 52, 53
Dravidian languages 22, 41–4, 57, 59
Dutch East Indies 135
Dutt, Guru 209

earthquakes 45
East India Company:

British 7, 11, 68, 135, 137–8, 139–48,
 152, 155–6, 159, 160, 163, 183, 207
Danish 135
Dutch 135, 138, 141
French 135, 141
Portuguese 135
Eaton, Richard 106, 109, 113
economics 8, 9, 11–12, 14, 15, 16,
 35–6, 51–3, 70, 77–8, 102, 108, 134,
 135–7, 138, 139, 140–2, 143–5, 175,
 202–03, 204, 207, 209
education 30, 34, 105, 124, 147, 148,
 161, 162, 163, 175, 191, 192, 193–4,
 196–7
Egypt 21, 34, 35, 36, 37, 39, 40, 68
Einstein, Albert 172, 176, 192
Elephanta 85, 99
elephants 38, 40, 74, 75, 76, 97, 104,
 105, 134, 165
Ellenborough, Lord (governor-general)
 108–9
Ellora 85, 99
Elmhirst, Leonard 173
Enfield rifle 155
English language 16, 88, 91, 92, 146–7,
 161, 163, 188–9
Estado da India 136, 139
Eudoxus of Cyzicus 102
Eurasians *see* Anglo-Indians
Eusebius 14
extremism (political) 165–7

Fabian socialism 16
Fairservis, Walter 41
Faizi 128
famine 12, 144
Farmer, Steve 33–4
Farrukhsiyar (Mughal emperor) 142
Fatehpur Sikri 128
Faxian 95–6
Fergusson, James 160
Fiji 162
firman 141, 142, 143
First World War 161, 165, 166, 178
Firuz, Nuruddin 108

240

31901055499539